CAMPUS IN CRISIS

CAMPUS IN CRISIS

Buell G. Gallagher

HARPER & ROW, PUBLISHERS
New York, Evanston, San Francisco, London

1817

Mr. Gallagher would like to acknowledge, with thanks, Jossey-Bass of San Francisco for permission to use the language and substance of the author's contribution to *The Troubled Campus,* which Jossey-Bass published in 1970.

FIRST EDITION

Designed by Sidney Feinberg

Library of Congress Cataloging in Publication Data

Gallagher, Buell Gordon, 1904–
  Campus in crisis.
  Bibliography: p.
  1. Education, Higher—United States. 2. College students—United States. I. Title.
LA227.3.G34   378.73   73–14261
ISBN 0–06–011402–9

To
Michael, Sharon, Buell, and Frank—
In Hope

Contents

cam·pus . . . 2: university, college, or school considered as an educational, social, or spiritual entity: the academic world.

in . . . c(1)—used as a function word to indicate a material, mental, or moral situation or condition . . . or an environing condition.

cri·sis . . . 3b: a psychological or social condition characterized by an unusual instability caused by excessive stress and either endangering or felt to endanger the continuity of the individual or his group; *esp*: such a social condition requiring the transformation of existing cultural patterns and values.

—Webster's Third New International Dictionary,
Unabridged (1969)

CAMPUS IN CRISIS

1

To Whom It May Concern

∾§ "I go my way with the assurance of a somnambulist, the way
on which Providence has sent me."
—Adolf Hitler, March 14, 1936

Interrupting one's reading to consult a footnote, said John
Barrymore in *Good Night, Sweet Prince,* is "like going down-
stairs to answer the doorbell on one's wedding night." In the
belief that making footprints is more important than consult-
ing footnotes, this book omits the familiar impedimenta of
pedantry in order to speed the reader on his way—toward
action. In deference to authors and publishers, a bibliography
of the principal works cited or quoted appears in the back
pages; but no numbered footnotes divert attention from the
flow of the text. This book is a tract for the times, not to be
consigned to the reference shelf, but to be read and passed
along to others.

Readers will disagree with the alleged dimensions of the
crises described. Some may feel that the argument is overstated, that it cries, "Wolf!" where there are only sheep and
dogs. Others will conclude that the author's apparent effort at
ultimate optimism is not warranted in the realistic light of
facts. Neither view fits what the writer has in mind. Taking
the commonly known facts of the campus and of the times, he
attempts to state the conclusions that the data themselves indicate. If the author's bias were to be stated, it might be ex-

pressed in his hope that there is still a little time remaining in which fresh thinking and comprehensive action may meet the demands of the human condition.

To whom are these pages addressed? Who are the concerned—or who ought to be concerned? Obviously, that half of the population stream that now enters college or university is concerned. The book is written, in part, about them. And to them. And for them. But these pages argue that teachers, administrators, and governing boards must bring a fresh perspective to their tasks if students are to be enabled to learn what must be learned. The writing of this book is, in fact, an act of concern; but it is written to share that concern with others.

The Times

Among the problems posed by our directionless and bewildering times are: the survival or demise of the species in history's moment of mortal peril; the influence or sterility of reason in an antirational or irrational age; the flowering or withering of compassion in a time of arrogance; the impotence or compelling power of affection in a day of ruthlessness—in short, the meaning of meaning, and whether life has any.

It is not that meanings have all been removed from experience, making life a treadmill between obscurity and oblivion. Nor is it that no one cares. It is that the meanings of life are under acrimonious debate, and that the disputants appear to care more about winning the confrontation than about discovering truth.

We are like a passel of cats, tails tied together, tossed over a clothesline: we claw each other and shatter the night with horrendous caterwauling, instead of asking who tied the knot and how it might be undone.

There are those who would smooth our animosities by appealing to pride in tradition. They resort to the sonorous recitation of what Reinhold Niebuhr once called our "national liturgies of self-esteem." They point to the traditional virtues by which we have disciplined ourselves and others, thereby subduing both the planet and the lesser breeds thereon, to be number one in power and wealth and prestige and enemy body-counts, and to stand like some self-anointed latter-day Moses, poised on Pisgah and taking sad self-congratulation in announcing that while our generation may not enter the Promised Land, where there shall be no poverty, no war, no disease, no caste of race or clan, no lung-choking or water-polluting effluence, no starvation or want—all these things and much more shall yet come to pass for our children, so that today must be content with the promise. So we promise. And promise. And promise. If only the old virtues were restored, and righteousness flourished, then everything would be all right.

But those who entreat us to return to the disused values and virtues of an earlier day succeed only in convincing themselves that error is truth, while alienating the oncoming generation. On the ears of the young—too many of them—the prevailing national liturgies of self-esteem fall as obscenities.

If there are any meanings to be discovered in our present moment of bewildered groping, these meanings do not emerge like a pillar of cloud by day or of fire by night to guide us. They are obscured or lost in the cacophony of reassertion and counterdenunciation. There may be genuine functional values to be found through recovering traditional virtues; but assertion and iteration do not make it so. The oncoming generation, in whose hands tomorrow lies, have long since ceased to listen. They turn elsewhere to find whatever meanings life is to hold for them.

If the values and virtues of the nineteenth century no longer commend themselves to younger America; if the proud achievements of the twentieth are looked upon with embarrassment, indifference, disgust, contempt, or fear; if breastbeating in behalf of the national self-image evokes not emulation but rebellion or desertion; if, in short, few younger hands are outstretched to catch the torch from a faltering older generation, it is fair to ask why.

Have the old meanings become meaningless? Or merely irrelevant? Or actual antimeanings? Or what? At a slightly deeper level: what meanings are now being learned and accepted? And still more deeply: how are meanings learned, and can they be taught? And what are they?

The plight of higher education results from failure to find answers to these questions, perhaps from failure to face them. Formulating a set of virtues through which we claim to have achieved cherished values, we attempt to induct young men and women into these virtues and commit them to these values, reciting the liturgies and reenacting the litanies of academe. Some of the younger generation concur. Others conform. All too many of the vigorous and lively among the Now generation tend to reject tradition, disregard the future, and live only in and for today. So, we adapt. We do not change.

The campus is very like a secular version of the contemporary church—torn between the traditionalists who claim that by intoning the old liturgies and performing the old rites the faith will be saved, and the revolutionaries who also deceive themselves in believing that the faith can be saved by jazzing up the ritual and modernizing the liturgy.

Beneath these conflicts of opinion and confrontations of life-style lie the real questions, the questions of the value of meanings and of the meaning of values, and of how either values or meanings may be learned, perhaps taught. This book invites to an examination of the hypothesis that the meaning of learning lies in the learning of meanings.

The Institutions

American colleges and universities are fighting for their lives. The dimensions of their financial difficulty are amply documented. They have become almost unmanageable. The over-extended university could, until recently, put its confidence in expected Government largess for support of its multiplying research activities. It is in deep trouble. The small college that seldom got a dime of government-sponsored research is equally straitened. Both public and private institutions, large and small, are threatened at the least with a serious reduction in the quality of their work. This threat includes probably all of the best-heeled upper third of the universities and colleges. An additional one-third are in more serious financial difficulty, forced to retrench and consolidate where they had hoped to grow or at least to hold their ground, threatened with deterioration in quality and also with cutbacks in size and quantity. The most precarious one-third of the institutions are within sight of insolvency, squeezed between rising costs and restricted income, facing a bleak future.

It is improbable that the American people will permit the entire congeries of private and public colleges and universities to go out of business; but it is likewise possible that the needed massive intervention of philanthropy and Government will not be timely enough to forestall further serious deterioration of at least half of the privately supported institutions—they will go public or cease operation. And the level of tax support for public higher education must rise at an exponential rate, far beyond anything apparently contemplated heretofore, if public higher education is to escape from the debilitating downward spiral into ineffectiveness. If the Federal legislation of June, 1972, is to be accepted as a forecast of the probabilities of the remainder of this decade, the future of higher education in the United States is ominous.

Perhaps that is as it should be. Why, indeed, should higher education be given special consideration when there are so many other problems pressing upon the nation and its people? Colleges and universities may be important, but so are hospitals and prisons and old-age pensions. Competing for its share of the welfare dollar, higher education comes as one of many suppliants. It is not looked upon as being an asset, a resource for meeting other problems.

The institutions of higher education fail to get the consideration they believe is vital. One good reason for this failure is the fact that those who dole out the funds hear the trumpets from the campuses sounding the alarums of financial trouble, but they do not hear the muted music that might tell of what the campus could do for the country.

Academicians talk fondly about the need for a reordering of priorities on a national scale. The hidden premise of their fond talk is the assumption that any rational reordering would give higher education a bigger cut of the financial pie. What is the objective justification for this assumption?

It is not enough to say that the American people have always looked with favor upon their colleges and universities. Too many unkind things are being said and printed about these institutions today. The old mystique no longer charms budget-makers and legislators. It doesn't warm the hearts and loosen the purse strings of alumni the way it once did. Not even an extensive excursion of collegiate athletics into the public entertainment field has turned the tide: there is no positive correlation between successful appearance on the television tubes or favorable bettors' listings and increased donations and appropriations. (When the president of the University of Oklahoma, some years ago, pleaded with the state legislature to "give us a library worthy of the football team," the result was not a new library but a new president.)

Alumni donors appear to be resuming something of their former level of donations, but at nothing like the level of generosity that preceded the years of anger and estrangement as the decade of the 1960s drew to its close. Legislators and governors are, in some instances, increasing the appropriations for higher education because colleges and universities are "home and motherhood" issues at the polls; but the watchdog stringencies that accompany appropriations spell academic austerity, not affluence. Increases seldom keep pace with rising costs, so the institutions appear ungrateful for them and are at a loss to explain satisfactorily to a bemused public that with more dollars they are able to do less. The general public, indeed, looks upon the colleges and universities without the congenial mixture of affection and awe that characterized the 1950s.

Nor is it sufficient to exhort those who are at ease in Zion to awake, defend their laurels, look to their defenses, and smite the Philistines hip and thigh. It is those same Philistines who must donate the dollars and vote (and pay) the taxes. Hip-and-thigh bruises do not make glad hearts, especially among those who already smart from other indignities. The standard of living of most parents and most taxpayers is not so much higher than that of most professors that the Philistines feel a moral obligation to support those who appear to them to loll in the groves of indolence. Most college dormitories provide living quarters more lavish than the homes from which most students come. And the general public still thinks that the academic life is an easy one, well enough paid for nine months of work in which teaching ten hours of classes per week is said to be a "heavy" load. The professor has three arguments going for him—June, July, and August. Let him try, for a change, to meet a payroll every month or bring home a paycheck every fortnight.

The public argument—and the institutions themselves have made it, and continue to make it—is the other way around. Students are lured to college and university with the claim, based on official "Government figures," that the holder of a baccalaureate degree will, on the average, earn during his lifetime in excess of $150,000 more than the holder of a high-school diploma. So, why shouldn't the student and his family pay for his education? Let them borrow. They'll get it back. Don't ask the overloaded taxpayer to add to his burdens in order to give lazy college students a free ride to riches. As long as institutions of higher education permit their recruiting efforts to include the siren song of future wealth, they will have an unconvincing story to tell to the Capitol or the Executive Mansion. When the embarrassed college president points out that tuition payments from students only take care of a small fraction of the costs of educating the student, the taxpayer responds not with a willingness to take up the slack but with a readiness to let the donkey carry its own load.

There was a time when snob appeal brought results in dollars. Before World War II less than one-fourth of the population stream went through the sluice gates of college admissions. An appeal to latent elitism in the average man gave him an opportunity to identify with the to-be-created elite through his generosity—and to feel like a nobleman himself as he gave. There was a time when legislators responded favorably to the public college that had achieved "excellence" —that is, had a record of educating only the exceedingly bright and promising; but that day is gone. The day in which a successful political career could be built on a reputation for generous support of higher education has come to its close. No matter how sophisticated the argument may have become, the public is also becoming sophisticated in seeing through the surface defenses. Elitism is snobbery, no matter how it is dressed up.

In the legislative chambers and governors' mansions, on Capitol Hill and at the other end of Pennsylvania Avenue, higher education is not seen today as having overwhelming sex appeal. Individual men of substance continue to come forward in significant numbers to give generously; but their total support does not increase at a rate commensurate with burgeoning enrollments and spiraling costs. In relative terms, philanthropy as a factor in supporting higher education is falling behind its previous levels. Not least significant in the declining effectiveness of sophisticated snob appeal is the fact that family foundations have replaced individual donors; and foundation executives, by definition, are not responsive to personal flattery. Not that this means any real diminution in the personal gratification that an individual gets when his gift goes through a foundation. Nor does this comment imply that vanity is a primary motivating force in philanthropy. The record to the contrary is clear. What this does mean is that the day is past in which a college president could "support Alma Mater by degrees."

The aspect of this general picture that calls for comment is not the fact that a great many donors still continue to give and that a great many legislators and congressmen continue to vote appropriations. What should amaze is the fact that, with colleges and universities no longer esteemed as privileged institutions for the privileged, philanthropy and Government continue to support institutions that still appeal to entering students on the basis of institutional allegations of superiority. The egalitarian necessities of a day in which more than half of the population stream flows through the colleges and universities should have led the institutions to abandon their former appeals to the impulses of elitism. Colleges and universities have mixed up their own priorities.

The full answer to the financial plight of higher education will not come from private donations. The load is too great. It will come, if at all, from taxpayers, by way of Congress and the state legislatures.

But help will not come in sufficient amounts over a sustaining period of years to a college and university world that merely appeals for help. It will come, if at all, to higher education that gives help as well—and is seen to be an asset rather than a liability. Only when donors and taxpayers come to believe clearly that colleges and universities are something other than expensive necessities will the financial future of higher education be brighter.

Better colleges and universities would be a nice thing. But so would better symphony orchestras and a nationwide network of the performing arts. And adequate day-care centers. And highways. And mental hospitals. And elementary and high schools. And sewers. And water supply. And unpolluted air. And clean rivers and lakes. And . . .

Men, at any given moment, attach higher priority to the things they value most. Some things can be neglected when others are more pressing or of greater value. Only the negligible is neglected. And what is negligible? Whatever is postponable among the pressing problems; and whatever is unavailable among the needed answers.

Financial problems are, of course, only the beginning of the list of difficulties faced by higher education. If it were not for such mundane matters as payrolls and laboratory supplies, college and university presidents and professors would see that the financial problem is not the real problem at all. The real problem is not that colleges and universities don't get enough money. The real problem is, why don't they?

Higher education has always been supported with an ampler hand when the people who put up the money were convinced that they were paying not only for something that needed help, but that that something was of inescapable significance. In earlier times, that idea was summed up in the "mission" or "purpose" of higher education. Contemporary parlance likes to call it "relevance." Colleges and universities have been established and have flourished precisely when founders and donors and taxpayers shared a belief that what went on within the ivied walls was very much worthwhile, more important than other things.

If higher education is to surmount its present financial crisis, and to master all the other internal crises that beset the troubled campus, these achievements will come only when supported by a clearly understood and widely accepted belief that the colleges and universities cannot be neglected because they are part of the answer, not part of the problem.

This is one of the dividends of insight deriving from the troublous 1960s. It is fair to say that in the 1950s and before, a simpler notion of the function of higher education sufficed. Our day requires a degree of sophistication because the case for higher education is considerably more complicated. It deals with something more than furnishing the minds and polishing the manners of the selected representatives of the younger generation. It deals with the stark realities of the human condition.

Those realities walk onto the campus each recurring September. They sit behind each desk of presidential worry, appear on the agenda of faculty meetings, stab the professorial mind out of its accustomed serenity, provoke the campus to an uproar, dominate the dormitory, scrawl offensive graffiti on the limestone, set the tone of campus life. The living reality of the campus is the human condition.

2

Civilization's Laundry List

&§ "One can try to guess at the point of no return—the time at which major ecological degradation might become irreparable. . . . Probably the firmest estimate is that regarding the depletion of oxygen in the United States surface waters. . . According to a 1966 report of the U.S. National Academy of Sciences, on the basis of present trends this will occur about the year 2000."

—Barry Commoner (1971)

The troubled campus is surrounded by a deeply troubled nation, in a profoundly troubled world. In most respects, the problems of campus and society are similar, if not identical, in scope and intensity. College is a microcosm of the world.

The logic of this fact therefore suggests that an assessment of higher education must begin with a brief review of the human condition.

Monumental Waste

Back in April, 1970, the undergraduate world was briefly concerned with the observance of "Earth Day." To a small fraction of the student population, the quality of the environment still continues to be a troublesome worry; and in most scientific circles, the integrity of the biosphere has become an important field of research and action. The academic world is becoming aware that what is at stake is not merely the quality of our environment. At stake is the survival of life in human form on the spaceship called earth. The supplies of oxygen, nitrogen, minerals, arable lands, fresh water, and open countryside are not unlimited. They are finite. They are exhaustible. And when they are used up, there isn't any more. This fragile earth with its frail ocean and its vulnerable atmosphere can no longer be exploited by a cowboy economy, exhausting each stand and then moving on to greener pastures. A finite environment is not capable of infinite nurture to man.

For years we have been warned. Rachel Carson, the Reinows, Wesley Marx, and a great many others wasted their eloquence. We waited until Lake Erie's commercial fish catch dropped from over twenty million pounds annually to less than eight thousand pounds before recognizing disaster. The world waited until the Caspian Sea had become a stinking cesspool, the Rhine an open sewer, the Hudson and the Mississippi sources of offending stench—and the productive coastal marshes had disappeared under bulldozed rubble and garbage or, polluted by human waste, had become breeding grounds for clams and oysters carrying the virus of infectious hepatitis. Only then came the realization that man must learn to be a husband to nature if he wishes to survive.

Now that the evidence is indisputable, it has become fashionable to take an interest in preserving the ecology. Your second-grader comes home from school talking about thermal pollution and committed to saving the biosphere. The Environmental Protection Agency has been established.

But we make progress slowly and irregularly. Witness the reversal of governmental advice on the use of phosphates in detergents: yesterday's boon became today's anathema and then was restored as tomorrow's probable lesser evil. Witness the exploitation of fish, mammal, and mineral wealth of the oceans by international competition, and the faltering ineffectiveness of governmental gestures at control. Witness the con-

trast between public discussion and governmental pronouncement about impending death by asphyxiation and ineffective
action by the automobile industry in curbing the noxious
emissions while trying to satisfy both stockholders and the
riding public. Look at the inconclusive conflict between the
advocates of mass transportation and the promoters of highways. Score, perhaps, one small victory for the faint, thin
atmosphere and the slight, thin eardrum in the defeat of the
proposal to build the supersonic transport; but remember that
a nation that insists on being number one in every field may
not forever maintain its reluctance to claim supremacy in the
skies.

The ambiguities of political fortune reflect the ambivalence
of our apprehensions. It would be a man of rare temerity who
staked his political future on an effort to save the environment
through the use of means drastic enough to make a difference.
The price of saving the ecosystem is the diminution of profits,
the lowering of real wages, the rise of costs to the consumer,
and probable limitation of consumption and production
through rationing. Or is it? Will not solar energy be harnessed to supplant dwindling fossil fuels? Already, in the case
of phosphates in detergents, the scientific findings have twice
reversed the field: what political careers could survive a succession of such reversals? Or, again, large contributors to
political campaigns are not always those whose ability to
donate derives from industrial or commercial processes free
of ecological endangerment. Finally, nearly every decision
about saving the ecology involves a trade-off of some sort, in
which many relative matters of degree of probability have
to be weighed against their counterpart arguments: convenience against contamination; personal leisure against ecological
exhaustion; conservation versus cheap consumer goods. Who
draws the line and where? What statutes and what enforcement?

Part of our bewilderment comes from the fact that it is only in the immediate past that the dimensions of our dilemma have become clear. Only since World War II have we become aware that the pace of technological change has accelerated exponentially. At least this much of Toffler's argument is irrefutable: *Future Shock* is already felt in the mounting piles of nonrecycled waste that are an end product of the no-deposit, no-return delivery system. The town dump has always been an eyesore and an offense to the nostrils; but the volume of today's refuse gives us a disposal problem not yet mastered. The speed with which the problem of waste has overtaken us is not, even now, fully appreciated.

If all of technological progress from the dawn of history down to the onset of the Industrial Revolution were to be represented by a column one foot high, then the succeeding two centuries or so that terminated with World War II could be represented by an additional two feet on the column; but to represent the growth of technology from World War II to the present would require that the column be somewhat taller than the Washington Monument. It is the speed of the relentless onrush of technology that sets the greater challenge to man's choice of priorities. The moment of effective choice passes before it can be seized.

And the catastrophe that now impends is different from every other that has confronted man since the dawn of history. There will be no recovery from this one if it comes. Always before, if famine or flood or war or depression took its toll, survivors could turn to a slowly replenishing Mother Earth and start anew. Not so today and tomorrow. The process of ecological pollution, degradation, and exhaustion is rapidly approaching the point of no return. In many important respects, that process is irreversible. When it has gone too far, there is no second chance.

But our technology symbolizes and enshrines some of our most dearly held values. We are proud of our ability to span the continents and oceans nonstop, satisfied with the ready comforts bestowed by a no-deposit, no-return delivery system of commerce and industry, ready to indulge our hard-earned leisure with the freedoms and enjoyment made possible by a technologically transformed society and culture.

Are we being asked to give these things up? Well, the short answer is that we must decide at least to restrict them sharply if we want our children and grandchildren to live. The values that we have come to accept almost as second nature, and which are the source of pride among us and envy among all the peoples of the underdeveloped nations, have to be reversed. Nature is not to be mastered and exploited; she is to be lived with in faithful husbandry. Life must be more precious than profits. Empathy for the whole earth must replace the greed of the prospector and the avidity of the strip miner. The future must take precedence over the present.

The Teeming Billions

What Paul Ehrlich calls *The Population Bomb* compounds the problem of monumental waste; too many people, with too little food, on a dying planet. Just as monumental waste will exhaust the ecosystem if it is not reversed, so the population explosion will exceed the food supply if it is not halted. Malthus was answered by the Industrial and Agricultural revolutions; but we are now obliged to reverse their relentless march. Neo-Malthusianism is not just a revival of a discredited nineteenth-century nightmare.

About 3,500,000,000 people now teem the earth. Of these, two billions are poorly fed—undernourished, malnourished, or starving. Compassion and the progress of medical science have combined to reduce the death rate with no corresponding reduction in the birth rate. Every thirty-seven years there are twice as many mouths to feed. At present rates of growth, there will be seven billions by the year 2007. But there will not be twice as much food, twice as much arable land. Unless the great excess of births over deaths is reversed within the two decades of the 1970s and 1980s, starvation will redress the balance. You and I will sit down to our ample dinners in the United States, tune in the evening news, and watch the starving die in living color.

For some time, we have watched death in famine, flood, earthquake, and war as mass disaster struck. This time, however, there will be a difference. Neither the practicalities of international power nor the realities of international war nor the urgings of humanitarian sentiment will permit the ten nations that now produce more food than they eat to survive peacefully in that day when the streets of a hundred other nations are choked with hunger riots. The population bomb is ticking. Hunger, the principal killer of men, might become the killer of mankind.

The United States is, of course, the world's largest producer. We are also its largest consumer. When a child is born in the United States, the impact of that one birth on the straining ecosystem is equal to the impact of fifty babies in India. That is the meaning of the differences in standards of living as consumption is converted into ecological impact. Differently stated: the people of the United States make up only 6 percent of the world's population, yet consume half of the world's production of goods and services. The population problem is worldwide; but the rate at which the American people devour food and destroy the resources of nature puts this nation in a special condition of peril. As the facts become more widely appreciated and the invidious gap in the rates of ecologically exhausting standards of living widens, why should the have-not peoples remain silent?

Population pressures compound the problems of a runaway technology. Do we choose to increase food production by even more extensive use of chemical fertilizers? Then how do we avoid choking the lakes with lush growth generated by the annual leaching of fertilizers in each watershed? In order to feed a starving world, do we permit all of the Great Lakes to become like Lake Erie, "thick enough to walk on, but not thick enough to cultivate"? Or, in order to save our lakes and streams from agricultural pollution, do we reduce our crop yield by abandoning fertilizers, only to find that the over-extended acreage can no longer produce without artificial restoration of its soil? Do we then permit vast acreage to lie fallow for a time, perhaps planting it to nitrogenous legumes plowed back into the soil, thereby not only reversing the process of technological change but also increasing the price of food on every man's dinner table? And how can a reduction in food production be justified when more than half the world goes to bed hungry every night? Agriculture has emphasized production at the expense of pollution. Pollution can be avoided only at the expense of production. The hard choice for the world has to be made between irreversible pollution and widespread death by starvation. This choice has to be made in the presence of an exploding population that demands a doubling of global food production every thirty-seven years in order to survive at present levels of malnutrition.

This problem has to be solved in the face of national rivalries and without effective world controls. If, for example, the United States and Canada were to combine their great bread-baskets to feed a hungry world, and were to do it by pushing production to maximum limits, leading to the eutrophication of all the Great Lakes, would the world be better off? If, instead, we coaxed our nascent joint conservation efforts to rescue the lakes by reducing the production of cereals, what other nations could be induced to pollute in order to produce the needed supplies? And for how many short generations would that shift of production keep ahead of the galloping rate of growth in the world's hungry?

If that set of problems were to be settled by some leger-demain of international arm-twisting, who will compensate the farmers in the abstaining nations as they are made to be content with a lowered standard of living? What urban areas are now prepared to absorb the additional millions who would swarm to them from a countryside whose formerly hospitable soil had been exhausted and could not be replenished through the use of prohibited chemicals? And the urban consumers of farm products—what share of their resultant higher food costs is to be absorbed by the families whose paychecks are never large enough? And what share of the farmers' loss would be recouped by public subsidy (say) through increased corporate taxes, a stepping up of the graduated income tax, or the imposition of a Federal sales tax or value-added tax? Can a nation achieve a healthy economy when national policy deliberately forces one part of that economy to be underproductive? And is decreased productivity of farmers essentially different from the suggested decrease in productive efficiency that might come from forcing the automobile industry to produce nonpolluting vehicles? The list of unanswered questions has no apparent end.

We are constricted within an ever-tightening ring of interrelated problems of population, productivity, and pollution in which, if present trends are not checked, the race between the survival of the species and the exhaustion of the ecosystem has only one presently foreseeable end result: a sharp reduction of the standard of living (rate of exhaustion of the ecosystem) in all of the advanced nations and particularly in the United States, until a world with wall-to-wall people starves to death on its garbage heaps.

While it might be said that, despite recession and unemployment, the people of the United States in the 1970s "have never had it so good," it is much nearer the whole truth to affirm that the oncoming generation will be one that "never had it so bad." And if it were to be argued that sermons about birth control should more properly be addressed to the peoples of the underdeveloped nations, let two things be remembered:

(1) the fifty-to-one differential in ecological impact of births as between the United States and India and (2) the tendency of advanced nations to rely on the underdeveloped areas of the globe to supply the needed green belt for earth, while those who have already pushed technological conquests over nature beyond the point of tolerance continue to drain the marshes, fill the lakes with algae, and pave over the fertile soil. Scapegoating is not the answer to the population problem. Birth control is.

Neither the affluent society nor the effluent society has a promising future.

Counterproductive Devastation

The rhetoric of the trade-offs gets quite angular when the discussion turns to expenditures for wars. The trade-off is posed as a choice between the use of restricted resources either to support life adequately while restoring the ecosystem or to pay for wars past, present, and future.

The dilemma used to be phrased as "guns or butter." In the crunch of circumstances outlined in the preceding sections of this chapter, that choice must be rephrased. It is a choice between extinction by starvation, asphyxiation, or poisoning *or* annihilation by guns, germs, and bombs. It comes down to this: unless ways can be found to reduce and then to eliminate the wasteful costs of war and the arms race, we will be unable to save the ecology and sustain life at humane levels. As long as expenditures for wars have to be taken out of the annual GNP of the nations, leadership is forced to vacillate between efforts to avoid first one and then the other of the twin catastrophes. The inevitable impermanence of public policy both illustrates and proves the point.

The balance of terror in the extent of overkill available to the principal military powers does not guarantee that full-scale warfare will never again be unleashed. The sudden finality of any all-out atomic exchange leaves little to be hoped for beyond the hour in which the fatal push button is pressed. On the day after Hiroshima, General Dwight Eisenhower exclaimed, "Now, perhaps, mankind may be blackmailed into peace!" His prophecy has not yet come true.

A searching and agonizing reappraisal of the value system of nationalism is in order. The posturing of professional patriots in high places and low does not provide the promise of permanent peace. It leads to brinkmanship diplomacy. Nor could the promise of enduring peace, if it were based on a frank declaration of the costs of that peace, win the support of the electorate. A citizenry that believes in putting the interests (or what appear to be the interests) of its own nation ahead of all other interests is not ready to be served by, and will neither elect nor follow, a leadership that proposes that the nations pay the price of enduring peace. That price is, at a minimum, the limitation of all national sovereignties to the extent necessary to make it impossible for any nation to wage declared or undeclared war on another. To make that limitation effective, it would be necessary to make sure that no nation retains or creates the ability to make war. It also means the establishing of the power and authority to enforce that denial of sovereign irresponsibility. Short of such developments, no responsible national leader in any country can honestly promise peace beyond sundown.

The Balkanizing of the globe prevents or inhibits the development of the sentiments of universalism in the patriot's breast. Outmoded parochialisms restrict horizons. The liturgies of national self-esteem are used to feed the ego needs of the common man. He is prevented from viewing his country as one nation among many: it must be first among all. First in everything good and last in everything bad, no matter what the facts may be, and regardless of the fact that there can only be one number one at a time. Nationalism, which Edward Shillito called *Man's Other Religion*, is, in many cases, his one true religion. Its loyalties and commitments override all else. Divided between more than a hundred national loyalties, mankind has little hope of lasting peace.

It was not always so. In a former day, when national self-interest could be followed to extremes without threatening total world destruction, the nation served an important purpose. The lesser loyalties of tribe or clan or dukedom or kingdom or birthplace kept men in continual warfare, interrupted by such things as the harvest and holy days. To correct these petty loyalties, the nation-state built larger and more compelling affiliations. Thirteen colonies became one nation. Germany emerged from a welter of baronies and kingdoms. The czars ruled from the Baltic to the Pacific. Nationalism emerged on the stage of history as a new and noble conception of man's destiny, a means of transcending petty loyalties and dedicating oneself to bold and noble goals. And because nationalism performed these functions, it was an acceptable transition stage in man's development. It was a necessary, and therefore endurable, evil.

The realities of atomic overkill have destroyed the validity of these earlier values. Nationalism is too costly a luxury to be longer entertained. In the Atomic Age, major war cannot be entered upon without total destruction. In the early years of the Atomic Age, one of its principal architects, Albert Einstein, used to say that he was not too worried over the probable onset of nuclear war, because one-third of mankind might survive. To be sure, he added, these would be the inhabitants of the less advanced portions of the globe; but after the radiation had died down, their descendants could dig among the ruins, decipher the artifacts, and begin the processes of civilization over again. In his later years, however, Einstein saw the cobalt bomb and then the hydrogen bomb replace the primitive instrument of Hiroshima. He recanted his limited optimism. He died without expressing any hope that mankind would survive the atomic displosion. He has been replaced, in the gallery of determined optimists, by the biologist who claims that he isn't worried over the coming holocaust because, while it is true that most of human and animal and vegetable life will disappear from the earth, the primeval soup will remain. The processes of evolution can begin over again. We have not heard what heights of optimism will greet the announcement that the laser bomb has been perfected.

If these comments are within a long sea mile of the truth, then we must conclude that the immediate, permanent, and total elimination of the possibility of international warfare is no longer optional. The alternative is catastrophe, so vast and thorough as to be beyond comprehension.

The burden of proof lies with those who reject this analysis. The weight of history and of contemporary fact favors the emergence of a world-inclusive organization with power to make crucial decisions that nation-states obey. This may not necessarily be a world-state (which could easily be afflicted with the imperfections of a nation-state); but it must be something more than a debating society in which differences are aired while history's course is actually determined by the balance of terror.

The difficulty is, in large part, that men and nations tend to address themselves to past difficulties, devising remedies that might have been adequate in a former day but are obsolete in new circumstances, rather than preparing for tomorrow. Thus, the weakly supported League of Nations that was devised after World War I did not enjoy support from the United States, and was clearly inadequate to the postwar world. As World War II approached its close, the United Nations emerged—an instrument that might have been adequate to the interwar period but which is not equal to the critical threats of the Atomic Age. The form and structure of a new relationship between nations that might be a less insecure basis of hope have yet to be created. About all we can be sure of is that whatever lessons are to be learned in this area must, this time, be grasped in advance of the onset of global war: there will be no opportunity to apply the lessons of experience after the atomic holocaust.

We are assured that the United States will never launch the initial nuclear assault, that ours will be only the now-familiar "protective reaction strike." But on that day when the Hydra-headed missiles roar from their underground silos, and blinding death sears the green earth to a smoking cinder, who will mourn man's passing? Perhaps a minor angel, fourth rank, fifth tier, may lean over the ramparts with compassion and (as another has put it) let fall

> A tear for the world,
> Cosmic erratum:
> Started with Adam,
> Ended with Atom.

Caste

Some call it "racism." It is that; but it is much more. It is easier, and more effective, to use an emotion-laden term than to be accurate. It makes the adrenaline flow to call another man a "racist." But scapegoating is never quite the whole truth.

The truth is that every child in America is born into and educated by a system of color-caste based on ancestry. The caste system determines—for white and black but not alike—how he will be born, where he will live, his diet, his early childhood development, his schooling, his friends and enemies, the ideals that dominate his life choices, what employment or entrepreneurial opportunities will be open at what remuneration, what probabilities of criminal or nonconvicted status lie ahead, what results may follow on acceptance or defiance of one's caste identity, whom one is likely to marry, into what caste his children will be born, and in what cemetery he is likely to be buried. The one thing over which no individual person has any control, namely, his ancestry, has an all-pervasive and dominant control over his life from cradle to grave. These things describe a caste system. Among the many characteristics of American society, racial caste must be identified as the greatest threat to, the longest existing denial of, the American principle of equality and the American profession of democracy. Racial caste is a value system. It is an unconscionable denial of the values of equality and freedom and brotherhood. In a word, it is un-American.

For a brief time, in the mid-1960s, the American people saw these facts and believed them. Sweeping legislation established civic, economic, and social equality, while educational equality was being pursued through the courts. Great expectations were entertained, magnificent dreams dreamed, dedicated energies enlisted. But the caste system was not to be easily discarded, as a snake sloughs its skin in the spring. Race riots swept like a prairie fire across the land. The dream began to fade a little.

In the first year after its publication (March 1, 1968), the *Report of the National Advisory Commission on Civil Disorders* (the so-called Kerner report) sold 1,700,000 copies. Some, at least, of these must have been read. But when two agencies jointly examined the results at the end of that first year, the picture was far from reassuring. There was a governmental promise of future programs for better housing in the inner city; but appropriations to get the programs off the drawing boards would have to wait on the winding down of the war in Indochina and the redeploying of new and more sophisticated weaponry, before adequate funding could be found. As for most of the other programs projected in the report, no progress could be found.

Meantime, what was happening in the racial ghetto? It was spreading in size, taking in more territory—but it was not taking in more people at the same rate of increase. Instead, whole areas of hard-core slums were being abandoned by landlords, vacated by tenants, and given over to the rats and junkies. Blight and abandonment pockmarked the spreading ghetto, the rate of deterioration significantly exceeding new housing starts. Overcrowding increased in the presence of increasing vacancies. The result? If the entire population of the United States were to be crowded together as tightly as central Harlem is packed, the population of the whole nation could be contained in three of New York City's five boroughs.

The trends that were evident in the first years after the Kerner report have not been reversed. They have persisted, intensified. Five years later, we are well on the way toward an America of 1985 that the report foresaw and deplored: ". . . an America of swollen metropolitan areas, black at the core and white at the fringes, with its problems . . . expanded beyond hope of solution." The report had called for the generating of "a new will." It had not been generated.

Other things had been generated, among them a surging new self-confidence and pride within the black caste. The new-found self-assertion created a thrust toward expected immediate change, a thrust that found no satisfying alteration in the glacial movement of social structures. The frustration of newly awakened hopes led to increased bitterness, even to wild episodes of black rage and violence, in the destruction of property, the burning of many inner cities, and the use of exaggerated rhetoric and symbolic acts.

Two organizational transformations illustrate the changing climate within the black caste. The Congress of Racial Equality (CORE), which had been founded in the 1940s as an interracial and pacifist thrust for equality of the races, now ejected its white membership en bloc and renounced its nonviolent methods. It became an all-black force, committed to using any prudentially justified means to achieve new power for the black caste, regardless of the effect of its methods upon what was once called "race relations." Secondly, the Student Nonviolent Coordinating Committee (SNCC) retained its acronym but changed its character, as "Non-violent" was revised to "National" in its name. Using both devious methods and deceit in its relationships with other civil rights organizations, SNCC displayed an excitingly provocative rhetoric and openly disavowed interracial cooperation and nonviolent methods. To underline the significance of these two organizational changes, a new group emerged, calling itself the Black Panthers. Lionized by the media, they became exaggerated symbols of the general fact that the black caste no longer accepted either the strictures or the stigma of caste.

In the early 1960s, massive nonviolent protest characterized the struggle against the caste system; but as the mood alternated between exuberant rejoicing over astounding legislative victories and deep despair over the relatively small changes in the actual status of the general run of members of the black caste, internal tensions grew taut. Demands were escalated. And the more the black caste agitated and demonstrated and pushed, the more the white caste retreated into a newly reenforced recalcitrance in which fear escalated into dread and former tolerance and benevolence were replaced by irritation, anger, self-righteousness, and counterprotest.

Nevertheless, even five years after the publication of the Kerner report, the trust of hope in the black caste is still directed toward an integrated society. Blacks still want into, not out of, the mainstream of American life. They proudly boast of nearly 3,000 black public officeholders who are the first fruits of the new registration and voting laws. They still continue their agonizing and ineffectual efforts to break the color barriers in the labor unions—particularly in the building trades. They press for adequate housing at fair cost near to available jobs.

But this time around, they are insisting that integration must be something more than tokenism in numbers and something other than a new adjustment within the patterns of inequality. They want integration, yes; but they want it to be an integration that breathes freedom and embodies equality—not a cat-and-canary merger. Continuing delay in fulfilling these desires feeds the forces of separatism within the black caste, thereby having a foreseeable but doubly frustrating effect because the spread of separatism actually strengthens the controls of the caste system, permitting the old separate-but-equal formula to achieve a new degree of respectability, as black acceptance and espousal of separatism negates the thrust toward equality in an open society while at the same time it permits the defenders of the dominant white caste to speak quite plausibly about "pluralism" and "Black empowerment" without threatening the solid structure of caste itself. Thus, many within the white caste who were beginning to move (reluctantly or gladly) toward an open society reversed their direction of movement and with a vast sigh of relief reassured themselves that blacks did not really "want in." The black caste became divided in its councils and equivocal in its actions, vacillating between the quickly fading satisfactions of black dominance in the ghetto and the mounting frustrations that followed on the realization that a caste-controlled society seldom relinquishes anything to black control or enjoyment until it is secondhand—financially bankrupt, obsolescent, and run down. With great hopes deferred and minor victories made empty for one caste, greater resistance and more openly aggressive hostility grew in the other, thereby both intensifying the damage done by caste and strengthening the system itself. As the thrust for freedom was met by the counterinertia of stasis, it appeared to the black caste that the nation's studied neglect had long since ceased to be benign. The seeds of an unprecedented disorder and division in the nation were being sown.

The first eruptions of that new divisiveness suddenly punctuated American history in the brutal murders of Martin Luther King, Jr., and Robert F. Kennedy. We shall never know whether accustomed lethargy and undisturbed indifference in the white caste, together with the controlling beliefs of the caste system, would have been enough to prevent significant progress in the dismantling of caste as the second year after the Kerner report began. The eyes of the nation turned away from the problems of racial caste and ghetto riots to stare with fascinated horror at the specter of violent death and generalized violence. The spirit of the vigilante and the night rider was abroad in the land. For a brief moment, Congress considered doing something about firearms, enacted a law designed to discourage sale of small arms to convicted felons, and hastily dismissed a matter for which it had no stomach.

A new Presidential commission was created, headed by Milton Eisenhower, to look into the causes and prevention of violence.

Violence

The new Presidential commission was appointed in June, 1968. It tried to be useful in illuminating the American scene during the campaigns of that year. Through a series of timely releases, Milton Eisenhower and his colleagues on the commission called public attention to the endemic character of violence in the history and traditions of the nation, made suggestions and proposals that forecast final findings, and tried to be of service to an apprehensive electorate as well as to parties and candidates. "Law and order" was a repetitive theme throughout the campaign period. The efforts of the commission should have been helpful. There is little evidence that they were.

When the final report, *To Establish Justice, To Insure Domestic Tranquility* (with fourteen supporting volumes) appeared in December, 1969, it was given adequate play in the news media. Its effect on the general public and official Washington had all the force of a marshmallow lighting on a featherbed.

There was greater public attention to a single photograph of armed black students at Cornell University than to all fifteen volumes of the commission's report. The report told the American people what they did not want to hear. An apprehensive citizenry wanted reassurance: they were told that reassurance had to be earned. Domestic tranquillity could come only if justice were established, said the commission. But the people did not listen. Instead, they demanded that somebody do something about violence in the streets.

The commission had said two things: that violence must be unrewarded (law enforcement), and that it must become unnecessary (a just society). The public response was: the violent must be repressed. In that difference, the task before the nation is described. The liturgies of national self-esteem have to be revised in face of the facts. America's homicide rate, for example, is nearly five times that of Canada, nearly nine times that of England and Wales. Such disparities reveal a disquieting acceptance of violence as an indigenous part of American life. The revisers of the liturgy do not move, however, from their defense of a society so prone to violence to make a constructive attack on the roots of violence in the American way of life. Instead, what we have heard are incantations of fear and belligerence, demanding counterviolence and repression.

Campuses felt the impact of this psychosis. During the academic years 1964 to 1969, when the mass media made a point of chronicling every campus disorder, carrying on one of the nation's more extended running stories with weekly roundups, readers and viewers became acutely aware of campus violence all over the nation. The years 1970 to 1972 saw a less intensive news coverage; but that served to hide the truth of a continuing story of campus violence. When, for example, the president of Akron University was held prisoner in his office, and the administration building was subsequently burned, a story that would have been played on page one all over the nation a few months earlier did not get reported outside a fifty-mile radius. It was the fall of 1970, and the news media no longer were interested. Meanwhile, campus violence continued to be a constant threat and a recurring fact, despite the highly sophisticated security devices and extensive security forces that many institutions had installed.

And around the world, campus violence also flourished—as if other nations were declaring that they could keep up with the United States in that one respect, at any rate. Violence has become a way of life for the student in India, Pakistan, France, Indonesia. Hundreds of universities were closed in Japan for the major part of an academic year because of student violence. Egypt has begun to vie with Central and South American devotees of the art of campus disruption. The Parisian newspaper *Le Monde* announced that violence had replaced debate on French campuses: "One speaks no more; one wishes simply to prevent others from speaking." Violence, said *Le Monde*, has "become a habit" in which "one hits out, joyously." The use of bombs and arson against property and people, not just against the police, began to be an accepted practice. And, of course, China endured the years of the Red Guard, when student violence was deliberately fostered to shut down all universities until professors and students could be reeducated.

What this has meant in the transmutation of campus values is all too evident. Vandalism has become a way of life for many. It has gone down through the high schools to the elementary schools. It is now an established pattern, accepted by pre-teen-agers. There are national associations of security officers for the nation's public schools. In a nation where violence is invoked to express discontent, and where counterviolence is the principal answer, hatred flourishes, anger rises, and contempt curdles compassion. The practices and procedures of vulgarity, obscenity, contumacy, derision, profanity, hyperbole, and epithet are, by now, strangers to few campuses. They are known to the courtroom. By negative reaction, the invidious alliterative allusion became a favorite medium of the Vice-President of the United States until a new image was thought to be useful around election time. Increasingly in the American scene, dialogue was replaced by confrontation; and on the campus, verbal and physical violence were preferred above other means of communication.

The Eisenhower commission proposed that violence be made both unnecessary and unrewarding. Instead, counter-violence was invoked throughout the nation. There is little indication in the statistics of crime as reported up through the winter of 1973 that repression has stamped out violence.

What it has done is to inflame the racial conflict. In a caste-controlled society, violence and racial animosity mutually reenforce each other. Our cities are becoming a kind of no-man's-land where the white worker and businessman surround themselves, while at work, with private armed guards, and at evening jump into their closed cars, lock the doors, and speed homeward on the freeways. Home is in an enclave surrounded by high wire fences, where neighborhood vigilantes or private police are on patrol. It would appear that we are embodying the spirit of apartheid, while reversing the details: the South African practice is to send the blacks to the enclaves outside the city. If these descriptions appear strained, let the reader visit his nation's capital. For that matter, let him look carefully at almost any of the urban centers of America. Instead of trying to correct the causes of violence, we move to protect the fruits of violence. We protect the iniquity of inequity by repressing the oppressed. We beat the victim until he bleeds, and then beat him for bleeding.

In the vain search for inner peace and social stability, we stubbornly refuse to abandon the racial caste system that is itself built on and defended by centuries of violence. In its continuation, caste is one of the causes of violence. On balance, we are not winning the struggle against caste and its attendant violence. There are constructive forces at work, some of them

Government-sponsored, others supported by private initiative
and individual courage. But in the years since the Kerner and
Eisenhower reports, we have lost ground. Such progress as can
be discerned is like sunlight glinting on a sea of blood and
tears.

We are aware of the trade-offs. We know that hard choices
have to be made—between racial caste and the open society;
discrimination and equality; freedom and repression; eradica-
tion of injustice and the self-generating circle of violence followed by counterviolence; mutual respect and joint contempt;
survival and catastrophe. We know what has happened to
earlier societies when faced with these choices if they chose
wrongly. Since we do not learn from history, our only hope
would appear to be in learning from contemporary experience.

It is fast nearing the point at which it will be too late for
experience to teach us. Will we wait until the uncouth replaces the couth in our set of values, and we revert to a frontier life where no man sleeps without his loaded pistol under
his pillow or ventures outside his door without his sidearms?

When we are told that one in every three persons in an
urban center like New York City will be the subject of some
crime against person or property before the year is ended, we
grasp for personal security. Another bolt is added to the door.
A guard dog is taken in as a household pet and protector. We
stay in at night, nurse our fears, build our hatreds, and watch
the violence grow—all the while demanding that They do
something.

It makes little difference that police statistics reveal that
crimes of violence are mostly perpetrated within each caste
rather than across caste lines. Each caste ascribes to the other
full blame for violence. Each caste claims an equal right to use
violence in self-defense against the other. "By whatever means
necessary" is the phrase. Militants in both castes use it. The
fact that the caste system thereby reenforces itself, inflaming

a situation that none corrects, does not escape our attention. We welcome it.

Violence is by no means limited to the caste system, either in its roots or in its expression; but without the continuing practice of official and unofficial violence, the caste system would be less strong. It might even be done away.

If repression has not cured the evils of caste, neither has it solved the problem of crime. In July, 1965, the President had established the Commission on Law Enforcement and the Administration of Justice, headed by Nicholas deB. Katzenbach. Its report laid out seven detailed objectives, warning that crime would seriously increase within the next decade unless sweeping reforms in the system of criminal justice were carried out, and unless patent injustices in the way society restricted opportunity and bestowed rewards unevenly were corrected.

The framers of the Constitution saw the necessary connection between domestic tranquillity and justice. Why is it so difficult for the American citizenry two centuries later to see it? Can it be that common usage has limited our conception of justice to the narrow field of criminal justice? "The underlying problems are ones that the criminal justice system can do little about," said the 1965 commission; but it took a bloody Attica to awaken the nation even to the problems of criminal justice. What will it take to open our eyes to the truth that a peaceful society will not emerge except as that society is fair? What dimensions of social upheaval must come before we see that only a just society has the right to expect to be tranquil?

There is an alternative answer. Totalitarian societies provide it. If we wish to give up freedom, we can stamp out violence, and by force maintain an unstable security; but in a free society, justice is the prerequisite of peace.

More than one hundred programs were launched from Washington during the Johnson years that were calculated to

build the Great Society. Taken together, these programs were
a promising beginning to the task of achieving an equitable,
fair society. We shall never know whether their continuance
and improvement might not, eventually, have brought a reduction in crime and violence. We shall never know, because
some of the programs faltered, others strayed, a few were be-
trayed; but mostly because the objectives of the Nixon Administration differ from those of its predecessor. In January,
1973, after slowing down the Great Society programs during
his first term, the reelected President proposed to scrap the
entire panoply of 113 programs, including the OEO and
Model Cities. We are, as a nation, a long way from fulfilling
the vision of the Founding Fathers. They knew that to enjoy
peace, a society must be just.

The Crowded Society

Today's America has no great, beckoning open spaces. Before,
say, World War I, vacant lands were plentiful. Aided by the
Homestead Act, families migrated westward, staked out a
claim, registered it, and proved it up by living on it. It wasn't
gold they were after. Just room to live and breathe. Alaska
now remains as the last, somewhat less hospitable, unoccupied
area of the nation.

There are those who enjoy freedom of movement. The
very well-heeled flit from summer home to winter residence
with the seasons. The very poor follow the annual crops
northward in one of the five streams of migratory labor, return to their winter lodgings, and set out with early spring
again. And almost five in every hundred of the population
now live strung out along the highways; but trailer-camp
dwellers are not the equivalent of settlers, any more than are
migratory workers. The geographical frontier is a thing of the
past.

Population now presses back upon the occupied centers.

Farm acreage declines, due to increased productivity of each artificially stimulated acre and the consequent abandonment of marginal lands. The small farmer gives way to the economies of agribusiness. With the perfecting of a machine for picking tobacco in 1969, the last remaining bastion of the small farm fell. In those remaining instances that require hand labor, migrants supply it, and the transients' shelter replaces the farmstead.

Where do the displaced go? To the cities. And what do they do? They do not stake out a homestead and prove it up through years of arduous self-denial to the point of proud ownership. They join the crowded slum dwellers in the asphalt jungles of the nation, a family or two to a room, waiting for work or Welfare, and largely without hope or expectation. In winter they suffer frostbite. In summer they sit all night on the stoop to escape the fetid tenement.

For all their crowdedness, the multitudinous millions of the nation are lonely. They have no elbow room, no place else to go, no freedom to move about or to think or to just sit in privacy. The little intimacies of private enjoyment are not available. The rhythm of man and nature is absent: man has penetrated nature so completely as to isolate himself from the natural world. No small boy squeals with delight as the dew of early morning bathes his bare feet in the tall grass. No little girl lies tranquilly by a small stream on a summer afternoon, idly watching a patch of white fleece scud across the limitless blue. Having crowded out nature, man has nothing left but the crowd.

The things that might make even a crowded life endurable are also crowded out of life for numbers of people. Half of the black male population under thirty is unemployed, has no hope of ever being employed. For them, there is no expectation that one will ever be able to come home on a Friday night, toss a fat pay envelope on the kitchen table, and watch the proud light leap in a wife's quick glance. The weekend holds no hope of an ample breakfast followed by the renewing of the spirit in a friendly church and the long, pleasant gossip with neighbors. The weekend is a long stretch of time during which the darkness protects the mugger and the daylight only reveals the overturned garbage cans in the gutter.

Crowded together in the ghetto, with several families using the same unsanitary sanitary facilities, they find no escape from the constant pressure of people, people, people. A mother keeps one bare light bulb burning all night to keep marauding rats from biting her sleeping children. A teen-ager listlessly hangs around until a rooftop interlude with the needle leads to another act of thievery to support his habit. A husband walks away from it all, knowing that desertion is the poor man's divorce. And everywhere people are rootless, strangers in the midst of a crowd, surrounded by others like themselves, all sharing the poignant loneliness of the crowded society.

The feeling of loneliness, purposelessness, rootlessness in the midst of the milling masses is not limited to ghetto dwellers. Since all things are relative, the experience of crowded loneliness has its degrees of presence among an entire population. Commuter's fatigue claims the suburbanite. The teen-age son has cut all the grass his young life ever wants to see, and his own variant of the universal ennui of youth prompts him to do his girl-watching at the shopping center in company with others of the lonely crowd of loners who have "no place else to go and nothing else to do." The plight of the suburban housewife is eloquently related in current fiction. Few segments of the population are as apprehensive, edgy, "uptight," as the insecure young adult suburbanite, with a mortgage, a daily struggle with the rush hour morning and night, the mandatory evening Martinis, compulsory weekend recreation, and compulsive weekday philandering.

Few have better stated the facts or summarized the conclusions of the overcrowded life than Toffler in his *Future Shock*.

There are limits to the adaptability of the human endocrine system. Excessive stimulation of that system results in permanent and irreversible damage to one's ability to react successfully to new and swiftly changing situations. Psychological trauma is equally evident, as the crowded world crowds in. The phenomenon of loneliness in the midst of the crowd is only part of a syndrome closely associated with a deterioration of one's ability to cope with excessive stimulation.

The malaise is more than loneliness. It may begin with the sense of being alone in a crowd; but it is a confluence of all the uncertainties and anxieties of a swiftly altering succession of transient and transitory experiences. The accelerated thrust of a burgeoning technology pushes man through a succession of experiences with such rapidity of transience and intensity of impact that the only real satisfaction he has time to savor is the anticipation of the next happening. And even that passes from him, because transience demands immediacy of the next experience. Waiting is an aching void. In a world of crowds and of crowding events, the one thing that ultimately cannot be tolerated by the raw-nerved victim is a moment of nonevent.

So, the wheel comes full circle. In an ecology that is exploited by an exponentially accelerating technology, we become consumers not only of the no-deposit, no-return delivery system in consumer's goods. In all other things as well, we make no deposits and expect not to return. Permanence is nowhere, transience everywhere. Novelty assaults the finite senses in infinite demand for reaction. Space is crowded, time is crowded, experience crowds. Acquaintanceship seldom is given time to ripen into friendship, so that noninvolvement becomes an accustomed shield. Sensitivity to passing people or to the onslaught of events can no longer be maintained. We walk through the crowd with unseeing eyes, ears closed, mind turned off.

We go home to sit silent before the TV, tuning out the

news, of course—we can't stand to hear about all that. With uncurious detachment, we observe others in trouble, not wishing to get tangled up in their lives. We have enough troubles ourselves. Time comes when release is sought through self-indulgence or complaint. Initiative is dulled. Projection becomes a ready mechanism of escape. We put the blame on everyone else because we can't cope with ourselves. Thus does loneliness become its own justification as it reaches its own peculiar peak of fulfillment. Not only are we lonely in the crowded society: we insist on being loners.

At the end of the road of loneliness one is confronted with the fact that it goes nowhere. There is no escape.

3

No Hiding Place

Some think they can run away from it all. That ultimate despair that would be signaled by a galloping suicide rate has not
yet come; but large numbers seek escape.

The Naysayers

Among all the varieties of escapists, the most naïve and obtuse
are the business-as-usual denyers of reality. They see no gathering storm. Everything will come out in the wash, they say.
They forget that *we* are the wash. Nevertheless, they persist:

If there is any real danger, it is not our responsibility. After all, we have done everything we could. We have made life good for our children, saving them from another Great Depression, giving them good homes to live in, with all the things we never had. Thank goodness our son and two daughters aren't like the kids down the block. Ours are straight. We keep them that way. We play with them and talk with them. They trust us.

Down the block—that's another matter. We just keep our kids home, although we do worry about what may happen to them in school.

Sure, there's a generation gap. But we don't holler at our kids. We want them to be happier than we were. The world is full of so many things that would make a king happy; and we see to it that our children do not want for anything reasonable.

Of course, just lately, we've wondered what's going on behind that locked bedroom door when the hi-fi is turned up loud and the room smells funny the next morning; but we trust our son. We *have* to.

It's a great country. Never before in history has any nation given of its blood and treasure unselfishly for the welfare of others, seeking no territorial aggrandizement, as we Americans have done. We came to the aid of a beleaguered Europe and saved it from the Nazis. We stopped aggression in Korea and in Vietnam. If it hadn't been for us, the world would really be in bad shape.

Look at the way we rebuilt a devastated Europe after the war! They don't appreciate us, although we don't see why. If they did, they would do something when our dollar slips on the international exchange. Didn't we save the franc and the mark and the pound?

As for all this scare talk about the environment, it needs to be put in perspective. If you want to be able to drive your car when you please, or get around fast in airplanes, you have to put up with a certain amount of air pollution. And they are working on it. The Environmental Protection Agency knows more about it all than Whats-his-name who writes those books.

There may have been a few excesses, due to industrial care-lessness or agricultural greed; but they can be remedied without all this shouting.

Look at all the new products in the drug stores and super-markets. Pretty near three-quarters of them weren't even on the market twenty years ago. That comes because some people have imagination and initiative and work hard. They don't just sit around and complain.

The scientists who say there won't be any life in the seven seas by the end of this century are mistaken. Other reputable oceanographers disagree, even though there is little chance that mariculture will give us answers if agriculture fails.

Demographers forecasting general starvation within twenty years are wrong, just as the Reverend Mr. Malthus was wrong back there a couple centuries ago. Already, the birth rate is dropping in the United States; and the Supreme Court ruling on abortion will now make overpopulation impossible—at least in *our* sections of the nation. We can't speak for the ghettos, where children are running all over the place.

As for the Big Bomb scare, it's there all right; and a pretty good thing it is to have it there. It has kept other nations from attacking us. It kept the peace in Europe. The prime minister of England said so. It has preserved world peace (except for a few brush fires) for a third of a century. We should be grate-ful to the men of the Strategic Air Command, up there in their circling planes and down deep in their silos. It may be a "balance of terror" that keeps the peace; but it keeps it. As long as the other nations know that we have a massive reaction capability that will destroy them completely, they aren't going to attack us. We have to learn to live with the risks of peace.

The race question is nothing new. But it won't be solved by pampering people. Our forefathers came over here, worked hard and saved, and got ahead. Let others do the same, instead of asking for a handout and a free ride on Welfare. And why do they want to put their kids in school with ours? Is it be-cause they know we are better than they are? They are wrong if they think that. We believe they are just as good as we are, and that they should be proud of themselves and want to stay by themselves, the way we do. So why do they want to bus their kids to our neighborhood? And we aren't about to let anybody force our kids to be bused thirty miles round-trip each day to some inferior ghetto school, either.

Everybody knows that the trouble with colored people is that their families don't function. Moynihan proved that. Their men don't support their women. Their women just sit home and have babies to get more out of Welfare. And we have to pay for it.

We have nothing against colored people. People like Ralph Bunche, we wouldn't mind living next door to. But if we made it the hard way, what's the matter with others doing the same? They should realize that riots and ripping off and mugging aren't the way to win friends.

Yes, we admit that sometimes we feel a little edgy. Things do get out of hand once in a while; and just now they seem to be upset some. But we don't use a lot of tranquilizers and we only pop an occasional pill and strictly as prescribed by the family physician.

Screaming won't cure things. These prophets of doom shouldn't get all that much time on the TV. Without them, we'd be a lot better off. The good old virtues of quiet and contentment should be cultivated.

Along with self-reliance and hard work, of course.

Unfortunately, the course of events will answer the nay-sayers. If that were all there was to it, they could be given their hour of equal time, and their plaints dismissed. That is not all there is to it.

Those who underestimate the peril of the human condition stand in the way of constructive remedy. By denigrating the men and women who warn of a diminishing future, they undercut all personal and social effort designed to avert catastrophe. They negate redemptive hope. Global and national crises will not disappear simply because the bland make themselves blind. Whether it be naïveté or obtusity or moral myopia that keeps them from seeing the gathering storm, the naysayers are a principal part of the problem. They are escapists.

The "Lumpenbourgeoisie"

The past decade has spawned what Toffler calls "the surfeit of subcults" among the younger generation. They appear mainly among the children of the white middle class, the children of the naysayers. They are the *Lumpen* who Webster's defines as

> an amorphous group of dispossessed and uprooted individuals set off by their inferior status from the economic and social class with which they are identified.

Dispossession is psychological, amounting to psychic trauma. It sometimes leads to disinheritance. Uprootedness is psychological and physical as well—not merely in dropping out, but in running away. A common trait runs through all of the cults and subcults. It is a sense of rejecting a society that is believed to be rejecting them. It is rootlessness, plus not wanting to be rooted. It is a feeling of inferiority that demands companionship only with peers, with those who also are rootless and rejected. Camaraderie makes all equals of each other, and togetherness makes the *Lumpen* equal to any.

Charles Reich sees all this as a justifiable and necessary revolution that will result in *The Greening of America*. The book is addressed to all of us, but it is an apologia for the *Lumpenbourgeoisie*. Three hundred pages are devoted to a restatement of the Marxian thesis together with a liberal admixture of contemporary insights into the meaning of the corporate state and galloping technology. It is a brilliant synthesis, erudite and urbane. The burden of it was said somewhat more succinctly than either Marx or Marcuse or Reich has put it, in the words of sixteenth-century Étienne de la Boétie: "Resolve to serve no more, and you are at once freed."

From his extended logical-historical-sociological-philosophical analysis and synthesis, Reich attempts to lead the *Lumpen* in a leap of faith. He asserts that what is needed to bring Utopia is neither the manipulatory power of procedures nor the power of politics nor that of street fighting, but "the power of new values and a new way of life." The assertion of faith has no connection in logic with the first three hundred pages of the book.

Indeed, if he were to have been faithful to dialectical materialism, he could not have made his particular leap of faith. He is doubtless correct in asserting that young America must somehow learn the skills necessary to identify and clarify, if not reconcile, conflicts in its own value systems. He correctly identifies this as the crucial effort. But he is wrong in attempting to ground this particular assertion of faith in the necessities of neo-Marxian analysis.

Lesser errors also flaw the book. There are many more varieties of the *Lumpenbourgeoisie* in the United States today than the single life-style that he advocates. The life-style and value system of the bronzed surfer is a compelling symbol for some; but not all, by any means. The black leather jacket of the cyclers, the denim–and–tennis-shoe costume of the campus, the variations on the theme of cast-off military uniforms or Camp from the (allegedly) Gay Nineties—the variety of costume alone is interminable. And the end is not yet in sight. Reich's beachcomber-surfers with their tanned bodies and free-with-nature attitudes may appear to him to be the best of the cults and subcults. They may be the only ones whose efforts will lead to the fresh start for America as he sees it. His book would have been more helpful if he had said so, and explained why. An irrational leap of faith is not enough. Utopia does not hang on a skyhook—not if it is to be taken seriously.

Reich puts his faith in the communes. There are thousands of them. They differ. And few last. Many have been disbanded because they had no defenses against the predatory violence that preyed upon them. Walden II has many copies, few successful emulations.

The parasitical position of the *Lumpen*, their refusal to be part of a productive society, their reliance on charity or checks from home or Welfare or scrounging in the garbage and the city dump for sustenance—the parasitical position of the *Lumpen* does not reassure a society that needs all the strength of its young. If some want to go through life as hitch-hikers, others have to provide the cars and drivers. Even Reich advises his ideal adventurers to return, once a month or so, to the comforts of a hot bath and a good steak at some motel. In this respect, he is very much like Thoreau, whose not infrequent visits back to the loaded table of the boardinghouse in town were thought by him not to be inconsistent with the idyllic intervals of asceticism at Walden Pond. But the remora merely attaches himself to the belly of the shark. He does not tell the shark where to go or on what to use his teeth. Not from those who withdraw from society will the leadership and strength for national renewal come.

The simplification of life is a central aim of the revolution that is to green America. Most of those who seek to simplify life succeed only in impoverishing it. They do not escape from life—only from its responsibilities. The lemmings are escapists.

All of which does not mean that, because Reich appears to fall short of a satisfactory prognosis for the American future, there is little use in talking about the *Lumpenbourgeoisie*. On the contrary, a very significant section of the college-age generation has been thrust into this category by the processes of home, school, and society. Alienated from what they consider to be the mainstreams of life, lonely in a crowded world, they drop out. Some run away. They reject the affluent society with its destructive effluents. They reject the racial caste that separates them from their black brothers and sisters, even though they are not always eagerly welcomed by their peers in the other caste. They eschew violence in international affairs, so they refuse military service. They will not use violence in interpersonal affairs, so they are brutalized and victimized by a violent society. They seek to escape from the general human condition; but in running away there is no escape.

The *Lumpenbourgeoisie*, as a part of the younger generation of the white middle class, most clearly exhibit the consequences of the malaise that pervades our moment in time. They are liberally interspersed with, and at times dominate, the remainder of their fellow students in college. There can be no successful coping with the problems of the campus that does not take them into account.

The "Lumpenproletariat"

The term is Marxian, the fact, American. The disenchanted *Lumpenproletariat* of contemporary American society is drawn mainly from the Black working class. Their emergence on campus in relatively large numbers is a result of institutional inadvertence stimulated by good intentions.

Responding to the idealism of the civil rights movement of the 1960s, college and university administrators and faculties undertook to redress long-standing imbalances in their student bodies. They recruited black students instead of waiting for them to come. Within one student generation, enrollments of black students in predominantly white institutions leaped upward 110 percent.

But there weren't enough "qualified" students to go around. Scarcely more than 10 percent of the population was black; and among that 10 percent, most were poor and poorly educated. The new recruiting devices and pressures quickly exhausted the list based on SAT scores. Competition between institutions for well-prepared black freshmen became even more acrimonious than the perennial struggle for athletes.

Large metropolitan institutions like the City College of New York had long welcomed the black student who could "make it." They took pride in providing extensive opportunities for the poorly prepared and the underachieving to come in by the back door of the evening session, where admission standards were less strict and courses and examinations could be repeated without penalty until the attainment of a stated average enabled the newly equipped student to transfer to the day session. And there were always a few black students who had managed to rise above the handicaps of indifferent elementary and secondary schooling, to enter as regular freshmen. Then came the new campus consciousness, a result of the civil rights movement, stimulated also by a new degree of concern growing out of the urban riots. And at precisely that same time, the same stimuli were leading the prestigious colleges and universities to make their own forays of recruitment into the ghettos, to lure the ablest students with fat scholarships and institutional mystique. The stream of able black students into the large urban institutions dwindled to a trickle. New devices for provisional admission and intensive remedial work were initiated, in a belated effort to correct at once the inequities of the public school systems.

All of this meant that a new breed of black college students was recruited. Whereas most of the black students in predominantly white institutions had formerly come from the numerically small black middle class (and from the homes of those who aspired to get into that middle class), the incoming black students now were drawn increasingly from the black working class. The colleges and universities were not prepared for the new breed of black student. They were unprepared psychologically. They were unready institutionally.

Psychologically, the new black proletarian on campus was

unlike his black predecessor. He did not aspire to climb into a white man's world. He was contemptuous of the middle classes, both white and black. Good manners, which had been the hallmark of the middle-class black *bourgeoisie*, were regarded by the newly arriving proletarian as signs of weakness and lack of race pride. He would not kowtow, smile, and feign a friendship he did not feel. He was in a strange new element, an academic world with its polite manners and correct grammar and competitive grading system, all waiting to catch him up. He came from the rigors and dangers and relaxed standards of the ghetto, where daily survival depended not on polite conformity but on eternal vigilance. The soft openness of the white man's campus confronted him with problems never before faced. He was uneasy, testy, belligerent.

The institutions, having put themselves to considerable effort in order to adjust entrance requirements, supply necessary remedial services, and guarantee financial support for the poorly prepared and poverty-marked black student, had naïvely expected (if they had thought about it at all) that the new flood of black students would be grateful for the fine opportunities that had been made for them. When brash rejection met their condescension, college administrators and teachers were shocked.

The new dimensions of self-awareness among the *Lumpenproletariat* emphasized the problem. The civil rights movement had awakened great expectations that were unsatisfied. Inner-city riots over a series of hot summers had enhanced their feelings of racial self-respect and intensified their antagonisms toward Whitey. In their high schools, back there in the ghetto, they had already learned the meaning of group violence as a catharsis and catalyst.

But this predominantly white campus was something else. Its standards of conduct, its modes of dress, its value system, its whole ethos and tone were white middle class. It was as though the institution were saying to the black working-class man and woman, "Welcome to *our* way of life!" The response should have been foreseen. It was not—and therefore when warm courtesy was answered with obscene expletives, mutual exasperation developed. The *Lumpenproletariat* found the campus even less congenial than did the *Lumpenbourgeoisie*.

A black student wrote home to her mother to complain that she was tired of being treated as Exhibit A of her race. She was fed up with the smiling little white co-ed who plumped down next to her just before class and said sweetly, "Now, tell me what it feels like to be black." There was no soul food in the cafeteria. Behind the desks of power and position on campus, there was not a single black face, and few among the full professors. The curriculum included a whole lot about ancient Greece and Rome, but nothing about ancient Africa.

The members of the *Lumpenproletariat* began to draw themselves together in self-protection. They sat together in the cafeteria—didn't the white fraternities and sororities do the same? They demanded separate dormitories—never mind that it was against the law. It was a white man's law, to be obeyed only when there was no alternative. On occasion, when exuberant white undergraduates engaged in heckling or other unkind exchanges, the black youth responded with his own weapons, trusted because ghetto-tested. His knife or his gun could be called upon. The whole nation sucked its breath shrilly when black students with guns stood straight and proud before the photographers that day at Cornell. *That* was something!

For all of this, the predominantly white campus was unprepared. Some administrators tried to meet the new violence with nonviolence. They found the devices of reason and dialogue were inadequate. Some tried to fend off growing uneasiness, until the moment of truth came and they called in the police. New deans and assistant deans were appointed over the

heads of their white colleagues, despite seniority and sometimes regardless of merit and qualifications, to create a new
institutional image. Black studies curricula were hastily improvised. Nothing worked. It was too late. The confrontation
had run its course up to that point: it had to continue to its
conclusions as the inner dynamics of the situation dictated.
Condescension had to be replaced by mature mutual respect
before black belligerence would subside. It was an angry time
on campus. It lasted for several years. Campuses will never be
the same.

In their own way, the *Lumpenproletariat* were running
away, trying to escape from a new reality with which they
could not cope. They had left the ghetto that spawned them
but were fish out of water on the white man's campus. So,
they read Eldridge Cleaver and Frantz Fanon and James Bald-
win and Albert Cleage and James Forman and William Brink
and Louis Harris and all the others in that excitingly fresh
group of young Black authors whose paperbacks began to fill
the shelves in the new bookstores. They banded together, ate
together, sang together, hoped together, and believed that
only black was beautiful.

They were spinning the threads of their own chrysalis, for
survival in an alien academe. They abandoned old hopes of
integration and became champions of the new separatism.
They created their own safe sanctuaries and escaped into
them.

The Revolutionaries

Some of the *Lumpen*, in both classes, developed a special quality of dedication and expectation that led them to fancy themselves as the vanguard of the new day, architects of the
coming revolution.

An oversimplification may here be introduced, merely to
make a point. Teodori's documentary history, *The New Left*,

gives five hundred closely packed pages of fine print to a descriptive record of the movement. Nowhere in those pages is that movement more accurately epitomized than in the words used by one of the movement's principal journalists and theoreticians. Having waged an unsuccessful campaign for political office, he was subjecting himself and his friends to his own extended and careful public analysis. He concluded with this comment:

> I think the main achievement of the campaign was that it was bold. Left liberal politics during the Cold War was characterized by fear, and our stance was arrogant. That's it.

Perhaps it is understandable that a movement that sees itself as attempting to destroy the arrogance of power should propose instead to stand on the power of arrogance. Certainly, no attempt to understand the posturing of the revolutionary romanticists today will succeed unless it takes as its point of entrance the feature that Robert Scheer deftly identifies. According to him, the distilled essence of the movement is its arrogance.

But no attempt to understand will be successful if, having identified arrogance as the dominant characteristic of the New Left, it then attempts either to write it off as irrelevant and ineffectual or to put it down with counterarrogance. On the contrary, the devotees of revolutionary thought have made an impression on the American campus that is bold and disruptive enough to warrant something more than indifference or arrogant disdain.

Many factors contribute to the growth and to the current resurgence of direct-action revolutionary efforts on the American campus. Among these factors, it is the offensive arrogance that most frequently piques college administrators and other Establishment-oriented figures; but what caused that arrogance?

Let the point be made by contrasting Robert Scheer with Frantz Fanon. In his *Wretched of the Earth*, the expatriate West Indian black psychiatrist stands in stark contrast to the American-born white journalist. Instead of Scheer's arrogance, Fanon gives his followers his own vision of the future in lyrical and deeply moving appeal to "a veritable collective ecstasy" of the new brotherhood. Old scores are rubbed out. Long-forgotten rivalries and hatreds are brought out into the open and exorcised. Forgiveness and reconciliation replace all quarrels and finally liquidate all grievances. Purging the traitor but welcoming the returning renegade, the revolution moves forward.

> Life is lived at an impossibly high temperature. There is a permanent outpouring in all the villages of spectacular generosity, of disarming kindness, and willingness, which cannot ever be doubted, to die for the "cause."

Out of the persecuted and oppressed colonial masses emerges "a confraternity, a church, a mystical body of belief at one and the same time." So prophesied Frantz Fanon.

Therein lies a principal difference, a sharp line of division, between the *Lumpenproletariat* and the *Lumpenbourgeoisie*, as expressed, respectively, by the revolutionary blacks and the white New Left. It is true that, in its beginnings, the New Left movement was motivated by deep moral purpose, by a heightened sense of outrage; but that it also made its great appeal to the ideal of the "Beloved Community," as the Port Huron Statement put it. The movement was nearly five years old before the Black Liberationists broke off from the white revolutionaries, leaving the latter to go their own way, somewhat perplexed and offended at being rejected along with white liberals. But while the Black Liberation movement went forward on the strength of Fanon's dreams of the mystical brotherhood, plus Garvey's pride in blackness, the whites of the New Left found it increasingly difficult to hold to their own version of the inclusive brotherhood. They had to make guerrilla warfare against the System, and particularly against selected personal targets in that system. Brotherly love is not the most advantageous psychological armor for waging fratricidal war. Thus it came about that, by 1967, the movement among whites had become arrogant, brittle, and fractionized; while the forces of the Black Liberation, looking only within the racial group for empathy, drew the brothers and sisters together in a "permanent outpouring" of mutually reenforcing affection and pride.

There are other differences, and some similarities, between the white New Left and the Black Liberation movements of the 1960s and 1970s. On the American campus, the two forces at times converged but never congealed. They had greater divergence than commonality of purpose; and in addition to their racial differences, they were separated by differences of class. They were both *Lumpen;* but one was middle-class, the other working-class; one white, the other black. Common disaffection with the Establishment was an insufficient bond.

In the 1960s, Students for a Democratic Society was the principal organ of the New Left on campus. Disruption, amply reported on television and in the press, was their main stock in trade; but an incredibly provocative series of national and international events fed the fires of discontent, while an equally incredible series of Establishment blunders on campuses, together with the bungling interference of angry politicians, increased institutional vulnerability. It must be added that not the least effective among all the factors that gave SDS and its affiliates their continuing viability, and which provoked Black Liberation to some of its more extreme expressions, in the years since 1968, has been the disdainful and arrogant alliterative rhetoric coming from high places.

The failing among liberals and conservatives alike—a failing that has characterized the whole Establishment, both its supporters and its loyal opposition—is a general tendency to write off the New Left and Black Liberation as being excrescences, not of the essence, instead of attempting to listen and to understand and to hold a meaningful dialogue about what troubles the alienated.

Faced with general rejection and general attack, both the New Left and the Black Liberation movements have reacted understandably. Up to the moment of this writing, neither of the two *Lumpen* groups has been open to overtures of reconciliation from the Establishment, even when approaches have belatedly been attempted. Just as any self-respecting person, on leaving employment involuntarily, shouts defiantly, "You can't fire me! I quit!.," so, when the *Lumpen* groups refuse to be coopted by an Establishment that has rejected them and which they have rejected, they are only reacting like human beings with self-respect. They walk out, looking for a place to do their own thing in their own way.

To be sure, they indulge in a great deal of rhetoric about what they will do when they get ready. The fantasy of revolution is fed by feelings of resentment. Whether arrogant words will be followed by desperate deeds remains to be seen in the history this nation is about to make. But as of the winter of 1973, one must evaluate both the New Left and Black Liberation essentially as movements of retreat and withdrawal into the world of fantasy and embittered rhetoric, rather than as movements with a promising program of action.

Such evaluation is neither moralistic nor ideological. It is pragmatic, empirical. Two considerations support the judgment: (1) a nation that is irrevocably committed to democratic ends and to democracy as process cannot forever refuse to yield to moral insistence from the outraged—there is hope *in extremis;* and (2) all the military power lies with the dominant, not the disenchanted. Revolutionary fantasies are likely to remain just that—fantasies. The realities of the situation expose the revolutionaries as actual escapists.

The Drug Nonculture

Interwoven with other variants, the life-style of drug addiction plagues the homes, schools, colleges, and the general society. It is not a phenomenon limited to any one class, race, religion, or national or ethnic group. Neither is it confined to any one section of the country (although it has its areas of greater concentration that contrast with other areas of tardier arrival). It has been returning from Southeast Asia with an estimated two out of every ten veterans. It was already waiting in the hometowns, in the high schools and the junior high schools. New York City has more deaths of teen-agers from heroin than from all the childhood diseases combined. Heroin is fast becoming the leading cause of deaths, nationally, in the fifteen-to-thirty-five age group.

Today's assignment for a high school student is not in the textbook. It is in the needle. Fewer users of heroin are found in college populations because, by definition, a heroin addict is a dropout from society. While he is still of compulsory school-attendance age, he is classified as a high school student, gets his fix at the school, even does some of his pilfering and thievery necessary to support the habit while at school. At the college level, there is a wider use of amphetamines and barbiturates than of heroin; but no knowledgeable college administrator denies that the drug nonculture has become resident on campus.

There is enough being written and said about the peril of pandemic drug abuse so that the statistics and medical arguments need not here be rehearsed. It is sufficient to note that one of the end products of contemporary society is the drug nonculture which, as it grows, threatens to destroy the cream of the oncoming generation.

Promoted by pushers and defended by its favorite gurus, the drug nonculture originated in the nation's youth. One of its original defenses was the assertion that the younger generation was only copying the example of its elders. The quoted aphorism ran thus: "The typical American is one whose daily intake of pep pills exceeds his daily intake of tranquilizers by just the right margin to enable him to make his weekly visit to the psychiatrist." If one's parents were into the drug thing like that, what's wrong with us kids doing *our* thing?

The cruel truth is that children *are* following their parents' example in many instances, as they seek escape from the bombarding stimuli of life, turning to soft and hard drugs; but this does not mean that their conduct is correct. It only gives it a specious defensibility. It indicts the older generation along with their offspring.

Moreover, the drug nonculture has now been around long enough for the production of its own young adults. And it pushes downward, through peer-group pressure and emulation, into the junior high schools—and below. The abusive use of drugs is no longer a matter of the younger generation appropriating the less desirable vices of its elders. It concerns individuals of a considerable age-spread, as it embraces their peers, from the preteens and early teens on up into the thirties, possibly the early forties. No generation, alone, can now claim that it is only copying its elders in trying to escape from a troubling world. The older members of the drug subcult are already parents themselves. More than five hundred infants born in New York City in 1971 had been addicted before birth. They were born as junkies.

Closely associated with the drug nonculture is an increase in the rate of crime. The habit requires an almost daily process of burglary and fencing, or of mugging and robbery, to supply the cash for the daily fix, since the junky cannot keep a steady job but must have a steady income. Of even deeper concern is the fact that no generally effective means of curing drug addiction has yet been devised. Heroic rescues are being made; but the numbers of youth annually entering the shadow world of addiction far exceeds the numbers salvaged.

Perhaps some nonaddictive substitute miracle drug will be found, which will liberate the addict in a way that methadone does not? This forlorn hope expresses one of the great delusions of our times. It expects ultimate answers to come from improved technology, in this instance, medical technology. It looks to men of science to produce the miracle cure. Not even Ponce de León indulged his fancy that extensively; but neither was he enslaved to the needle.

The greater tragedy of the situation is not only the loss of so many of the youth of the nation. It is that persons permanently addicted—whether to heroin or to some substitute like methadone—are people whose will to resist has been destroyed. The human condition demands a supreme assertion of the will to achieve. Members of the drug nonculture are not, and cannot supply, the conquering legions of the new day.

Instead, they are escapists, in the fullest sense of the term. They find a means of avoiding the drab and meaningless round of life, or of eluding the irritations of awareness of insoluble problems. But the problems persist. The addict does not find escape. He has intermittent oblivion, punctuated by the craving for another fix. And the problems remain.

For each person caught up in addiction, his plight is actually an expression of the general crisis of values. The trade-offs are all too clear. Whether to fill the void of an uneventful day, or to escape the sounds and smells and sights of a repulsive environment, or to identify with his peers, or to defy authority, or for whatever reason, the addict makes his choices. A twenty-year-old in Harlem says he shoots horse because he can't stand the smell of urine in the stairwell and the stink of garbage in the kitchen. An eighteen-year-old in Scarsdale says she does it because all her friends do. A high school senior in Missoula says he uses drugs because they are there, and because They say he can't. The life-style and value systems of the straight and the square are held in contempt.

The Establishment has not yet found an answer. Drug addiction continues. It grows. Escapism victimizes the person and weakens the nation.

Some few graduates from addiction have learned to live without drugs. They exhibit the heroic resolution without which the human condition will remain perilous and become pathetic. They are living refutations of the canard that the needle is the way out. Sometimes an individual person acts alone in winning his way back to society. More often, his return is made possible by membership in a reinforcing group.

Religious Apocalypticism

One group that has a remarkably effective rate of success in rescuing drug addicts is the movement familiarly called "Jesus Freaks." They usually prefer "Jesus People." Intensely evangelistic, this fundamentalist movement proselytizes vigorously. It has drawn its members almost exclusively from the *Lumpen-bourgeoisie*, and primarily from that part of the *Lumpen* that had become engulfed in the drug nonculture.

Apparently, the movement is of great assistance to its recruits in helping them to kick the drug habit. In more than fifteen hundred communes of the Jesus People from coast to coast, former drug addicts mingle with those who never were addicted, as the life of the community supplies their intellectual and spiritual needs. Their physical needs are met by the bounty of rejected parents, the Welfare rolls, the charity of local merchants, and daily scrounging and begging.

These are escapists, running from the drug nonculture, from parental domination, from a school or college experience that turned them off, from a complex of social problems they do not wish to face. An apocalyptic hope sustains them. Taking literally the eschatological sections of the New Testament, they await the Second Coming of the Messiah. Some have set the date. They engage in dedicated self-purification, awaiting the Day of Deliverance. None of the communes of the Jesus People has made a notable record of serving or salvaging the sorry world around them.

If the movement only saves a few thousand from the ravages of drug addiction, it will have served a useful purpose. Let it not be condemned as being of no value whatsoever. If—wild hope—the Jesus People should manage to supplant the drug nonculture entirely, that would be no small achievement. Or, if a more modest contribution were made, if only a few hundred thousand of our children were to be saved from the living death, that contribution to the general welfare would leave a grateful nation forever in their debt.

But if that were to be all that the Jesus People accomplished, it would not suffice. The dilemmas of the 1970s and beyond would still remain. Hamelin's children followed the Pied Piper —but so had the rats before them. Our children follow a piper and leave us with the rats. The *Lumpenbourgeoisie* who are siphoned off into the Jesus People's movement are lost to us and to society. The drug addiction and the alienation syndrome remain, together with the causes thereof. The problems that now confront us will destroy all of us—the Jesus People included—if all of us together do not solve them.

Saved from drugs? Yes. But saved for what and to what? To another form of escapism, another means of avoiding moral responsibility. The essential act of will has been made, but made for socially irrelevant and extraneous, even antisocial, ends. Like their forerunners in the first and second centuries, the Jesus People substitute eschatology for ethic. They escape from a cult that made opium the religion of the people by joining another cult that makes religion the people's opiate.

The fault of communes does not lie in the organizational pattern of communes as such. The contemporary commune is not necessarily made irrelevant or antisocial by being a commune. The *kibbutzim* of young Israel prove the contrary. The Beloved Community of the gathered can be the strength of a society, if the commune is organically linked to that society by a common sustaining purpose and by the practice of that purpose.

Neither is the commune, as such, made irrelevant by its temporariness. The wagon train drawn up in its nightly protective circle, or plodding its dusty miles westward, proved the contrary thesis. A commune formed for a defined temporary purpose can pass off the scene without loss when its aims have been reached, because the original expectation of something else at the end of the road was what gave the journey meaning.

Nor is it a Utopian hope that necessarily makes the rural retreat invalid or unviable. There was virtue and value in Oneida and Hopedale, Nashoba, the Wisconsin Phalanx, the North American Phalanx at Red Bank—and many more. Brook Farm and Icaria, Equity and Utopia (Ohio) and Modern Times (Long Island) each had qualities that the communes of today's *Lumpen* lack. Delta Farms at least proved that money could be raised in New York City to support an interracial farm in Mississippi. But the *Lumpenbourgeoisie* of today have no Utopia, in either sense of the word: they lack both a defined objective and a lively hope of actualizing the dream. Especially do the Jesus People emphasize the vulnerability of the commune that has no earthly expectations of success—they are the precise opposite, in this respect, of the Shakers and the Hutterites. For today's *Lumpen*, Utopia is beyond life, not in it.

Nor does withdrawal from the general society always invalidate a commune. Religious monasticism has been its own justification through the centuries; but enduring monasticism is rooted in social purpose, in something more than survival. It is an exaggeration, perhaps, but not an unfair caricature to suggest that the contemporary commune of the *Lumpen* resembles nothing quite so much as a den of Cub Scouts tenting overnight in the backyard, savoring the thrill of being outside the protective parental roof after dark while still enjoying Mom's milk and cookies, and all the while pretending that each alley cat is a crouching tiger, each mutt a slavering timber wolf. Pretense or self-pity makes a feeble foundation.

It may be that some of the communes will survive, as Brookdale did not, but as monasteries do. It may be that there is a durability in the life-style not demonstrated at Haight-Ashbury. The Woodstock Nation has yet to prove that it is America's bright future, or even that it offers a viable future for the *Lumpen* themselves. Rebels without a cause, whose Utopia is escape, whose communal society is dysfunctional and whose values turn out to be dysvalues, their rejoicing is too loud to be permanent, their tears too salty to be transient. Many a commune offers a friendly pad to a runaway on the move; but there is nothing socially redemptive in the hobo camp.

Almost by definition, the yearnings of the *Lumpen* are destined to be disappointed. Since it is in the transience of the event that they search for meanings, when the happening is over, it leaves emptiness. Only a deeper frustration and a wilder longing remain, unsatisfied and insatiable.

The secular variety of the commune requires for its viability a high degree of the virtues on which the established society is allegedly built—hard work, self-discipline, obedience to rules and regulations. A community in revolt against established society has great difficulty in using the virtues it rejects. Some communes resolves this inner contradiction, achieving a dedicated cohesiveness that gives them continuity. Most do not. They founder on the rock of anarchy because they choose anomie.

The religious communes of the Jesus People avoid some of the pitfalls into which the general run of voluntary communities of the disenchanted children of the white middle class fall; but their variant of monastic life is vitiated by its apocalypticism.

Escapism generates its own defeat. It is also fraught with social disaster.

Romanticism

Some try to escape the human condition by embracing a romantic faith in technology. These persons are not a revival of the Technocrats of the 1930s. That earlier breed of naïve sophisticates put its faith in a controlled technocracy in which the Technocrats were to be kings. It was a blend of naïveté and totalitarianism: naïve in believing that all the major problems could be solved through technological control, and totalitarian in the exercise of its proposed controls. For example, since it was known that a razor blade could be manufactured that would last for fifty years, why wasn't it done? Because manufacturers wanted to stay in business and continue to make profits. To market the indestructible razor blade would be to cut the future market to that small group of adolescents who annually began to shave—once all the shaving adults had been supplied. This was contrary to the whole profit system. Therefore, the indestructible razor blade would never be marketed. Technology could supply that blade; but capitalistic individualism would not permit it. Destructive waste was essential to the system. What was needed was for the whole productive system to be taken over by the technocrats. Perfecting a perfectible technology, they could supply man's wants without waste and without ostentatious consumption. Their society would, of course, have to be fascistic. But the trains would run on time. There would be no more Depressions.

Today's true believers do not turn to socialism or fascism to bring salvation through technology. They appear to believe that there is nothing basically wrong with the technological revolution, except that it hasn't gone far enough or fast enough. Technology, they say, needs not control but liberation.

For example, politics must be kept out of decision-making. Technological truths should indicate choice. Item: When it is necessary to make a trade-off between clear-cutting the forests of the Bitter Root Mountains and selective-cutting at greater cost, the decision ought not to turn on a politician's judgment regarding the probable effect of increased lumber costs in holding back the number of housing starts in an election year. The technology that can cut the trees in great patches at lesser cost can also prevent erosion of the denuded mountains, forestall pollution of the trout streams, and institute a scientific system of tree farming that will ultimately produce more lumber more quickly and at less cost. The opinions of the Committee on Environmental Quality and the hopes of political candidates should not interfere, through the secretary of the interior, to make the decision on the basis of short-run political expediency.

The Gargantuan machines that strip vast acreages of mid-America to produce cheap coal can also be harnessed to restore land contours, replenish the fertility of the soil, reclaim the acreage for cultivation, make the land habitable again. Technology, used for social ends, uninhibited by extraneous forces of politics and morals, can solve our problems. So runs the argument of the romanticists.

They overlook, or deprecate, the importance of ecological balance. Particularly, they do not fully credit the importance of differences in the time scale as between the natural processes of the ecocycle and the artificial processes of a forced technology. They seem to believe that today's and tomorrow's technology can provide man with a working substitute for nature. Within, say, twenty years (they appear to believe), technology could repair the damage and redress the balance of ravaged nature, when seventy million years or so have been required since the Pleistocene Age to create what a single season's cutting of timber or of strip-mining destroys.

The most systematically developed defense of this romantic faith in technology is presented in the turgid and involuted prose of Buckminster Fuller. Since the globe is, in fact, a spaceship, man ought to take command—not just ride on it, with due concern for preserving its resources; but take command, use those resources in their limitless possibilities as technology foresees those possibilities. That man has the capabilities to do this, Fuller seems never to doubt. That technology could, if released, insure limitless expansion, he appears to believe. He advocates a holistic approach to the ecosystem, using science and technology in their fully developing potentials, directed by the wisest insights that technological man can invent. Fuller extols the endless extensibility of technological process, affirming that man ought not to deny himself anything that can be made possible. There are for him no limits to the total population that can be accommodated on the globe: after we've occupied it all horizontally, we need only to begin piling up vertically. New technological answers will always be ready as new problems of ecology emerge.

Fuller's ideas tumble across the pages in torrents of complexity, half a hundred notions all trying to be expressed at once in a single sentence. That is his method of grasping reality. He comprehends totalities in all the complexities of their intricacies. He uses simultaneous expression of these totalities instead of linear argument. The resulting prose style is opaque. It therefore gives the impression of being profound. In this one respect—the opacity of his prose style—Fuller is like Marx. In both cases, readers are intimidated into believing that something that is so complex in its statement must be profound.

Not so. Man's dilemmas will not be answered by a galloping

technology via the exaltation and veneration of the synergistic omnirational coordinate system. Step back a moment and get a holistic view of Fuller's Utopia. If he were to be fully understood, and his opinions were to prevail, the globe would be a pleasant place for industrious ants, possibly for robots. Not for men. The geodesic dome does not a congenial Utopia make.

Those who allegedly follow Fuller's lead are, in their own way, taking a "trip" not too different from the escapist dreams of their acid-head compatriots who substitute psychedelic fantasy for concerted attack on the ills that beset us. Ideation, fantasy-structuring, verbalization, particularly when done with considerable showmanship and personal charisma, become diversionary rather than redemptive. To offer alleged insights and putative solutions that are more rhetoric than remedy is to be as misleading as the Robinsonadia type of Utopianism.

The solemn and somewhat ponderous sensitivities of Lewis Mumford come much closer to the truths of experience and the realities of the ecosystem than do Fuller's dramatic fantasies. Those who expose the dangers of a rampant technology are rendering a greater service to contemporary man than those who encourage the unlimited extension of the technological revolution.

Escapism, even on a grand and global scale, is still escapism.

The Refugees

As mechanization and industrialization made small farms marginal, and agribusiness supplanted the farmstead, rural citizens fled to the city. The number of farmsteads in the nation has been cut in half during the quarter-century ending in 1970. A disproportionate percentage of those fleeing from the country to settle in the cities have been black, the most easily displaced with the least to lose.

Arriving in the metropolis, they have aggravated the human

condition in the already congested ghetto. The ghetto has expanded, block by relentless block and neighborhood by changing neighborhood, as fleeing whites left for suburbia. And this locust plague of ex-urban runaways has settled down first in the nearer and then in the farther interstices of the suburbs, mile after stretching mile along the newly built Federally supported highways. All the old balances are destroyed, faster than new equilibria can be devised.

Let Long Island represent the nationwide problem of the suburban sprawl. Levittown and its numerous replicas gave young-marrieds their "chance in the country." A modest plot of grass to trim, a struggling tree or two to promise a future time of shade. A winding dead-end street safe for the children. The nearby superhighway to take the breadwinner to his work and bring him home again. Gone were the dirty and crowded and dangerous city streets. Gone the leaden sky and the sulfurous air. With a job and a mortgage and high hopes, the ex-urbanite settled in.

Others also settled. More and more, they came. The glutted superhighways became extended parking lots during rush hours. Burgeoning families increased the school tax. Public utilities were strained beyond capacity. So, opposition to further development began to mount. As always, the latest arrivals were the strongest opponents of those who came just behind them.

The crisis of the water supply illustrates the entire point. The developers' dream and the ex-urbanites' Shangri-la promises to become the homesteaders' nightmare. Nassau County, that portion of Long Island that is nearer to New York City, is more densely settled than its neighbor, Suffolk County, the eastern portion of the Island. In the last two years, the residents of Nassau County have begun to be alarmed over a receding water table. They fear that the time is not far off when the annual rainfall will no longer supply the needs of a growing Nassau County population. To impound fresh water anywhere on the mainland and pipe it to Nassau County at a price consumers could afford appears unfeasible. Likewise, desalinization of seawater is too expensive. (Only the United States Government at Guantanamo Bay can afford such luxury.) Nassau therefore turns to Suffolk County, asking that an equitable sharing of all the water table of the entire Island give respite to Nassau County's needs. The folks of Suffolk will have none of that. Already, they get up earlier to commute farther at greater expense and effort, merely to enjoy the same degree of amenities of suburban living as their Nassau friends. Suffolk must look to its own future needs, when its own growing population will require rationing of its own limited water supply.

Jacob and Laban solved the problem of a limited water supply by erecting a cairn at Mizpah as a no-trespassing sign, and each taking his flocks and herds in an opposite direction to find new water holes. But Jacob and Laban were nomads, not refugees.

Nowhere is the option of Mizpah open to today's refugees. Tied to jobs, they cannot commute beyond the point of feasible daily round trips. They are mortgaged to specific pieces of real estate. They are no longer nomadic. As refugees from the city, they must now stand and fight. Long Island's water dispute is but one example of the anxieties of megalopolis. Water, soil, and air are being preempted by refugees arriving from the city. The actual boundaries between city and surrounding towns exist only on maps. Former political divisions have become anachronistic. Megalopolis stretches from Boston to Richmond in an unbroken succession of occupied territory, dotted by hamlets stubbornly defending themselves as last havens of retreat, and punctuated by congestions of population that once were proud cities. Within each city there is the decaying and decadent inner city of misery, thronged with its refugees from the farm.

Everybody is a refugee, trying to escape. He moves when

he thinks he can improve his lot, can find an opening, can borrow the down payment and keep up the mortgage, can stand the commuting. If he can't become a refugee, he stays where he is and feels like a cornered rat. The inner city is uptight. Suburbia is uptight. None is immune from the uneasiness of the decade. All would welcome an escape. The mentality of the refugee rules.

No one is immune, because there is no escape. The open frontier is no longer out there somewhere. The more the refugee runs away, the more he finds that the nomadic age is past. Water holes are too small and too few, herds and flocks too large and too many. Problems multiply. The statistics of the situation appear in the public media with mesmerizing regularity. The simple, irrefutable fact of life in the 1970s and beyond is that there is a diminishing amount of unoccupied living space either in the city or outside it, and consequently no easy place in which to run away from the troubles of urban life.

Flight to the islands of the South Seas or the Great Barrier Reef? Not for many of us. To Australia? Are you ready for the rigors of the outback and for the upsurgence of Australia's aboriginal population that will greet you with that continent's variation of the race problem you are running away from? To Canada then? Or Alaska? Perhaps a few millions could be absorbed. They probably will be. For those few millions, the day of difficulty may be postponed a few years, provided the Eskimo does not claim his full birthright and provided that English- and French-speaking Canadians find a viable future together. Well, then, Central or South America or Africa? Doubtless a number of the independently rich can live there in opulence amid poverty until the day of reckoning catches up to them. That leaves the Far East, where the most densely populated areas already teem.

Then why not send the surplus population as pioneer spacemen, to populate the galaxy? The proposal is redolent of the

1920s, when those who wanted to send all Negro Americans "back to Africa" discovered that if they were to take the combined merchant marines of America and Europe and have them ply ceaselessly between New York City and African ports, they would not quite be able to take care of the annual *increase* in the population of Negro Americans. Spacemen departing for the nearest star would, instead of relieving the crush of people on this earth, have to replenish their own generations during the extended journey.

There is no escape. There is no hiding place. Not in denying the existence of the problems. Not in copping out into the *Lumpenbourgeoisie*. Not in dropping out into the drug nonculture. Not in joining a mind-blowing eschatological movement. Not in singing the sirens' song of technology. Not in fleeing from the inner city—or to it. Not in running away to anywhere else than where we are.

No Hiding Place

Realization that there is no escape from problems that are real, that press, and that are potentially fatal leads some persons to turn and face them. Others, when they find that they cannot run away, go from skepticism to cynicism, pessimism, resignation, despair.

The student generation that populates the campus in the early 1970s is a harbinger of the decade. It has among it many who turn from active involvement and activist agitation to introverted self-analysis. The campus is ominously quiet. Some students in their passivity appear almost sullen, withdrawn into the inner cities of refuge. University administrators who have only begun to adjust satisfactorily to student demands that the institution become relevant to the human condition now find themselves required to reverse the field, to use the institution to shelter students from the human condition. In this longing for the soft protection of the institutional cocoon, escapists are yearning to return to the womb. They are wishing they had never been born. Not yet.

But no institutional chrysalis will answer their problems. They are not islands, entire unto themselves. They are parts of the whole. Whatever threatens or diminishes any man, threatens and diminishes all. There is no escape.

It is precisely because the campus has within it many resources of resilient hope, other than its institutional pinions that shelter the refugees, that a reexamination of the institutions of higher education is imperative. Will they discover that they, too, are escapist, refusing to face the human condition?

4

Planting the Groves of Academe

Each college or university looks back proudly to its origins, fondly recalling its particular legend of a time when there were giants in the earth and the ground trembled gently to their tread. Selected archetypes will illuminate this inquiry.

A Founding Father

Born, baptized, educated, and ordained an Anglican, John Henry Newman (1801–1890) became a Roman Catholic at the age of forty-four. At age fifty-three he accepted an invitation from the Irish bishops to go to Dublin as rector of the

Catholic university about to be established there. He left his native England, but brought with him his scholarly prejudices, his religious predilections, and a consuming passion for justice.

Arriving in Ireland, he was challenged by those whom he called "wise and good men." What possible use could there be in his mission? "There is no class of persons who *need* a University," they said. Their syllogism ran thus: A university is for the gentry only. All the gentry in Ireland are "strangers," Protestants from England. Therefore, a Catholic university in Ireland has no possible clientele. His counselors questioned, "Whom will you get to belong to it? Who will fill its lecture rooms?"

Father Newman had his answer. On its surface and in most details, the new institution would appear to be very much like Oxford, which had trained him and where he had taught. The one noticeable difference would be the dominant position of theology among the disciplines. Newman conceded that "an academical system, formed upon my model, will result in nothing better or higher than in the production of that anti-quated variety of human nature and remnant of feudalism, as they consider it, called 'a Gentleman' "; but he had an additional goal. In Great Britain and Ireland, he declared, Catholics had been "robbed, oppressed, and thrust aside for centuries." They had not been admitted to an education that would have equipped them with "the qualifications withal, social and intellectual, which are necessary both for reversing the forfeiture and for availing themselves of the reversal. The time has come," he thundered, "when this moral disability must be removed!"

And where would he get his students? "We will give them lectures in the evening," he replied. "We will fill our classes with the young men of Dublin." To the working-class young men, who were employed by day and could study only at night, he would open the university's halls by the light of the flickering wick. Not the sons of the gentry of today but the fathers of the gentry of tomorrow, would be his students. A radical overriding purpose infused his *Idea of a University*.

The Evening Classes (Newman's own capitalization, reflecting his own emphasis) began as the university opened; but they died quickly, due to poor publicity, bad weather, and faculty recalcitrance. But Newman made up in stubborn perseverance what he lacked in administrative foresight. He kept at it. By the end of the second academic year, the Academical Senate had come around to his point of view. The Evening Classes were formally authorized, established with their own set of bylaws. And as the fourth academic year began, young working-class Irish Catholics thronged the lecture hall to hear the rector address them. Knowing where his potential scholars were to be found, he had set about to make the university available to them on terms and under conditions they could meet. He had done this deliberately for a revolutionary purpose. He intended to use higher education to prize the locks and hinges off the gates of the gentry class, to provide open entrance by educated working-class young men.

To his mind, the hidden agenda were just as important as the more obvious purposes of the institution. In this opinion, the founder of Dublin University was not different from those who laid foundations at many other institutions. They, too, had their own dualities of purpose.

Definitions and Distinctions

Few persons claim to know the meaning of the terms "university" and "liberal arts college." Those who claim to know, disagree.

In this discussion, and for the remainder of this volume, we shall refer to a university as being a collection of colleges and professional schools authorized to grant professional and advanced degrees and carrying on research. We shall use the term "liberal arts college," to refer to an undergraduate insti-

tution authorized to grant the bachelor's degree and which has
no separately organized professional or commercial schools
described within the covers of its own catalog. These pragmatic differences reflect with reasonable accuracy current
American usage. These definitions do not, however, guarantee
that a particular institution will fall easily within the categories
as defined. The purpose of the definitions is to provide tools
for analysis rather than to classify individual institutions.

The choice of terms is arbitrary, but not without logic. In
Roman law, the term *universitas,* from which "university"
appears to have been derived, means simply a corporation, an
entity that, whether made up of only one unit or of several, is
treated under the law as though it were a single unity. All the
homilies and commencement speeches that attempt to read
additional meanings into the word are just that. "University"
is one of Humpty Dumpty's portmanteau words. It can be
made to carry whatever baggage of meaning a speaker stuffs
into it.

The University of Paris was the first to lay claim to an ex-
clusive right to use the term in defining itself, and thereby to
begin to read extraneous meanings into the word. All the
others (Padua, Salamanca, Cologne, or whatever) failed to
embrace *all* the arts and sciences, said the academics of Paris,
whereas we include them all, thereby becoming truly universal and therefore being the first and only genuine university. Arguments of this sort, not limited to medieval
Europe, account for an occasional practice that equates university with universality, making variety, inclusiveness, diversity, bigness, even heterogeneity, synonymous with university.
It is enough for us in these pages simply to use the term to
designate an institution that offers degree work in several professional courses of study and the doctorate in at least a few
disciplines, while also carrying on genuine research. Current
usage does not yet demand that, in addition to advanced teaching and research, an institution wishing to call itself a univer-

sity must engage in extensive service to the nonacademic world. Such service may, indeed, be included in institutional aims; but it is there because it was put there, not because the definition requires it.

As to the term "liberal arts college," in American usage it is usually limited to institutions granting only undergraduate degrees, although such colleges occasionally are found offering master's degrees, even doctorates, without surrendering their earlier identification as colleges. In the Middle Ages, Europe saw many centers of learning flourish in which the seven liberal arts were taught: the trivium or elementary division included grammar, rhetoric, and logic, from which students progressed to the quadrivium—arithmetic, music, geometry and astronomy. These institutions were commonly called universities (i.e., corporations), despite the fact that they taught only the liberal arts. In the present-day United States, it is not uncommon to find an institution that calls itself a university but which, in its present stage of development, is to be recognized as performing the functions only of a college. Naming institutions is sometimes like christening a child: they are given adult names and expected to grow up.

The confusion of nomenclature reflects not merely a lack of precision or of clarity of definition. It expresses the vagaries of the academic mind under the influence of institutional pride. Aristotle was speaking of possessions, not of fields of study, but the quotation bears on the latter as well:

> Of possessions, those are useful, which bear fruit; those liberal which tend to enjoyment. By fruitful, I mean which yield revenue: by enjoyable, where nothing accrues of consequence beyond the using. [Rhetoric, i.5.]

In short, the phrase "liberal arts" might better be "enjoyable arts"—as opposed to useful arts. The knowledge gained in the pursuit of the liberal arts is knowledge for its own sake; its enjoyment, not its utility.

It is possible, however, to teach the liberal arts illiberally, that is, for their utility. They become the means of getting a degree or of fulfilling the prerequisites for entrance into graduate school, or a ticket to a good job. To teach the liberal arts for the purpose of enhancing earning power rather than of sensitizing the student to life's meanings is not to teach liberally. It is quite possible to teach liberal subjects without liberalizing or liberating the student. Rote learning, tedious lectures, computerized examinations, and grading on a bell curve will do the trick. It is possible to make tedium out of the enjoyable arts and to give the liberal institution most of the characteristics of a penal institution.

Nevertheless, reclassification in accordance with the degree of faithfulness to definitions of meaning is not here proposed. Such an attempt would be foredoomed to failure because it would amount to invidious name-calling. If an institution wishes to call itself a liberal arts college, let that wish be honored, provided only that the college is authorized to grant the bachelor's degree and is not a vocational or professional school. What is not to be taken for granted is the inference that every self-styled liberal arts college is, indeed, liberal or does, in fact, produce liberal and liberated graduates.

So, also, with the term "university." If the institution is made up of a cluster of professional schools (probably also including an undergraduate college of liberal arts), if it engages in research to a significant extent and grants degrees beyond the bachelor's level, it has the right, in American usage, to be called a university. That does not guarantee that its offerings encompass a universe of knowledge or that its graduates will be everywhere at home in the universe of the intellect. It does not imply that the several disciplines are organized into a single, interrelated system or synthesis, a universe, where all the parts would derive their full meanings through their interrelationships and men would explore universal meanings by interdisciplinary dialogue. It is true that in the world of nature what we call a universe is made up not of unrelated stars and galaxies but of bodies and groups of bodies that have their full meaning in their interrelationships. Each star sheds its light on all others, receives light from all others, is known by its position and movement relative to others.

But a university? At least one president has laconically described the institution over which he presides as a cluster of buildings held together by a common heating plant. Another, with greater candor, finds that the only common element that gives unity to his university is the annual struggle over the budget, which reflects the fact that the curricula of the several schools within the congeries are determined primarily by interdepartmental treaty and the whole university is held together by common and united opposition to the administrative control of the budget.

An encouraging dividend on candor is the tendency to rechristen institutions, giving them names or nicknames that more nearly describe their characters. Or the intentions and prejudices of the christeners. Thus, Clark Kerr's "multiversity" is a term coined to fit the institution that is a sprawling and diverse agglomeration like the University of California at Berkeley, held together by skilled mediation between warring factions. "Communiversity" is the name that the University of Wisconsin at Green Bay prefers: it expresses intentions of campus-community interrelatedness and involvement. The future of this process of renaming or nicknaming is bright. Why not be more precise in describing a fact or in symbolizing an aspiration? "University," except as it signifies a corporate entity, is no guarantee that universality of meanings and relationships or explorations into the whole universe of knowledge will be found at the institution bearing that name. Both purpose and performance may be narrowly conceived and indifferently realized, yet the institution has the right to call itself a university.

The upshot of this digression over definitions is this: there is no necessary connection in practice between what an institution is called and what it does—not, that is, with reference to the *interna* of the institution. In its external appearance and its formalized degree-granting authority, the institution can be recognized and given an appropriate name; but its hidden agenda, its actual purposes and functions (whether recognized and announced, or only implied by performance) may vary widely.

When, therefore, someone suggests that it would be improper to include a suggested function or purpose in a given institution because it is a college, or because it is a university, the answer is clear: proposed departures should be assessed each on their own merits, not on the basis of a preconceived notion that derives by definition from the name.

The point is worth a little elaboration. Just as Father Newman had a revolutionary purpose in mind when he went to Dublin, so, too, with many other founders and builders—and diverters.

American history supplies many examples of the founding of institutions of higher learning under the guidance of some overriding impulse not unlike the example of Father Newman in Ireland. Dartmouth College is an outgrowth of Eleazar Wheelock's (1711–1779) missionary efforts among the Indians. It owes its original endowment to the eloquence of an Indian alumnus, the Reverend Samuel Occum, and its name to the beneficence of the Earl of Dartmouth, who was enlisted in the fund-raising effort.

In 1833, following the disastrous schismatic disputations over slavery at Lane Seminary in Cincinnati, Oberlin College was founded in the wilds of the Northwest Territory for the express reason that its founder believed that the races and sexes ought to be educated together. Coeducation was then a scandalous idea, not elsewhere practiced.

In 1847, Townsend Harris founded the Free Academy (the nucleus of what has become the City University) of New York to bring "the sons of the mechanics classes" into the same classrooms as the sons of the well-to-do. His purpose was "to try the experiment" that might discover whether boys of humbler origin could not learn just as well as their more fortunately born classmates. Harris antedated Newman by five years in this revolutionary idea of higher learning, although Newman was first, by half a century, in starting an evening school to reach the working poor.

As the Civil War ended, dedicated New England schoolteachers, like an army in petticoats, moved alongside the Freedmen's Bureau to establish schools and colleges as well as universities for the illiterate ex-slave. They faced the formidable task of convincing a skeptical nation that black former slaves were educable in the same manner and to the same advanced levels as were their white former masters. Their detractors sneered at the image of a Negro reading Cicero while stumbling down the furrow behind a mule. The founders of schools for the freedmen were undeterred. They proved their case. The caste of color continues to be challenged by half a hundred or so colleges and universities that were started for that purpose.

One of the side issues that has diverted higher education through the years is the argument as to whether special groups ought not to be given special education. The controversy raged, as between the followers of Booker T. Washington and the followers of W. E. B. Dubois, for fifty years. It is not yet laid to rest. It is revived in connection with the current interest in things African and black within the Negro caste. The controversy almost precisely parallels another, namely, the question of what kind of education is "proper" to women.

Should not women be given a different education because they are different? They are biologically different, perform reproductive functions different from men, occupy a different social position, and perform a distinct social function. They are "anabolic rather than catabolic." It would be wrong to educate woman away from her true nature, to ruin the delightful qualities of femininity by forcing upon them a masculine mold. Women are, of course, known to be inferior to men in pure mental capacity. They are more intuitive than logical. Therefore, if they must be educated (and, of course, we are all for it), let them study poetic myth rather than scientific data. Emphasize art, literature, the biography of the saints; but omit metaphysics and ontology, and include only the most elementary levels of chemistry and mathematics. In economics, man should study production and management, woman consumption. Teach women domesticity because they are suited to it. And that is where they belong. In short, make sure that they are taught to stay in their place. So ran the arguments against the higher education of women during the nineteenth century and well into the twentieth. Those who argued for the higher education of woman as a device for changing her social status were naturally to be found on the other side of the debate.

In examining the declared purposes and actual performance of several archetypes of higher education, it will be useful to keep in mind the fact that it is possible to use each of these archetypes for purposes other than those suggested by their general format or characteristics. As we have seen, the real purposes of the institution may be to support social stasis, or to promote social change. These real purposes may be promoted effectively, in a well-coordinated effort of curriculum, teaching, and institutional process; or they may be promoted indifferently because of the lack of coordination between aims and methods.

There is nothing startlingly new in these facts. They are brought to attention, however, because they are commonly overlooked—and yet are of basic importance.

The Liberal Arts College

Let the oldest come first. When it was authorized by the Massachusetts general court in 1636, it had no name and those who sought the charter were uncertain whether it should be "a schoale or colledge." They did know, however, what its purpose was to be. ". . . dreading to leave an illiterate Ministry to the Churches, when our present Ministers shall lie in the Dust," they wanted to establish an institution to train clergymen. Fourteen years later, the official charter then issued went beyond this initial purpose, dedicating the college "to the advancement of all good literature, arts, and sciences," and to "the education of the English and Indian youth . . . in knowledge and godlynes."

The prototype of the American liberal arts college was founded as a professional school—in today's nomenclature, a theological seminary. What Americans generally today recognize as a liberal arts college was originally intended to be a professional school, with incidental benefits of "knowledge and godlynes" accruing to any who might be educated therein but who later entered some vocation other than the clergy.

The example has been widely copied. In most cases, as at Harvard, church sponsorship has meant church control, at least in the initial phase. Harvard, however, had an additional feature not available to any subsequently chartered institution. It was sponsored by both church and state. The Puritans looked upon the Massachusetts Colony as a theocracy, and they made no separation of church and state. It was natural for them to use the public treasury to support the training of young men for what was acknowledged to be the noblest profession. The colonial court made the first grant from public funds: four hundred pounds in 1636. Three years later, the legacy of the Reverend John Harvard gave the little seminary 780 pounds, 260 books—and his name. Joint church and state support, together with increasing private benefaction, continued. The last direct subsidy to Harvard from the public treasury of Massachusetts came 198 years after its founding. In this one feature, namely, joint support by church and state, Harvard was unique. That uniqueness underscores the decisive influence of a particular professional perspective in shaping the character of the liberal arts college prototype.

Harvard College, founded as a theological seminary, went

on to become a university, adding numerous professional and
graduate schools to the original nucleus and establishing the
Divinity School (1819) as one of a growing cluster of professional schools. The mantle of the liberal studies then fell upon
the undergraduate college, thus passing on to a secular unit
within the university the responsibilities of the liberal education tradition for the culture and training of undergraduates.

That general process has been replicated, in many modifications, in all parts of the nation by most of the four hundred
denominations of Protestantism as well as by Catholicism and
its religious orders. Throughout the nineteenth century and
well into the twentieth, the typical American liberal arts college had been founded and nourished by the church, had kept
the liberalizing studies (especially the "dead languages" and
the classics) as its central core of concern, and was commonly
presided over by a clergyman who also taught the required
courses in mental and moral philosophy to seniors. Governing boards tended to be dominated, if not controlled, by
churchmen who called the tune long after the church ceased
to pay the piper. Reenforced by secular trends in society (and
therefore within the faculty and student body), liberal colleges became less and less sectarian, then less and less religious
and more and more secular in their intentions and in the content of their curricula and the shaping of the weekly round of
activities. The general progression of institutional life from
piety to eclecticism to secularism is illustrated over and over
again.

An illustration of the way founders look upon their efforts
was given at Madison Square Garden in 1972 when the Reverend Oral Roberts, founder and president of the young institution that bears his name, cheered his basketball team to
victory in the first round of a tournament and then exclaimed,
"This was a victory for God!" He was not quoted as having
said that God was defeated when his team lost in the next
round of the tournament.

Both in its Harvard prototype and in most of its subsequent

manifestations, the liberal arts college was designed to serve a single profession, the clergy, and also to offer to the secular world graduates who were "liberally educated." The liberal arts college has been the manifestation of a life-style, intended to promote a deepened commitment to an accepted system of values. The catalog called it "building character." An original emphasis on the training of young men for a special professional pursuit has broadened into a concern for the quality of mind and life of all men and women of whatever vocation or none.

Not that every liberal arts college has, at all times and with compelling success, been completely successful in exemplifying or promoting the value systems of that life-style. On the contrary, changing social conditions, new intellectual climate, revised mores, clashing ideas and ideals within and among the family of the nation's colleges and universities, the growth of scientism and the vulgarization of the culture, together with the declining social influence of the church itself, have brought extensive changes in the philosophy and practices of collegiate life. Any church-founded institution that has been in existence long enough to outlive its founders by a generation or so tends to respond to what are called "broadening influences." Something of the original flavor and ethos is lost. The liberal college becomes eclectic. Nevertheless, it can be said that, even when it has become an omnium-gatherum, the liberal arts college still tends to be a place in which, in their better moments, faculty members and administrators pay honest homage to their heritage. Even though they might not wish to return to the restricted horizons of a former day, they admit to a quiet nostalgia for a time when life's values were clearly known and convincingly taught, when the college had a controlling central purpose to which all subscribed.

The liberal arts college, originally intended as a professional school for the ministry, enshrines in its ideals and sometimes exhibits in practice the liberalizing and liberating influences and values of a life-style in which rigorous intellectual discipline, active cultural appreciation, and a sensitive moral conscience converge in the self-disciplined man or woman in pursuit of learning for its own enjoyment. A system of values, however loosely defined or indifferently held, is still alleged to permeate the institution. Its teaching of literature, language, science, and the arts is believed to result in "the development of character." Its graduates are expected to contribute to society not only by being good citizens, self-supporting and successful in their chosen careers, but, also and most importantly, just by being cultured persons. Not so much by doing, but just by being, the liberally educated person is to justify his existence and reflect glory on Alma Mater. In the Aristotelian sense, enjoyment, not utility, is the measure of the value of a liberal education, both to the educated person and to society. The shades of the founding fathers would add, ". . . and to God."

Colleges for Teachers

Many of the college-trained did not enter the ministry. A large proportion went into teaching in the common schools and academies. It was not until Horace Mann and James G. Carter combined forces in Massachusetts in 1838 that teacher-training institutions were established under public auspices. To Horace Mann must go the credit for devising what has become the most widely copied American social intervention, namely, the universal compulsory free elementary public school. It was James Carter who was to become known as "father of the normal schools," which were established to provide the teachers for the developing public school system. Slowly at first, then rapidly, as the public school movement swept the nation, normal schools were established to supply a need that the graduates of the liberal arts colleges could not meet.

Carter's normal schools in Massachusetts set the pattern that was widely copied throughout the country. Students were to be prepared to teach in the ungraded common schools by mastering the range of subjects they might be expected to teach, together with whatever could be improvised at the normal school under the heading "The art of teaching."

A little later, and particularly in the Middle West, as public high schools supplanted the private academies and there came to be an effective demand for high school teachers, state after state began to establish normal schools. Some of the earlier normal schools, like that at Albany, New York, were converted into state teachers colleges and began to confer degrees. By the time of World War I, there were nearly fifty state teachers colleges in the forty-eight states. The decade of the 1920s saw the number more than doubled. While many a small-town high school still continued its "normal department" whose graduates taught the one-room rural schools, the state teachers colleges began to catch up with the pace of expansion of high schools, urban elementary schools, and the newly arrived consolidated school, which used the splendid new gasoline-powered buses to bring farm children into a critical mass where learning might better flourish.

Complementing this development of the state teachers colleges, separate departments, schools, or colleges for teacher education were developed in the liberal arts colleges and the universities. All aimed to supply teachers for the elementary and secondary schools, leaving the training of teachers for the colleges and universities to the graduate schools where, in turn, it was assumed that anyone holding an advanced degree in a discipline was automatically qualified to teach in his field of competence in any institution of higher education. In the teachers colleges and in their counterparts within the liberal colleges and the universities, the curricula for teacher training tended to be similar: mastery of the subject matter one might be expected to teach, together with a proliferating series of courses in "the art of teaching," later to be known as "pedagogy," then as "education."

The period since World War II has seen most of the state teachers colleges develop into, or be renamed as, units of a state university system. Teacher training may continue to be a central function, but the infusion of the liberal curriculum and the addition of most of the paraphernalia of collegiate life (including coeducation of the sexes) have substantially altered the character of the original normal schools.

The education of teachers has always suffered from something of an inferiority complex in the American family of institutions of higher education. Widely publicized studies have spread the idea that they tend to draw their students from the lower half of the spectrum of collegiate abilities as measured by such devices as the Scholastic Aptitude Test. In their own defense, the teachers colleges have pointed out that the teaching profession was grossly underpaid, so that the abler students did not aspire to it; that many young women went to college and trained as teachers while actually searching for a husband (making the profession of teaching their second choice); and that legislatures and governors tended to favor the big name institutions with the fiscal support that the teachers colleges needed also but did not get.

Whatever the reasons—or excuses—for the feelings of superiority on the part of other types of institutions, the struggle for respectability by teacher-training institutions has been a principal feature affecting their growth. Among other things, this struggle has, at times, stimulated the proliferating of a formidable variety of methodological courses, in an undisguised but misguided effort to prove that "education" is a respectable academic discipline. Lacking the glamour of the liberal heritage or the prestige of big time athletics, the teachers colleges have been forced to demonstrate their excellence by other devices. They have had to become first-rate in doing what they were designed to do—educate for the teaching profession. Not a few have done just that.

Yet, in the galaxy of American higher education, the planets and stars and satellites of teacher education have not always shone brightly or orbited steadily. The principal cause of their uneven performance lies in their failure to clarify their own self-image. They have wrongly assumed that, to be professional schools, they must move away from the liberal arts college tradition and emphasize their narrower specialty, "education." They have failed to recognize that the liberal arts college is, in essence, a training school for a particular profession; and that that profession is historically and actually very close to their own. Instead of taking their cue from the cultural aims of the liberal arts college, they have tried to be like the schools training for medicine or law or pharmacy. Perhaps it may be that they have not fully sensed the importance of their own task in furthering a value system instead of multiplying the minutiae of methodology.

To be sure, the liberal educational institution had originated under the ethos of the church and therefore had a heritage of ethical aspiration and cultural appreciation. On the other hand, teachers colleges have been predominantly sponsored by public sources, secular and nonsectarian. Their desire to become established as "fully professional" led them to look elsewhere than to the liberal arts college for their model.

The teachers colleges have shared a dilemma that the parents of public school children also faced. Desiring to have their children "properly" educated, parents (and the school boards on which they sit) have appeared to believe that right attitudes and good conduct could come from proper discipline and respect for authority, together with the rituals of the flag salute and school prayers. Verbal repetition and outward conformity were supposed to inculcate the attitudes and habits of good citizenship. And although Abraham Lincoln had impulsively inserted "under God" in his Gettysburg address, the constitutional separation of church and state made it difficult indeed for the public school to go much beyond bare rituals in an effort to teach young children a system of values. When the Supreme Court refused to condone the use of prayers and

Scripture in the public schools, teachers began to feel less pressure toward teaching ethical values. But both teachers and parents were worried.

Elected officials, and those running for office, like to say (particularly in election years) that God ought to be restored to primacy in the schools. In so doing, they are playing on the very real anxieties of parents and teachers in the deepening crisis of our day. There is an understandable desire to restore the old litanies and perform the old rituals in the hope that incantation may revive the flame of faith and perhaps even recall the moral restraints of yesteryear.

How can a secular institution, one which cannot lawfully show a preference for any religion or for none, supply the students' need for ethical guidance and self-directed moral living, while American society moves away from these ancient standards? Religion exists only in some sectarian expression; but if ethical and moral values are to be promoted in the public schools, stripped of sectarian religious reference, what is left for the teacher to do? There have been significant efforts by teacher-training institutions to introduce ideals and practices that might lift the level of life or enrich the meaning of civic virtue. These efforts have uniformly been resisted or suspected or inhibited by influential sections of the American public.

For example, when the nation was experiencing the Great Depression of the 1930s, a lively controversy within the teachers colleges centered around the question "Dare the schools lead?" Should educators try to reform society? A resounding answer came back: No! You don't dare! So, they didn't.

Or, again, since the *Brown* decision of 1954, desegregation of the public schools has increasingly become an all-absorbing problem in the public schools. The teacher-training institutions, which had learned in the 1930s that they were not to take the lead in changing society's values, did not generally emerge as the front-line defenders of integration. They did not sufficiently train their students for the new role of the integrated school. Isolated instances of well-conceived efforts to integrate faculties and student bodies in the teacher-training institutions themselves—and to do it with equality, compassion, and justice in mind—can be cited. Some of these efforts were relatively successful. But school boards and superintendents still did the hiring and firing. The record does not indicate universal support by parents and taxpayers of those boards and superintendents that paved the way for successful integration of the races in formerly segregated school systems. Notable exceptions stand in bold contrast to the general practice. If, then, taxpayers and parents and school boards and superintendents wait on the courts to force them to do what the Constitution requires, what part might the teachers colleges play, other than to train their students to conform to general practice? And by the time that busing had become the emotionally charged political issue of the 1970s, it was too late for the teachers colleges to assume a leadership role. Like their sister institutions, the colleges for teachers mirrored prevailing values of the general culture.

Colleges of education will not escape from their secondary position in American higher education until they cease to apologize for being professional schools. Medical schools do not wait until the general public approves new techniques in surgery or chemotherapy before training interns to use them. A profession is supposed to lead, not be led. But for teachers colleges, the truth lies in a paradox, namely, that they can become true to their professional purpose only by realizing that their profession has at its heart the liberal educational tradition with its emphasis on a value system. The question before the teachers colleges is not whether they can do a good job at professional education, but what that good job might be if they were to do it.

The element that is most lacking in the teacher-training

institutions is also lacking in other professional schools. The difference is that what is left out is, in the case of the schools of education, the only element that could lift them from the vocational to the professional level, namely, a convincing, profoundly understood, clearly enunciated, winsomely taught, and fully exemplified system of values. If the liberal arts colleges can continue to draw strength from memories of their own once-great traditions, cannot the institutions for the education of teachers also draw deeply from the wellsprings of democracy?

The University

The American ideal of the university had its origins far from the puritanical restrictiveness of Harvard Yard. It was not at New Haven that the new pattern was conceived, even though Yale College was founded by men who had been unsuccessful in their efforts to unseat the strict Calvinism that controlled the Cambridge institution. The tree of freedom, whose spreading branches would be for the protection of all learning, took root in a cultural soil quite different from that on New England's rock-bound coast.

Before his death, Thomas Jefferson directed that the legend on his tomb should record only three items from a remarkably full life. His two terms in the Presidency of the nation were to be ignored. His Cabinet membership under Washington, his ambassadorship and governorship were not to be mentioned. None of his many notable achievements such as the Louisiana Purchase were to be recorded. Only three items were to be included: that he was the author of the American Declaration of Independence and of the statute of Virginia for religious freedom, and that he was father of the University of Virginia.

Whether or not the University of Virginia as Jefferson conceived and built it was the first institution in this nation that had the right unquestionably to be called a university, none can doubt that no other institution up to that time (and few since) have a more genuine right so to be known. Jefferson's earliest venture in public service was concerned with the bettering of the elementary education situation of the colony; his final years were devoted to establishing, full blown, his grand design for a university for the state.

He had the personal equipment necessary to the task. His broad-ranging interests and accomplishments included most of the liberal and useful concerns of his time. He was well-versed and at home in the fields of aeronautics, agriculture, architecture and building, botany, education, ethnology, geography, geology, government, invention, languages and literature, mathematics, medicine and surgery, philosophy, plantation, religion, and zoology. He was an accomplished violinist with a lively intellectual understanding of the plastic arts. His interests and his knowledge were encyclopedic. It was no accident that he came to know the friendship of the French Encyclopedists and to read extensively from Condorcet. (Rousseau and Montesquieu, he eschewed.) His mind was selective and eclectic, but broad and unfettered. He was a Renaissance man.

More importantly, he had the strong courage of the democratic spirit in the marrow of his bones. His faith in the common man was a passion that ruled all his thinking and writing and action—provided only that all men were educated. To Jefferson, education did not mean mere literacy. Literacy must be consummated in liberation. His words were: "I have sworn upon the altar of God eternal hostility against every form of tyranny over the mind of man." His faith in education was one with his belief in democracy, fire-tempered steel corrected by profound compassion for humanity.

He had the practical ability to translate his vision into enduring living reality. He designed each building for the new university, in accordance with a grand scale all others were to envy and to emulate. He personally supervised the construction of each building, right down to the last finial. Within those buildings were housed a faculty that he personally gathered—mainly from Europe. He devised the curriculum and wrote the governing statutes for a university that was to operate along lines far more advanced than any other then in existence, anticipating the twentieth century in many respects. The curriculum was completely elective. The faculty were all equals, departmental chairmen being elected in rotation. Students attended lectures and completed examinations under an honor system, and student discipline was also under a system of honor. There were no religious tests for admission or for anything else, and no religious practices were permitted. As he fought for the Bill of Rights in America's basic document, so he constructed a university that would teach those rights by embodying them.

He was flawed, because he was human and because he was the son of a wealthy landed gentleman of eighteenth-century Virginia. Jefferson's will provided for the manumission of only a few of the more than 140 slaves in his possession. He arranged that the territory north and west of the Ohio River was to be reserved as free soil; but in the lands to the south of that river, slavery was to be permitted. The best he could do with the perplexing problem of the Indian was to devise the reservation (which some will say was worse than genocide, but which others will see as a humanitarian concern for peoples who would otherwise have become extinct as the frontier was pushed westward). The fuller truth is that, despite his own limitations and shortcomings, his doctrines and his life put into motion the forces that ultimately were to destroy the undemocratic institutions of white supremacy, institutions within which he was imprisoned, along with his generation. Today, the university he fathered is racially integrated and moving toward equality of the races in an open society, at a pace that challenges the Old South, even as it falls far short of Jefferson's ideal of full equality of all men. Today, the nation whose basic faith he enshrined in chiseled words is going through a second Reconstruction Era, a development that was precipitated by men who took Jefferson's ideas seriously enough to act upon them. The *Brown* decision of 1954 is, in its essence, nothing other than the full affirmation of Jefferson's convinced belief that the Creator has made all men equal.

The ideal of the American university includes within it the ideal of American society.

In addition to all these things, Jefferson also foreshadowed another development in American higher education. He included agriculture in the curriculum. It was inevitable that he should do so. He had inherited an estate of nineteen hundred acres and increased his holdings to five thousand acres by the time he was thirty. The death of his father-in-law doubled that acreage. He managed it. He knew well, and loved, the practical business of farming. He was a confirmed lover of rural life, detesting urban centers as "sores upon the body politic." His agrarian outlook colored all his political attitudes. It was the basis for including agriculture in a university curriculum. Not until 1862 did the nation catch up to his practical vision.

The Land Grant Institution

The first Morrill Act (1862) set aside Federal lands to support in each state and territory

> at least one college where the leading object shall be, without excluding other scientific and classical studies, and including military tactics, to teach such branches of learning as are related to agriculture and the mechanic arts, in order to promote the liberal and practical education of the industrial classes in the several pursuits and professions of life.

With the passing of the second Morrill Act in 1890 and the Nelson Amendment in 1907, direct Federal subsidies were annually added to the basic land-grant endowments. From the beginning, the states were required to share in supporting their land grant colleges and universities, and state support has turned out to be the main source of support for the Federally stimulated network of institutions of higher education.

These institutions have profoundly altered the course and character of American higher education and of the nation itself. "Practical" concerns have become as respectable and as legitimately academic as "liberal" studies. Manual and commercial arts have taken their place alongside the classics as academic disciplines. Domestic science and stock-judging are regular catalog listings. The practical business of making a living takes its place in the hierarchy of academic values on a par with classical preoccupations. ". . . to promote the liberal *and* practical education . . ." said the Morrill Act. And, finally, while the egalitarian documents of American democracy do not recognize a class of gentry, Congress unabashedly refers to "the industrial classes" and sets about to provide higher education for those whom the established institutions for the elite did not serve. The American Revolution was immeasurably advanced by this act of tampering with social structure by educating the children of the farm and of the working class.

In reality, the land grant college movement turned out to be the first great Federally sponsored antipoverty program. Directed to the needs of the rural poor, this new type of "cow college" was to become the source of rural well-being and the channel of extensive governmental effort to ameliorate the plight of the rural poor. A panoply of supplementary and complementary services, agencies, and programs was created over the years, mainly administered within the Department of Agriculture, designed to work through the land grant institutions to serve the rural population. Experiment stations perfected new seeds and new strains, developed hardier breeds, evolved new methods and materials. County demonstration agents carried the word and showed the way. Short courses in the winter months brought farmers and their wives to live on the campus, to see and wonder and learn. Extension services carried the latest and most promising innovations to grange and farmstead. Branches of the land grant institutions were established, to bring the services within reach of horse-and-buggy travel over dirt roads. Cooperative marketing was sponsored, to be followed by credit unions. Rural electrification came. And the boys and girls who proudly displayed their 4-H membership on the farm's front gate, when they finished high school, went into residence and study at the colleges that had served their families during their youth.

Grinding rural poverty has been replaced by a satisfying way of life for millions of American farmers and their families. American life is frequently thought to be barren and sterile out there in Ruritania. Much of it is. Had there been no land grant colleges or their equivalent, the rural situation would today be unbelievably worse.

Deficiencies are not hard to identify. For example, the tendency to serve the rural population and to champion its interests over those of the rest of the nation has not always insured a balanced and objective approach to the farmers' needs in the light of the whole nation and its people. Item: Extensive use of chemical fertilizers, promoted by the Department of Agriculture with the full support of the land grant institutions and their experiment stations, has made a dead sea out of Lake Erie and made the soil so dependent upon its annual artificial renewal as to make the situation almost irreversible. Item: Pockets of poverty remain, almost untouched, throughout the rural South and in Appalachia. Item: The plight of the tenant and the migrant remains too far from the center of attention, while successful farming and its sequel, agribusiness, appear to profit out of proportion to the generalized and inclusive aims of a democratic government and its educational institutions. Finally, the cultural aspects of the curriculum and the institutional ethos have not infrequently fallen short of the "practical *and liberal*" aims of the charter.

On the other side of the ledger, credit must be given to the land grant college movement for (1) greatly strengthening higher education in all states and territories, (2) bringing the practical questions of vocational and professional concern into the normal ambit of academic life, and (3) helping to build a new fabric of rural community and family life, replacing poverty and despair and isolation with a measure of hope and decency and achievement. The snobs of academe may smile amusedly at mention of "the ag schools." The graduates of the land grant institutions laugh all the way to the bank.

Not the least important dividend of the land grant college movement was an accident of Northern patriotism in the person and influence of Representative (later Senator) Morrill, Republican of Vermont, first elected to Congress in 1854 as an antislavery Whig.

The Public Colleges for Negroes

Congressman Morrill's bill was voted into law at a time when the nation was locked in fratricidal war. For Northerners, antislavery sentiment had become almost synonymous with patriotism. If the Southern states were to benefit from the land grant endowments, they were to be compelled to provide higher education for Negroes as well as for whites. The language of the Morrill Act therefore required that "at least one" institution should be established in each state or territory. If they wanted one for whites, there must be one for Negroes.

Safeguards to insure a just distribution of Federally supplied funds were written into the legislation and its enabling regulations. So far as can be determined, the distribution of Federal funds in each of the seventeen segregating states meticulously followed the legal requirements, distribution being made in accordance with population ratios within each state or territory. From its establishment in 1867, the United States Bureau (later, Office) of Education was made responsible for administering the Federal land grants in the states and territories. Almost alone among all Federal programs prior to very recent dates, the administration of the Morrill Act funds expressed a sense of justice within the prevailing inequalities of the nation.

That does not mean that the land grant colleges for Negroes in the seventeen segregating states were, in fact, equal to their sister institutions for whites. It means that the small portion of total annual funds for each state that came from Washington through the United States Office of Education was equitably apportioned between the Negro and white institutions. The story is wholly different within the states themselves, where marked differentials in state appropriations have been the rule. And when attention is given to all the programs operated through the Department of Agriculture, in cooperation with the land grant colleges and universities, the discrepancies between the services to and through the institutions for whites and those for Negroes become shamefully clear. Experiment stations, whether one or several in the state, were always attached to and operated under the jurisdiction of the white institution—never the Negro A&M. All the county agents were attached to and functioned as arms of the faculties of the white institutions. These practices meant that the Negro institutions remained bare skeletons of teaching faculties, while the functions of research and demonstration fleshed out the white institutions, giving them both prestige and power. The only known exception to the otherwise universal practice of racial discrimination in public higher education throughout the South, prior to 1954, is in the distribution of that small portion of the sustaining funds of the land grant colleges that derives from the first and second Morrill Acts and the Nelson Amendment.

Nevertheless, the fact that there are seventeen publicly supported institutions of higher education open to Negroes is due to the Yankee sentiments of wartime antislavery patriotism in 1862. Most of the seventeen segregating states had two institutions for whites, the state university and the land grant college; but only one for Negroes, the land grant college. Except for the Morrill Act, there would have been none for Negroes.

There would, of course, have been normal schools for Negroes, since the public schools were being established for both races (separately) and, in many states, whites were forbidden by law to teach in the public schools for Negroes. The normal schools followed the general development, resulting in state teachers colleges for Negroes throughout the South.

Everybody knew, and acknowledged, that the institutions for Negroes were not equally well-supported, enjoyed lesser consideration in the legislatures and the governors' mansions, were held in lower esteem, even though they were defended as "separate but equal." It remained for the United States Supreme Court to affirm in 1954 that schools for Negroes are not, and cannot be, the equal of those for whites so long as separation is enforced. It still remains as an item of unfinished business on the American agenda to bring the public institutions founded for Negroes up to anything approaching the level of excellence of those provided for whites. With the possible exceptions of West Virginia and Missouri, the predominantly Negro institutions lag far behind. The founding of institutions of higher education for Negroes in the seventeen formerly segregating states is due to the passing fervor of a wartime Congress. The nurturing and survival of these institutions, together with the teachers colleges for Negroes, is a triumph of frugality and compromise under conditions of indignity and neglect.

The Community College

More than any other segment of American higher education today (more than the land grant institutions themselves), the community colleges reflect and express in the 1970s the practical concerns of the land grant tradition. The land grant institutions themselves have grown into large multipurpose agglomerations, serving a broad spectrum of educational concerns as well as the continuing practical concerns of the population. Their 4-H Clubs are now found in the inner city as well as on the prairie: they still continue their original mission of direct practical service to the poor. But the elaboration of research and teaching in the sciences and arts generally, the development of the full-blown "university" image, and the passing of the years have brought the land grant universities far from their "cow college" beginnings. The community colleges have emerged as the inheritors of the mantle of the Morrill Act—without the Federal subsidy. This fastest growing segment of American higher education is not so much a new variety of higher education as a new way of packaging it and making it available to an additional sector of the population. The land grant tradition reaches its urban phase of growth in the community colleges.

The land grant emphasis on technology, agriculture, applied science, and the professions has been translated by the community colleges into strong support for vocational and technical proficiency of the commuting city-dweller, together with direct service to the practical needs of the people of the surrounding city and region.

Service to the commuting student and the part-timer at the community college has deemphasized the country-club aspects that are present in much of American higher education (although not a few of the proliferating junior colleges in California have managed to outdo their four-year rivals in their lavish provision for the recreational aspects of student life). The low-tuition (or no-tuition) policy of the community colleges has brought them within reach of the poor in a manner and to an extent that even the American high school did not demonstrate until after World War I. California has the most extensive network of community colleges, presaging the day when (except in the most sparsely populated rural areas) a low-cost or free two-year institution of postsecondary education will be within commuting distance of the home of every college-age person in the nation.

Curricula in the better community colleges tend to be pragmatically determined, according to the industrial and commercial demands of the area, embracing the practical and vocational studies that may be of utility within the region. These practical offerings are accompanied by general and cultural courses of study and by continuing adult offerings.

With 781 community colleges in existence in 1970, the Carnegie Commission projects the need for an additional 230 to 280 such institutions by the end of the present decade. Presently enrolling some two million students, the two-year colleges serve about 30 percent of all undergradutes of the nation. About half their students are adults, over twenty-two years of age, most of these with strong vocational and professional motivation, seeking to qualify for a better job. Among the students who are of the usual college-going age, the same theme of professional and vocational motivation is strong, although the so-called "transfer programs" that lead on from community college to the pursuit of a bachelor's degree at another institution sometimes tend to be more prestigious than the "career programs" on a local campus.

Within the decade of the 1970s, nearly 200,000 additional teachers (including replacements) will be needed for the community colleges, according to the Carnegie Commission's estimates. These teachers will be graduates of the colleges and universities that have been accustomed to serve a clientele somewhat different from that which the community colleges reach. There is little reason to assume that the four-year colleges and the universities, as presently oriented and operated, will automatically produce teachers who are qualified to do what community college teachers ought to do. There is, as yet, no evidence that the commission's recommendation for an expanded program of Federal training grants to provide teachers adequate to the task will meet with Government approval and support in time to be of any real use in this expansion crisis. There is every reason to believe that the average university-trained holder of a doctorate will be quite incapable of providing the quality of teaching and counseling that the community college undergraduate needs and deserves.

The community college movement that began so hopefully in Joliet, Illinois, in 1901 and has developed into the most dynamic segment of American higher education deserves to be saved from engulfment in the institutional vagaries of the System. If foresight and courage can be coupled with essential dollars, and with freedom both from external interference and from unfortunate emulation of the four-year establishment, the community college could become the leaven in the lump of American higher education. Education has, at times, been the yeast of democracy. If care to details and attention to basic values were to prevail over institutional pride and one-upmanship, the community colleges might prove to be as important a development for this century as were the land grant institutions a century ago. It would be a major loss to the nation and its people if these institutions, which by 1980 are expected to enroll 40 percent of all undergraduates in the country, were to repeat the errors and copy the mistakes of the institutions serving the other 60 percent.

The Research University

The founding of the Johns Hopkins University (1867) and the discovery of the Norddeutscher Lloyd passage to graduate studies introduced American higher education to a substantially different set of educational purposes, a contrasting life-style and mode of thinking academically, which were to have an almost revolutionary effect upon the institutions of higher education and, through them, upon American society. Science came of age, and scientism replaced theology as queen of the sciences.

Scholars tracing the history of science customarily go back to Plato's Academy to find the source of antiscientism. Before him, all philosophers had concerned themselves with the "natural" world, that is, the earth, the heavenly bodies, the universe. Plato turned philosophical inquiry inward, to a consideration of the working of the human mind and an examination of the results and processes of human thought, to what came later to be called "mental" and "moral" philosophy, as distinguished from "natural" philosophy. In the history of Western thought, the relationship between natural philosophy on the one hand and on the other mental and moral philosophy —that is, the distinction between science and religion—has been a constantly recurring theme.

When Charlemagne decreed (787) that a school should be established in connection with every abbey throughout the empire, the trivium and the quadrivium became the curriculum, and theologians became the teachers. The Schoolmen attempted to keep reason and revelation together in an uneasy harness. Their compromise may be paraphrased: it is impossible to know what can only be believed, and immoral to believe whatever can be known. This formulation had the advantage of keeping the barrier between reason and revelation flexible; but it proved to be so flexible as not to be a barrier of protection for the faith against the pressures of inquiry.

The medieval universities, as they emerged, took their conceptions of knowledge and their ideas of education from the Scholastics who had survived through the Dark Ages in their monasteries. The underlying assumption dictated by theology to the Scholastics and by them bequeathed to the early universities was that all knowledge and all truth were one, since the Deity was one and He was the source of all knowledge and all truth. A constant effort was made to reconcile the conflicting notions of nature and of morality, an effort that reached its climax in the writings of Thomas Aquinas.

In the Thomistic synthesis, all of knowledge and all of faith were woven together in a seamless fabric. Theology was queen of the sciences and all truth was a single universe of discourse and concord. The synthesis of the *Summa* held together the warring elements of philosophical thought, reconciling all differences and subjugating all knowledge to the discipline of faith.

There was also a hidden agenda in the Thomistic effort. It was an anxious desire to preserve the crumbling feudal system from disaster. All societal relationships had come to be regulated by the hierarchy of obligations and loyalties between lords and vassals, from about the ninth century onwards. Safety of person and security of property depended upon the reciprocal binding power of the feudal oath. So did tenancy and livelihood. The feudal system gave order and stability to life. But lesser fiefdoms were threatened by greater ones, just as the larger kingdoms clashed with each other for supremacy. New mercantile and trading influences, sheltered in their own walled towns, began to threaten the power of lords in their castles; the burghers emerged as another class, vying with the nobility. Confusion of jurisdictions and powers led to constant warring (interrupted, of course, by the planting and harvest seasons, and by holy days). With the kings and nobility fighting over the scraps of a disintegrating empire, and with an upstart merchant class asserting itself and a restless peasantry held in serfdom by force, the feudal system began to crack at the seams. Chaos threatened. Some authoritative cement for a tottering social structure had to be found. It was provided in the Thomistic synthesis, and given the most powerful sanction of the day: God's will. Every man was born into a station proper to him. He was bound in that station by his oath of fealty. This was what God had ordained, since He was the Creator and Sustainer of the universe. The Thomistic synthesis of all knowledge and all faith was also a seamless coat of mail, encasing and protecting the feudal system. It served to prolong the life of feudalism for at least two centuries.

The coat of mail turned out to be a straitjacket. The price of social stasis was paid in coin of intellectual stagnation. This was too great a price for simian man to pay. No fixed intellectual system could forever contain his inquiries. Through the Voyages of Discovery, the Reformation and Counter-Reformation, the Industrial Revolution and the Enlightenment —four hundred years of struggle—science fought to be free from theological controls. One by one, and then in clusters, the ideas and conclusions of Aquinas were challenged by the awesome conclusions that new discoveries indicated: that the earth was round, that it moved in an orbit around the sun, that blood circulated instead of pulsed, that the human body was a "machine," that gravity, though unseen, was an irresistible force, that man could observe the heavens with a telescope to learn through observation what errors of faith had been committed. Relying not on revelation but on reason, man turned to observation and reflection as pathways to knowledge, pushing back the boundaries of revealed truth until God was about to be bowed out of His universe. Man could know without resort to faith. The more he knew, the less he had need of faith to supply the interstices of ignorance. The Thomistic synthesis was no longer the answer.

René Descartes set about to save the faith from the onslaughts of science. Wherever he went, he could always be seen with a copy of the *Summa* under his arm. To save the faith, he proposed that science should be cut loose from theology, that separate spheres of competence and jurisdiction should be assigned to each, and that each would then be safe from the attacks of the other. Descartes died believing that his work had been accomplished, that he had saved the faith by giving science its freedom.

The Cartesian compromise was gladly accepted both by the

Church and by men of science. All knowledge was to be divided into two parts, and all inquiry governed accordingly. To the Church and religion went the domain of First Causes, Ultimate Ends, and the World of Souls between. To science went everything else. The compromise succeeded.

And, be it remarked, so did science. Free at last from the restraints of theological assumptions, presumptions, and restraints, science launched out on its own with vigor. The work of Descartes ended with his death in 1650; but the seventeenth century witnessed the labors of Bacon, Galileo, Kepler, Harvey, Snellius, Desargues, Cavalieri, Fermat, Von Guericke, Torricelli, Wallis, Pascal, Sydenham, Boyle, Huygens, Barrow, Hooke, Willoughby, Newton, Leibnitz, Römer, Helley, Stahl, and Boerhaave. That same century saw the early colonizing of America, witnessed the profound upheaval of the Thirty Years' War on the continent of Europe and the rise and fall of Cromwell in England. As the last vestiges of feudalism were being swept away, men were moving boldly on new frontiers of geography, of political and social organization, and of the mind. A new adventurous spirit of learning and inquiry was being born.

Through the eighteenth and nineteenth centuries, that bold spirit delved ever more deeply into the theoretical bases of science and moved with amazing effectiveness to apply the newly acquired scientific insights. The Industrial Revolution began, blossomed, spread, and changed the face of commerce, industry, finance, and government. Political revolution in America and France in the eighteenth century, and on the Continent in the mid-nineteenth, helped to unsettle old restraints. Everywhere, and in every phase of life and learning, it appeared that man was on the move, ever inquiring, ever discovering, ever succeeding, ever liberating. Science became as liberating as its liberated devotees could make it.

No wonder that Father Newman in 1854 exploded in anger, saying to his young institution, "Whether or no a Catholic

University should put before it, as its great object, to make students 'gentlemen,' still to make them something or other *is* its great object, and not simply to protect the interests and advance the domain of Science!" He inveighed against Bacon, defended revelation as superior to scientific inquiry, fought his rearguard action. It was a losing battle. The future of higher education was to lie with science, with a new and startlingly different life-style for academics, a new and self-secreted set of values.

In America, philanthropist Johns Hopkins had appointed the trustees for his newly incorporated Baltimore institution in 1867. Only with his death in 1873 did his fortune become available for use. The trustees promptly consulted with leading educators, as they designed the curricula and the infrastructure of the new university. Among those consulted was Andrew D. White, president of Cornell University.

White had been a member of the New York State legislature in 1862 when the first Morrill Act was passed by Congress. Together with Ezra Cornell, a fellow member of the legislature who had made his fortune in the fast-growing telegraph industry, White decided to ask the state of New York to designate as its land grant institution a new university that the two men would establish. As Ezra Cornell put it, the new university was to be a place "where any person can find instruction in any study." In addition to this broadest of all charters, the institution was to avoid control by any religious sect or by nonreligion, through the makeup of its governing board. No one sect could have a majority on the board, and neither could the board have a majority of persons of no sect. Persons of every religion and of none were to have equal consideration for appointment and advancement in the faculty.

White had not chosen the most auspicious moment for his bold declaration. Darwin's *Origin of Species* had been published only six years previously. Darwin's theories had violated the Cartesian compromise. Whereas devout men like Jefferson had accepted that compromise and retreated from Theism to Deism as science progressed, Darwin now challenged the right of theology to supremacy in the area of First Causes. Science now invaded the reserved areas on which religion had expected to stand undisturbed. The churches were shocked, the clergy sputtered and thundered, and the politicians reacted obediently. The press and the religious denominations descended upon Albany in bitter denunciation of the proposal to dethrone religion in the establishing of Cornell University. After three years of struggle, the legislature finally granted the charter; but that was only the beginning of an extended running fight.

White was appalled at the severity of an attack that he believed was as unwarranted as it was unexpected. "I simply try to aid in letting the light of historical truth into the decaying mass of outworn thought which attaches the modern world to mediaeval conceptions of Christianity, and which still lingers among us—a most serious barrier to religion and morals, and a menace to the whole normal evolution of society," he protested. In his own way, White was trying to be a latter-day Descartes, endeavoring to save the faith by cutting science loose before both were destroyed. He wrote:

The flood is rapidly rising, the flood of increased knowledge and new thought; and this barrier . . . though honeycombed and in many places thin, creates a danger—a danger of a sudden breaking away, distressing and calamitous, sweeping before it not only outworn creeds and noxious dogmas, but cherished principles and ideals, and even wrenching our most precious religious and moral foundations of the whole social and political fabric. My hope is to aid . . . in the gradual and healthful dissolving away of this mass of unreason, that the stream of "religion pure and undefiled" may flow on broad and clear, a blessing to humanity.

He was later to write a monumental defense of his position in *A History of the Warfare of Science with Theology in Christendom* (1896).

From the perspective of a century later, White's proposals seem both modest and appropriate. He rightly saw that if religion did not withdraw its impedimenta from the pathway of science, both the obstructions and the faith itself would be swept before the torrent. He proposed a new relationship of tolerance and coexistence that was to be of mutual benefit. Both pure and applied science were to thrive, and so was non-science. Cornell University was to be a place "in which the study of literature, ancient and modern, should be emancipated as much as possible from pedantry; and which should be free from various useless trammels and vicious methods which . . . hampered many, if not most of the American universities and colleges." He had taken accurate aim at the tradition-bound institutions of higher education. He correctly argued that neither science nor religion would prosper unless everything that trammeled were struck off—no matter what might appear to be the resultant dangers.

To promote these general purposes, White and Cornell agreed that the new institution would be characterized not only by undergraduate excellence but also by advanced instruction and research. White stuck by his principles and waged his fight for a full quarter-century, continuing as a member of the board of trustees after his retirement from the presidency of the university. This was the man whom the newly appointed trustees of the Johns Hopkins University consulted as they shaped their own designs for Baltimore.

Progress at Baltimore was unhindered by sectarian back-biting or political interference. Beholden to a sole benefactor (and he in his grave), the trustees had given no hostages either to politics or to the Church. The faculty at the Johns Hopkins University were free to pursue any research in any field and to disseminate their findings without fear. Scientism had found sanctuary.

The most notable departures in the teaching method at Baltimore were the replacement of lectures and recitations with seminars and laboratories. There was an undergraduate college of arts and science, but the chief emphasis was to be on graduate and professional schools together with a vigorous research effort. Research was the center of all else, and long before the "publish or perish" doctrine was conceived, an impressive quantity of publications annually came from the pens of Johns Hopkins professors.

The essence of the new university lay in its single-minded devotion to the scientific method. Almost literally, the researchers at the Johns Hopkins University followed the injunction of their British contemporary Huxley to "sit down before truth as a little child." It is true that Huxley himself appeared to some to hedge a little when he served (briefly but effectively) as a member of the newly constituted London School Board and in that position insisted that the Bible should be taught in the common schools. His reasons were pragmatic. He, like Aquinas, wanted to preserve the social order from disintegration. He wanted the Bible taught because it was great literature, but even more because he saw no other way by which "the religious feeling which is the essential basis of conduct, was to be kept up, in the present utterly chaotic state of opinion in these matters, without its use." The solution to the problem at Johns Hopkins was brilliant. Included among the great names on the faculty were Gildersleeve (Greek), Haupt (Semitics), and Harris (Biblical philology). The basic disciplines of theological study were directly embraced within the circuit of scientific research, along with all others. The position of dominance was reversed, theology becoming one among many instead of *primus inter pares.*

But if the trustees took their principal guidance as to general structure and purpose from Cornell University, it was from the German university that they imported their idea of research. Meticulous examination of carefully isolated bits of selected problems was to lead to fitting another small piece into the expanding mosaic of knowledge. All broader conclusions were to be held in suspense pending further insights. The precedent caught on. American undergraduates began to flock to Germany for their graduate studies. Holders of German doctorates thronged the American campus. The research university was in the process of being created in the United States, with the Johns Hopkins University as its stellar example and with scores of newly trained research professors fresh from their German studies settling in everywhere.

In the research university, the scientific spirit and method were to be everywhere in control. In whatever field or discipline, ideas were to be accepted only when they derived from experience and observation and could be verified by repeatable experiment. All a priori assumptions were to be questioned. Judgments were to be suspended, preconceived notions set aside. Reason, not intuition, was to guide inquiry and supply rationale. Values—those curious congeries of habit, mores, preference, custom, and superstition—were to be treated like everything else and tested along with other things; but since they were not readily amenable to the methods of scientific analysis, values must be in suspense for a time. Ethics became the relative study of relative values, the promotion of none.

The star that shone brightly from Baltimore quickly became the envy of many a professor or president who stood, rope in hand, waiting for the moment to hitch a wagon. Not until the excesses of the value-free technology (a principal fruit of scientism) began to come into a degree of critical disrepute in the 1960s because of a sudden concern over the pending exhaustion of natural resources and the imbalances of the ecosystem did the risen sun of scientism begin to wane. Scientism had hardly missed a stride in its onward rush when a temporary flurry of national disquiet followed the implosion over Hiroshima. The research university, fountainhead of scientism and custodian of the future of a scientifically managed world, had become the dominant fact of American higher education.

The Technological Institutes

The newly emancipated scientism not only dominated the American university, it also created its own special variety of institution.

In Boston, William Barton Rogers incorporated the Massachusetts Institute of Technology in 1861, but the onset of the Civil War interrupted his efforts. With the end of the war, he found the needed fiscal leverage in the Morrill Act. M.I.T. became a land grant institution. Rogers was a brilliant scientist and president of the National Academy of Sciences. Under his leadership, the new institution was dedicated to scientific pursuits to the exclusion of all else. By omitting the arts and humanities and social studies from its purview, M.I.T. avoided being embroiled in the raging controversy over evolution and the attendant exacerbating and debilitating struggle between science and religion. It was a decisive stroke of pragmatic genius by which Rogers and M.I.T. avoided the diversionary skirmishes that occupied White at Cornell. Furthermore, Rogers had the full advantages of a private institution with public support, protected by the land grant status of the institution. Before long, the institute had outgrown its Boylston Street buildings and had relocated on the Cambridge side of the Charles. Its original curriculum consisted of two branches of engineering plus chemistry and architecture. It quickly developed toward a score of engineering departments plus half a dozen scientific disciplines, added graduate work leading to master's degrees and doctorates, together with vigorous research in most of those fields. The practical success of the Rogers formula is exhibited by the fact that a century after its founding, the institution derives more than 90 percent of its annual budget support from the Federal government, mainly in the form of grants to support research; and at the same time, M.I.T. is independently controlled.

Similar institutes sprang up and prospered elsewhere; but this success has had its price. The deep concern over social and humanitarian values that erupted all over the nation during the Great Depression had its impact at the institutes of technology. No matter how excellent technicians their graduates might be, the technical institutes felt impelled to show an interest in the humane and social studies. Strong doses of these latter were injected into the M.I.T. curriculum and scientists and engineers were urged to stress the social obligations of their professions. It is probable that the technological institutes saw the inadequacies of specialized scientism at an earlier date than did the more inclusive institutions. The universities were still haggling over the warfare between the sciences and the humanizing studies, and their angular conversations had the effect of perpetuating rather than correcting the inadequacies of scientism. Thus, for example, it was not until the late 1940s that graduate students at the University of California in Berkeley (an institution which had taken on many of the characteristics of an M.I.T., particularly in its involvement with the science of the atom) revolted against an increasing narrowness of Berkeley's scientific offerings. Graduate students in physics, unable to obtain faculty sponsors or to pursue their studies in any field other than atomic physics, left the department and went into other fields such as political science.

Other great private institutes of technology such as Carnegie and California had experiences with their curricula not dissimilar to M.I.T.'s. But the prestige of the big research and graduate institutions, supported by increasing Government largess for research, led many a college or university (like Stanford in California), after World War II and especially during the post-Sputnik phase of congressional generosity, to extend themselves in the directions pioneered by M.I.T. and developed by Berkeley and others. The spirit of rationalism, coupled with the obvious prosperity of contract research both theoretical and applied, eclipsed all else on the American campus. Even the smaller liberal arts colleges developed a kind of presidential game of one-upmanship in making their trips to Washington—not only because Federal dollars for research might spell institutional solvency, but because institutional prestige went along with announcements of the grants and contracts. But Federal dollars were available primarily from the National Science Foundation, the Institutes of Health, and the Department of Defense. The imbalance in institutional interest and offerings that resulted from soliciting Federal monies for research in the scientific fields has left a permanent impression. That influence has scarcely been corrected by the tardy creation and modest funding of the National Foundation for the Humanities.

The Arrival of Scientism

The process seemed inevitable. It began with the natural sciences, physical and biological. In geology, astronomy, mathematics, chemistry, physics, in botany, zoology and ethnology (later, anthropology), the inductive method denied the validity of intuition and revelation, kept theory subordinate to observation and experimentation, permitted inference only subject to verification. While it is true that the great advances in physics in this century (the theory of relativity and the quantum theory) were first projected as theoretical speculations, it is also true that they were not accepted fully until experimental verification had validated them.

Seeing the physical and biological sciences forging ahead, and stung by the accusation that they were not also "scientific," the social studies took on the obligation of becoming scientific. That is to say, they moved away from deduction toward induction, from analysis of the qualitative aspects of life to the measurement of whatever could be quantified. They became less normative, more descriptive.

The difficulty lies not in the fact that the social studies attempted to become scientific, but in the fact that they adopted what should have been adapted. In the behavioral sciences, psychologists found themselves studying man from whom the psyche had been excised, sociology was becoming sociometrics, anthropology was retreating from evaluative comparison to descriptive empiricism. Economics discarded the a priori methods of Adam Smith and David Ricardo and Karl Marx to take on the coloration of half a dozen quarreling schools of thought whose principal common characteristic appears to be heavy reliance on computers. Political science, while retaining its affinity to history as a discipline and to philosophy as a fellow traveler, has become essentially the handmaiden of politics. What has happened in each case is a subtle but comprehensive shift away from the original *raison d'être* of the discipline. What started out as the marshaling of empirical data to support a proposed movement or to fulfill a desire (that is what Smith, Ricardo, and Marx did) by gradual change has become the amassing of data to describe a process. What was future-oriented, with the expectation of making a difference in human affairs, has become past- and present-oriented, with no larger ambition than that of studying what is going on.

If it were true that man is interested only in where he has been and not in where he is going, the social sciences might be said to be fulfilling their function. If, indeed, men were like ants or bees or elephants in all respects, then the methods of the biological sciences would be adequate for the social sciences. But the progression of scientism from the natural sciences to the social sciences, with insufficient adaptation of method and spirit, has produced in the colleges and universities a set of so-called social sciences that are not scientific and are less than social. They are less than social because society is a totality of relationships that can be understood only under a total scrutiny—never within the isolated purview of one or another of the disciplines subsumed as social sciences. They are not scientific because they do not adequately deal with all of man, including his systems of values, his motivations, his beliefs and preconceptions as *actual empirical data*. Such things are set aside, held in suspension, relegated to the "softer" fields of philosophy and the humane studies. Not being readily amenable to treatment through experimentation, and not being easily quantified for measurement, human values are not welcomed *as data* by the social sciences. Let the humanities have them.

Meanwhile, the humanistic studies and the arts, to whom the world of values has been delegated by default, are refusing to deal with matters that are unamenable to scientific method. Scientism has moved in on the humanistic studies as well. Let the point be illustrated by a few references: the fondness of a current school of philosophers for using the computer count of word usage as a tool of philosophical analysis; the degeneration of the study of languages into the abstract and abstruse areas of linguistics, also by means of computer counts. A typical example of the end result of the process is the assertion of the president of the Modern Language Association, that largest and most influential of all scholarly organizations in the humanistic fields, before the 1971 meeting of his association. He told them that the teaching of literature was no longer a legitimate objective for American higher education.

The overarching and undergirding framework of scientism in its institutional model is value-free university. Let the vulgarization of the culture be noted as revealing the extent to which the humane studies have become unhumane in an age when the suspension of values has created a vacuum that evokes vulgarization.

It is not that we bewail the transmutation of music into musicology, of art to criticism, of history to current events, and political science to politics. Transmogrification might conceivably lead to mutation and the emergence of some superior or less specious species. What is regrettable is the loss of standards of reference and of evaluation. Each discipline is left open and vulnerable to whatever spurious and unverified vulgarisms manage to seize the center of attraction, get translated into quantified respectability (with footnotes, of course), and to project their authors and sponsors into some new pinnacle of acclaim in the quickly passing review of academic irrelevance. The degree of immediate relevance, as measured by the amount and intensity of current interest, turns out to be the actual measure of irrelevance as each passing moment is succeeded by another. Nothing endures, either in meaning or in the meaning of life.

The fuller significance of the triumph of scientism in and through the value-free university can be seen in better perspective if we turn from history to the contemporary. There is a newly emergent campus force that has risen in revolt against the uncritical and uncriticized assumptions of scientism. It is not a resurgence of the mesmerized liberal tradition, which is still pursuing its false destiny by trying to become a value-free copy of scientism. But man being the complex and paradoxical contradiction that he is, there should have been no doubt that a countervailing force would rise to challenge the value-free research university. It did rise. It is here. We shall call it the existential university.

5

Trouble in the Groves

~§ "Radical historical moments like ours—characterized by extraordinary intensity of change, inertia and threat—call forth equally radical responses."

—Robert J. Lifton (1961)

"You taught me language; and my profit on't
Is, I know how to curse."

—Caliban, as Shakespeare gave him words in
The Tempest (1612)

Just when it began, no one can say with certainty. Reich, in his *Greening of America*, dates the moment of promise (as he sees it) with "a few individuals in the mid-nineteen-sixties." That date might serve as well as any, were it not for the fact that the roots go a little farther back in time.

As to what it may mean, there should be no disagreement: the value-free university has been challenged. It means that liberalism—as an expression of the widely tolerant skepticism of scientism under which technology burgeoned and science reigned; as the suspended judgment with a passion for patience; as the philosophical defender of noncommitment and noninvolvement; as the assertion of reason, suppressing all emotion and distrusting intuition—is accused of being bankrupt. It means, further, that academic freedom, cornerstone of the research university, has come into disrepute. The value-free university has been declared valueless.

The Crucible

The conviction that the value-free university is without value was not born overnight. It was nurtured through successive academic years and their intervening summers, as students became active in the civil rights movement of the early 1960s and then returned from their summer's confrontation with the cattle prod and the fire hose and the jail to find that their fight for justice and freedom was encouraged by Alma Mater only for so long as it took place somewhere else.

The decade was ushered in by four black students in Greensboro, North Carolina, who got the curious idea that a store that sold them toothpaste standing up should also serve them hamburgers sitting down. The decade ended with death by gunfire at Kent State University and Jackson State College. During the decade, the Berkeley syndrome developed and spread, the essential ingredients of that syndrome being (1) an intensifying absorption with racial injustice in the United States, (2) a gradual realization that surface injustices and hostilities actually indicated deep cleavages of caste that were repulsive to the democratic tradition and the ethical impulses of American youth, (3) an alienation from established authority and the agents and agencies of law enforcement, which were seen to be on the side of injustice. The national climate was prepared for the reception of the new perspective by the prairie fire of urban rioting that spread from Harlem and Rochester (1964) through Watts (1965), Chicago and Cleveland (1966) to Tampa, Cincinnati, Atlanta, Newark, and Detroit (1967), and burst into final conflagration in 1968 with the murder of Dr. Martin Luther King, Jr. The movement itself went through intensifying stages of development, from the sit-ins, freedom rides, freedom marches, wade-ins, and pray-ins, with their emphasis on nonviolence and interracial teamwork; through the voter registration drives (with three martyred students lying beneath an earthen dam outside Philadelphia, Mississippi); to confrontations of violence and clashes with police and military forces. The decade saw the National Guard used to open up the University of Mississippi to entrance by a Negro student. It also saw the National Guard shoot students to death. There was the murder of Medgar Evers, of four little girls at the Sixteenth Street Baptist Church on a Sunday morning in Birmingham, of Martin Luther King, Jr., on a Memphis balcony, and of Robert F. Kennedy in a Los Angeles kitchen corridor. Disillusioned over delayed school desegregation, resistance to the black vote, and tardy action by the Federal Government in the fields of employment and housing, a newly militant black force veered away from biracial nonviolent struggle and began to rely on Black Power with implied separatism. White liberals found themselves no longer welcome in some sections of the civil rights movement, and withdrew in dismay from the struggle for equality and justice, or began to be exercised with pangs of fancied guilt and contributed to the new separatism in the name of reparations and "black empowerment." Along the way, satellite movements for liberation developed: Gay Liberation, Women's Liberation. The Indian and the Chicano were emboldened to action. Suddenly, almost without warning, ecology came into the common vocabulary of concern.

Running through the decade, as a continually recurring theme and a point of constant emphasis, was revulsion to the war in Indochina. As American armed forces increased from a few thousand advisers to half a million ground troops with their massive support from air and sea, Selective Service call-ups grew larger. Anxiety on campus mounted. There is some truth in the allegation that the college campus was used, during the 1960s, as a means of escaping the draft. Those who couldn't afford to go to college, or who lacked the academic qualifications, could be drafted; but we who are in college have only to keep our bills paid and our grades up to be safe. It was like the 1860s, when the son of a rich man hired the son of a poor man to take his place in the draft. The difference was that by 1960 the price had gone up a little.

Not all undergraduates felt completely easy in their minds about their privileged position on campus as compared to others who had been drafted. Stung by guilt, the student resented his situation. He blamed the war that threatened to engulf him. He blamed the college that sheltered him. And he resented the fact that his first task in college was to keep his grades up so that he wouldn't be drafted. Imperceptibly at first, then quite openly, and finally with brazen shamelessness, college youth wrung from their empathetic professors a compassionate concern over their academic standing. By 1967, no professor willingly "poured napalm on a boy," which meant that he gave him at least a C no matter what his grade should have been. Academic priorities were reversed and made to serve draft-postponement purposes: grades became the supreme objective. Learning could wait. The whole educational process began to be vitiated and held in something less than full respect. Some professors entered openly into collusion with their students: their classes were thronged.

When the draft calls grew quite large, Selective Service began to talk about taking men into the armed services during an academic year instead of waiting for the end of a term. To do that, it was proposed that men should be called up in reverse order to their rank in their class. At that point, agitation against the giving of grades and the ranking of students according to grades embroiled faculty members as well as administrators in an exacerbating debate over whether or not to cooperate with Selective Service by furnishing information about a student's rank in class. Some faculties solemnly voted not to supply such information to Selective Service. Many seriously considered abandoning the grading system altogether: there would then be no higher or lower ranks. At the City College of New York, two or three junior members of the instructional staff became minor folk heroes overnight with their solution to the dilemma of giving grades that might lead to differential ranking of students: they gave everyone an A. Women students found themselves directly embroiled in the agitated controversy when they were told that *all* students' grades, including those of women, were to be counted in determining the class rank of any male student. Should conscientious co-eds deliberately flunk or work for low marks in order to give their men a better chance? Agitation against ranking of students and the giving of grades to determine who might be drafted reached paranoiac proportions.

On-campus expressions of the military Establishment became targets of student and faculty antagonism. The R.O.T.C. was vilified, held up to ridicule and contempt, mocked and derided. Its quarters were vandalized or burned. Defense-related research, especially if it were "classified," became a favorite target of demonstrators and writers in the student press. With each academic year, certain industrial concerns were selected as that year's special targets: when their recruiters came to hire seniors, the representatives of the "military-industrial complex" were the subjects of bitter demonstration, mass opposition, physical attack.

Simultaneous reporting by press and television kept each demonstration before the public, making all campuses one audience and greatly multiplying the impact of each action. One widely publicized instance sums it all up. When Secretary McNamara visited Harvard University in 1969, student mass action and rudeness prevented him from completing his mission in peace; but when the president of the university attempted to evoke formerly reliable sentiments by appealing to civility, his applause came from *The New York Times*, not from the students. They laughed at him. If there had remained any doubt, it was now clear that the student of the 1960s no longer wanted to be known as a gentleman.

The feeling-tone of the times also revived the latent pacifist movement that had been dormant since the early thirties when the Oxford Pledge swore students around the world never again to fight "for Queen and Country." Pacifist opposition to war in general was intensified by revulsion against the particular war in Indochina. The bloody antidraft riots of the 1860s had their counterpart in the campus demonstrations of the 1960s. As the peace movement gathered force, it drew to itself all the radical and revolutionary campus groups, as well as all the anti-Establishment energies, in a united front that gave many a small group of dedicated activists a potential campus following of major proportions. Any incident, real or manufactured, sparked a sit-in or launched a demonstration, a take-over, or a strike. College and university presidents knew they were sitting on volcanoes, not so much because all presidents supported the war in Indochina (not all did), but because the handiest on-campus target was that man behind the president's desk.

Academia had become paranoid. Not until the blood of students stained the ground at Kent State University and Jackson State College did the fury of the seizure pass. With the approach of war's end and the winding down of the draft system, the intensity of the activity subsided. One final spasm of activity brought an estimated 100,000 to demonstrate around the Washington Monument while the President was being reinaugurated. As the war limped to its halt in an uneasy truce, it left a constricting scar of antagonism, bitterness, disillusionment, and distrust across the heart of academia. All through the decade, opposition to the unpopular war furnished the tinder and fed the fires kindled around all other issues that crowded the troubled campus through these times.

Applying the Heat

Throughout these developments, institutions were changing—but never fast enough to keep ahead of student demands and expectations. Earlier requests for meaningful dialogue became angry insistence on confrontation instead of talk. Violence and counterviolence, including guerrilla warfare and the use of troops to buttress police, turned the pleasant groves of Academe into something more nearly resembling the Argonne Forest in 1918. Discussion, reason, the democratic process, all were casualties. The institutions were alternately besieged, tolerated, or held in contempt.

A new life-style was being born. A new breed of college student emerged. He did not glow with gratitude simply because he had been admitted to candidacy for a degree. He questioned whether a degree was worth getting. He ceased to value the degree because he began to reject all the values it symbolized. Told to be objective, to suspend his emotions, delay making judgments, tolerate those who disagreed with him, defer his satisfactions and defer to authority, he cried out in incoherent rage. Why didn't the institution *care!* Look at what is happening! We are people, persons, human beings—not IBM cards with numbers. Do Not Bend, Fold, or Spindle Us! We are not excited about the white-coat path to a Nobel prize: it was scientists who gave us the atom bomb and invented napalm. What else will they give us today?!

The new student was not enamored of a civilization that condoned rat-infested slums and permitted urban blight and decay. He did not stand in awe or admiration of a technology that took men to the moon and back, because that same technology left several million dollars worth of choice garbage on the moon each trip, and that technology was unable to ingest its own waste on the earth. He began to believe that the American Dream was really a nightmare.

By the end of the decade, as a recent study has shown, three in every ten college undergraduates of the nation said they wanted to live their adult lives somewhere else than in the United States. For that sizable fraction of college students, alienation had reached its provisional climax. They rejected the whole thing.

And since the whole of contemporary America, including its universities, was allegedly bankrupt, the values of that society and of its institutions of higher education were discarded. The Now generation had arrived, with its own evolving values, its own changing codes (uncodified), its own readiness to strike out in different directions toward a new and different day.

The central virtue of scientism and liberalism was "tolerance." The Now generation labeled it "hypocrisy" and rejected it. A new absolute was erected and called "sincerity." On that new absolute stood the new superstructure of the "new intolerance." This new intolerance could be disarmingly genteel, but it abhorred the ideal of the gentleman. Never for one moment could the Now generation relax its own basic ruthlessness: that was its own protection and shield against a hostile world. Ambivalence in conduct became normal; logical contradiction, expected. Idealistic pronouncements about the Beloved Community alternated with the thrown half-brick or the Molotov cocktail. Wanton vandalism blossomed into guerrilla warfare, to be interspersed with long rap sessions or just quiet sunning on the green. Rejecting the mass processes of the multiversity, the Now generation nevertheless readily resorted to mass demonstration and mass revolt. Alternating between periods of activism and intervals of waiting, rejecting the prevailing values of the Establishment but not yet sure what, if any, values ought to be established, and pushed toward the new experiences of each moment by the terrible urgencies of that Future Shock Toffler delineates, the college and university student of the 1960s and early 1970s does not find his answer in any of the models of higher education available to him.

The humane and liberating studies, originally intended for

an elite, do not have universal appeal or applicability when the student population includes (as it now does) a larger proportion of the total population stream *in college* than had graduated from the *eighth grade* at the turn of the century. A system of higher education believed to be right for an elite fraction is now under ever widening pressures. Neither the parietal rules nor the paternalism of the classical college evokes enthusiasm or empathy from the Now generation.

The practical studies for vocation and profession likewise provide no answer: affluence and personal security, the goals of professional and vocational education, have proved to be elusive for many—vacuous when attained. Poverty haunts the nation. Its middle class is insecure and apprehensive. The professional and vocational institutions that were especially designed to serve as ladders of upward mobility found themselves standing like staircases in half-ruined castles, leading to nowhere.

Finally, the research university, institutional expression and embodiment of scientism, has become the supreme object of exasperation and contempt because it is both the source and the expression of all the values that the Now generation rejects.

In order to reject the institutions and the values that the institutions symbolized, it was necessary to reject the authority of both institutions and institutionalized values. If it was right to oppose authority when it was on the wrong side of the civil rights issue in the South, then it was equally correct to oppose authority in the North (and especially on campus) when that authority was wrong. If civil disobedience was a virtue when practiced by Martin Luther King, what made it a vice when practiced on campus by undergraduates? Here was one more instance of the hypocrisy of the academic Establishment! So, don't yield to authority on campus any more than off. Just as the police dogs and truncheons did not turn us around down South, so, also, we ain't gonna let nobody turn us around up

North. Demonstrate. Sit in. Lie in. Take over. Bring the institutional juggernaut to a grinding halt. Disregard authority
whenever you can. Disobey it always.

But keep the cops off campus. We know that prexy wants
peace, not violence. We know that academic tradition has always said that the campus is a sanctuary, where the civil authorities are kept out. Academic discipline won't hurt us: they
can't expel the whole student body. If any of us get caught,
we will say that all of us are equally guilty, and demand that
all of us be punished. Remember Spartacus! We can handle
this stuffed-shirt institution and its hypocritical automatons.
They're a pushover. Just keep the cops out of it.

And when the cops did come—police brutality! It's simple.
When arrested, go limp. Make them drag you to the paddy
wagon, and dress so as to be ready to be roughed up. Perhaps
you squirm a little at the right moment and get clubbed? It'll
be on the six o'clock news all over the networks. Do it a few
times to make the cops look bad. Next time, they'll be mad
even before they get here.

All too often, they were.

But when you get in trouble, don't take it lying down. Get
a lawyer. The rest of us will work the mimeographs. We'll
demand universal amnesty as the first concession. The administration doesn't want trouble, so they'll cave in. If they don't
cave in, we have another issue, one that will get the whole
campus behind us—free speech.

The actual language, of course, was never quite that polite.
The unprintable obscenities that became standard language
over the bullhorn were calculated to irritate the nostrils of the
administration and delight the ears of the rebels. The filthy
speech movement was born. It became at once an integral part
of the spreading Berkeley syndrome. After all, it was an up-
roariously funny way to unsettle the equanimity of the administration.

Unsettling the administration's equanimity led easily to

unbalancing the equilibrium of authority—and that meant that institutional authority itself was in grave peril. The spirit of liberalism, which permeated and guided most campuses and their administrators, was not prepared to deal with the new campus mood of contempt, disdain, and contumacy. Liberalism's spirit of tolerance, in the earlier stages of campus revolt, invoked its accustomed readiness to empathize with the rebels —the classical liberal is one who can defend everyone but himself, and does. When dealing with other liberals, liberalism is protected by the rules of civility; but the newly emergent campus forces were illiberal: they played a different game, by quite different rules.

The institutions of higher education were in deep trouble. In a single semester—spring, 1968—student protests and campus unrest (something more than mere petitioning and agitating) broke out on 232 campuses. The climactic year of the decade exploded in incidents of major importance on more than half of the nation's campuses—incidents that included arson in more than two hundred instances, and which in more than half of the confrontations featured interruption, disruption, or complete cessation of academic pursuits for periods of time running from a single day to several weeks. Fully reported on television, radio, and underground communications, these campus disruptions were front-page news for the press. Each new outbreak of violence fed the fires of public criticism, with off-campus forces (especially politicians and officeholders) beating out a mounting crescendo of caustic comment and alarmist denunciation.

Under these pressures from within and without, the frail fabric of institutional authority crumbled. Court injunctions were used instead of presidential pronouncement. Police supplemented—and then replaced—campus guards, to be followed by the state troopers and the National Guard. The processes of criminal justice took over. Campus authority over student life was in eclipse. Soon it was gone altogether. The charges preferred against students, and for which they were arrested, arraigned, tried, convicted, and sentenced, ranged from simple misdemeanor to first-degree felony, from trespass to kidnapping and arson. (The accusations of homicide were leveled at the peace officers and militia, not the students.) Slowly, then suddenly, the institutions of higher learning discovered that they had, by default and inadvertence, lost control over what had once been matters of on-campus discipline. The life-style of students became in fact a matter of *sui juris*. Authority? What authority? The campus no longer had any to exercise.

Destroying authority was only incidental to larger ends. There was the tyranny of the required curriculum: it must be overthrown. That little matter of the grading system: it gets us in trouble with the Army, remember? And the faculty has too much power. And, oh, yes, pot. And sex. And a few other things like that stinking Rotcy. How long do we let Them tell us what we can't do!

In all these ways, and many more, the gentle groves of Academe were troubled.

The Existential University

Not all college students during the 1960s were rebels. Not all were escapists. Not all were revolutionaries. Not all joined the Now generation. Probably the larger number, by far, were none of these. They were just young people who were going to college when all this came along.

Whether the squares or the freaks will win in the long run is not an open question. Neither will. Both will continue to cohabit the campus; but both will be modified by intergroup osmosis and mobility. The resultant campus society will be something different, if not new. It will, in turn, finally begin to produce its own stasis. And against that, a future generation will arise, using, for example, the crew cut and polished shoes as symbols of *their* declaration of independence from the sloppiness of their undisciplined elders who got that way back in the 1960s and 1970s.

But, long before that day arrives—and *if* it is to arrive—there are still a few struggles to be entertained.

Growing up inside the institutions of higher education, or just off campus, is a new type of higher education. The existential university is being created by persons of all ages who have become members or *aficionados* of the Now generation. Disenchanted with their role as spectators, they demand the right to become involved, at the same time that they refuse to be co-opted in that involvement. They wish to participate; but only on their own terms. Lacking the restraints and controls of the traditions they have rejected, freed from the claims of morality and contemptuous of the requirements of law or authority, the Now generation is creating its own values and its own life-style. They want to be "relevant," to make a difference, to say yes to life, not death, as they see it. They are creating the existential university.

They began by abandoning the past and attacking the present while despairing of the future—precisely because they had first despaired of the future, which had been determined by the past and bequeathed by the present. For them, immediate and unmediated experience replaces vicarious observation and rational analysis. Involvement, voluntary involvement, replaces authority. Emotion and intuition, even revelation, supersede reason.

They demand that life begin to mean something here and now. To that end, education (which is all the life they have just now) will have to be made over into something that has genuine meaning here and now—not somewhere else and later on. And since the meaning of each successive moment is unique, and each different "now" takes place in a different "here," the meanings are always different. There are no eternal verities, no permanent values. There is not even a discernible continuity of meaning in history. Whatever is to be accepted as the meaning of any moment of experience must be subjective, not objective. It must be vivid, real, intimate, personal. It must happen right now. To me. So that I can feel it. That is what "relevant" means in the emerging existential university.

The existential university tries not to take a fixed shape or structure. If it should happen to find itself engaged in a project, it begins at once to search for an unproject to engage in. Structure is a trap, to be avoided. Authority uses structure. The existential university, existing in many forms and structures, attempts to be formless and unstructured. Any effort to classify it in a scheme of structural models is therefore useless. Indeed, it is less a structure than an attitude. It breaks out from the established structures of higher education wherever it can make the opportunity. It is found in greater numbers, flourishing in greater variety, on the campuses where the liberal tradition or the research emphasis has prevailed. It gets its best start where the two are combined, or where they coexist without combining, in a contradictory and vulnerable paradox of tolerance. The campuses that attract primarily professional and vocational students are less susceptible to the existential virus, because student self-selection has given them a larger proportion of the squares than of the freaks.

As a result of its aversion to being structured, the existential university often penetrates existing structures with its attitudinal revolution. A particular class or course of studies may be a good beginning. Whole departments, perhaps schools within a larger university, are changed in character. When it is true to its genius, the existential university emphasizes the present happening as being the real meaning of the learning experience. Such matters as logic, syntax, the meaning and use of appropriate words, appreciation of literature, the history of thought, rote learning, or memory exercises are deemphasized or excised altogether. Tests, examinations, and grades are abhorred. Competition between students is anathema—share the wealth! To be admitted to the existential university, a teacher must cease to instruct. He becomes a fellow experiencer, sometimes a resource person, never a dictator of what ought to be the learning outcomes. Almost any important or unimportant facet or characteristic of the established college or university is automatically suspected, resisted, or rejected. Whatever is part of what has been will be of little use in serving our experience in what is.

Frequently, the existential university strikes out in new directions, that is to say, in pursuit of some curricular notion that is not in the catalog. Who wants it, if it is there already? That means it has been. From Zen Buddhism to ethnic dance, an almost random series of exploratory experiences gets established, frequently to die a quick death rather than to become embalmed in the half-life of the accepted curriculum. Permanence is a contradiction of the transitoriness of meaning. What counts is the feeling-tone of the passing paraders.

Emphasis is upon self-understanding, self-realization, self-expression, rather than upon the mastery of any so-called subject matter. When this emphasis is coupled with the denigration of form and structure, the result is an attitude in which the student progressively impoverishes his vocabulary. Since each new experience is beyond words, words should not be used in an effort to capture meanings. Meanings can be neither captured nor conveyed. They can only be experienced. Only the ineffable, the inexpressible counts. When one has been there, he does not need to tell others who have also been there; and unless you have been there, you have no way of understanding anyway. There is no need to try to reduce experience to thought and language in order to communicate, because experience cannot be communicated when it is so reduced. "Like, wow!" tells how you feel. The real meanings are not rational, therefore cannot be confined in rational terms or rationally communicated. The deemphasis of the rational processes and the refusal to use accurately defined words to convey careful meanings are essential components of the attitudinal syndrome that rejects both the liberal educational tradition and the research university.

Membership in the existential university is in continual flux, with students moving in or out, or partly in or partly out. Numbers are usually greater at the beginning of a term: less as the examinations in regular courses approach. Resistance to authority dictates rejection of structure, so that the existential university is amorphous. Its vitality derives from its fluidity. Its attractiveness depends upon the absence of demanding discipline.

The existential university is not to be confusingly identified with the experimental college. The latter is a frequently used device of the Establishment, designed to bring new ideas or different practices into an institution. Famous examples like Alexander Meiklejohn's at Wisconsin in the 1930s have flourished. The Great Depression saw many experimental colleges spring up, both in the W.P.A. and outside it. The experimental college is an accepted part of the campus scene in a respectable number of institutions today.

On some campuses, where the administration and faculty have not preempted the opportunity by setting up an experimental college, the existential university moves in, calling itself an experimental college. Hence the occasional confusion. In these instances, the experimental-existential college will keep structure and formality to a minimum and attempt to promote free exploration reminiscent of Ezra Cornell's ideal: "A place where anybody can study anything he wants." The similarity ends with that sentence. The existential college is randomly developed. It moves from interest to passing interest, as the inclinations and whims—or deep yearnings—of its participants suggest. Anything more formal would be a violation of its essential spirit, and that spirit *is* the existential college. To the existentialist, it is more important than logical form, continuity, permanence, or objectives. The spirit of freedom (as it is understood) blows through the existential university. There are to be no compulsions, no requirements, no restrictions, no inhibitions. Follow the spirit of experience wherever it leads, whenever you feel like it.

Therein is the heart of the matter of its challenge to the research university. Huxley, giant precursor of scientism, would have had all preconception and all emotion set to one side, all involvement held in abeyance, all subjectivity eliminated, in order that with a completely open mind man might follow truth. But Huxley set all else aside in order to free the rational processes. The existential university sets the rational processes aside in order to free everything else. With intuition and emotion, through revelation and ecstasy, meaning is to be experienced in following the spirit of experience. And what is that spirit? It is not to be imprisoned in language, not to be reduced to words, not to be trammeled or captured. It is the first, fine careless rapture uncaptured. It is the inexpressible, beautiful, fulfilling feeling. The butterfly is to be enjoyed as it flits colorfully from shadow to sunlight, hovering, then darting off randomly and unpredictably. It is not to be caught in a net, chloroformed, pinned under glass, and classified.

In the existential university, there is a sense of sanctuary, of escape from a world that is too much with us, laying waste. There is balm for the wounded heart, severely bruised by the angularities and harshness of a fixed curriculum with its invidious grading system. There is a feeling of equality among equals, as the *Lumpen* of the world gather together. There is leisure and relaxation for those who are tired of the treadmill. There is an end to confusion and the coming of the moment when ". . . all my lines lie parallel within me." If there must be an effort to express meanings through words, let it be done in poetry, not prose. Poetic license lets words be used as one feels them to be helpful at the moment of utterance, not as those meanings are cramped into the confining pages of Webster. And poetry should always be spoken, in order that its inflections and emphases may be the better savored.

In the existential university, poetry is preferred to prose partly because poetic meanings can be quite different to two different listeners, partly because poetry is not expected to be a precise carrier of precise meanings: it is expected to be what it is, a poetic interpretation of meanings undefined. The best poetry is therefore formless itself. It follows neither logic nor rhyme nor reason. It lets words come together on the page and say whatever they say, as the poet permits the existential moment to speak through him.

It was no passing aberration that led Plato to distrust all poets. Champion of the use of clear logic and precise definition, he used mental processes both oral and silent to discover and to convey meanings. He would have crowned all poets with garlands of wool and ushered them out of town. The liberal arts tradition, in its aversion to the precisions of scientism, has not fully shared with Plato the scientific aversion to poetry's imprecision. The liberal tradition has drawn strength from Plato's emphasis upon man and mind as opposed to observation, and in that it has welcomed the original antiscientific thrust of Platonism. It has drawn even more heavily from Aristotle. But within the liberal tradition, poetry has its primary place as a means of conveying meanings both rational and emotional. In the liberal tradition, poetry adorns the meanings it conveys. In the research university, poetry exists to be analyzed. In the existential university, poetry cannot be analyzed. It neither adorns nor conveys meaning. It *is* meaning. If the existential university followed the rules of logic, it would logically conclude that the best poetry (that which carries the most meaning) uses no words at all. It does actually begin to approach this state when, as with Ginsberg, everything is resolved in the resonant "Om."

When life's meanings are found primarily in the afferent rather than the cognitive and rational processes, human relationships take on a special quality. To "relate" to one another becomes very important, especially when no words are exchanged and the quiet silence spreads its welcome pinions. Each feels his relatedness to each other, and the fewer words that accompany that feeling, the more authentic it is felt to be. (Much the same quality of experience comes, not through shared silence, but through shared stimulation of the senses, as in the room that is thunderously reverberating with acid rock while colored lights bathe the scene in riotous confusion.) Words may precede or follow the moments of interpersonal communion, but communication through language is not to be substituted for communion. Understandings are immediate. They come at once, and they need no mediator.

Externals tend to be minimized in the existential university. Differences of race or nationality or sex—sometimes even of age—fade away and are ignored or forgotten. Mutual trust becomes very precious. "Sincerity" is the touchstone of human contact. The naked spirit greets others, unadorned and unashamed, gladly communing. After that, mere communication is very mere indeed.

Being antirational and hence frequently irrational, the existential university sees no contradiction between its unreadiness to use the form and structures of contemporary society and its readiness to identify its own membership by conformity to its chosen life-styles and standards. Modes of dress and hairdressing, of eating and sleeping and drinking, of smoking, of relaxing or working, tend to become more or less standardized within the community as the existential university identifies itself and its membership. Conformity to the mores of the *Lumpen* is not felt as something forced upon one: it is the badge of membership, gladly worn. When their fellow students and their professors and administrators look upon these external signs of the existential fellowship and accuse the existential university of establishing its own tyranny of conformity, they err. They fail to grasp the fact that it is not conformity they are witnessing. It is communication. Gesture, dress, vocabulary, life-style, all should be viewed not as the externals of a new conformity but as a declaration of group independence from the tyrannies of Establishment conformity.

Not all who adopt the externals of the existential university are bona fide members of it; but those who are members can readily distinguish between the hypocrite and the sincere adherent. "Sincerity" is the touchstone, and on that rock is founded the Church of the New Intolerance. The demands that are made on the psyche of the insincere who try to get accepted into the existential university are the SAT scores of that institution. Just as the research university tells its entering freshman to check his emotions with the registrar and postpone his satisfactions until after graduation, so the existential university tells its potential convert to open up his spirit, his emotions, and his feelings. As for his mind, either blow it or leave it at home on the closet shelf. The existential university rejects the primacy of reason and exalts the freedom of nonreason.

From that rejection (and acceptance) flow a series of consequences: (1) exclusiveness—if you insist on intruding reason and logic into our relationships and explorations, you are a doubting Thomas: go back to the loneliness of the research university; (2) parochialism—we have no compassion for those who do not like us and will not be like us; (3) self-righteousness—we know what is best for us and for the world, and in that feeling of rightness we make no apologies for feeling righteous; (4) inner peace—we have excluded the problems that bothered us, and found peace within ourselves; (5) quickness to anger—stop doing evil and begin to do good as we understand it, and do it right now; (6) transience—don't expect me to become a slave to anything because I'm on a trip that goes right on to the next thing right away; and (7) sensitiveness—because I feel rather than think, I keep myself open to experience (and I *do* know the difference between sensitiveness and sensitivity, but don't throw definitions at me).

Few members of the existential university will completely accept the foregoing paragraphs in their entirety as being an accurate or adequate grasp of truth. The only reply that can be given goes along these lines: until someone who is inside the existential university violates his own commitment to unreason and becomes rational long enough to use words and sentences and paragraphs of prose in their proper sequence and connotation and thereby give us a rational statement, we are forced either to abandon the effort to understand the existential university or else to supply the language ourselves. The mirror may be faulty, but there has been an honest effort to hold it steadily and to report the reflection faithfully. It may be true that the existential university cannot be described in words, since language is a rational tool; but those of us who are accustomed to use language to convey thoughts as well as feelings should not be too severely faulted for attempting to understand what we see and to report it as faithfully and honestly as we can.

There is, nevertheless, a certain quality of the existential university that finally defies all effort to define it and put it into language. Perhaps it might be suggested by calling it the appeal to the primitive. Prehistoric man had no language of words. He used the language of gesture and grunt. And since, without language, thoughts cannot be communicated, only feelings, he communicated his feelings and felt no lack of something more. The existential university is, perhaps unwittingly, attempting to return to a more primitive time when the Noble Savage roamed free. Certainly, one of its basic motivations, though not necessarily defined, appears in its constant effort to escape the complexities of our time, to reduce life to its simplicities, to reduce the conflicts and turmoil and tensions and ugliness and pollution and busyness to simpler terms of personal relatedness in the bonds of unspoken and unspeaking mutual trust. Thoreau's Walden beckons.

There was a time when the nucleus of the emerging existential university fastened its attention on the use of mind-blowing drugs, beginning with the psychedelic LSD and moving on to more esoteric heights. It was hoped that one might find through the trip what could be found no other way. The existential emphasis is open to the suggestion: tune in, turn on, escape to reality. Here was the completely and absolutely existential Thing! No need to be logical or to use the laborious processes of reason. No need to deny emotions or defer gratifications. Drop out of what bores or aggravates and enter the world of the ineffable. Seize the day. Seize the hour. Let the moment rule. As the lonely shepherd boy responds with leaping heart to the pipes of Pan, so the existential emphasis is open to the induced trip.

If persisted in, this emphasis within the existential university could destroy it and its membership, leaving nothing but a generational basket case. And who would then be presumptuous enough to assess the blame and point the faulting finger? Would it not be enough to know that much of the potential intellectual and moral leadership of the nation had dropped out into the gray shadows of slavery to the needle and the pills?

The existential university is, on most points and in most of its expressions, substantially different from and frequently at loggerheads with both the research university and the liberal education tradition, as well as with the particular practical goals of vocational and professional education. The existential university is on a collision course with all the other ships in the academic flotilla. For that matter, all the others in our little fleet seem to be sailing without general orders.

And there are so many human beings on board.

Through the 1960s and into the 1970s, the several traditions and modes of living that (to change the metaphor) have cohabited the campus have behaved less like human beings than like animals. They have, at times, been at pains to try to destroy one another. Each speaking its own accustomed vocabulary, talking to itself but about the others, has expressed the spirit of the Mock Turtle's arithmetic: Ambition, Distraction, Uglification, and Derision. Cohabitation has not brought conviviality and creativity. It has not been even a common-law marriage. It has spread distrust, contempt, conflict, misunderstanding, academic fratricide.

The confrontation has brought out the worst, not the best, in each. From the tradition that calls itself liberal, it has elicited the repressive restraints of a Puritan heritage rather than a liberating faith in human perfectibility. From the research university it has evoked a defensive reassertion of pride in technology together with a stubborn reliance on whatever is rational, to the exclusion of anything emotional, instead of the quiet humility of the inquiring mind. From the practical and vocational emphases in higher education it has drawn a stout reassertion of the cash value of higher education rather than a recovery of the moral commitment of the Morrill Acts to the alleviation of poverty and the correction of injustice. Finally, this warfare in the groves of Academe has led the existential university to lose sight of its own reason for being, to skip dizzily from one moment's fad to the next, running through the gamut of the great causes of mankind like so many truncated and unrelated items in a standard college curriculum—as though the great ideals were like so many childhood diseases, each to be contracted temporarily in mild form in rapid succession, with resulting total immunity from all. From civil rights to antipoverty crusade, to antiwar, to the Pill, to pills, to Gay Liberation, to Women's Lib, to ecological balance, to the population bomb, the existential university has blithely skipped, careful not to get permanently involved in any. What might have been the great awakening on the American campus, an awakening to a clear and compelling vision, has petered out into an embittered rush to hurry through the immediacy of each issue without lingering long enough with any of them to see it through. (Even the most nearly persisting emphasis, the opposition to the war in Indochina, turns out now not to have been an effort to do away with war at all—just an effort to get American troops out of Vietnam.) So it has happened that the campus of the sixties provoked the worst instead of evoking the best, in each of the life-styles that coexisted as distrustful strangers.

But what might happen if the best of each tradition were to be drawn upon in a common effort is worth a passing thought. Suppose that the warmth and immediacy of the existentialists, the moral idealism of the liberal tradition, the patient doggedness of the research tradition, and the practical concerns of the land grant tradition were to combine in a single effort to remake higher education. What might bring this about?

If the picture of national and global peril that was limned in Chapter Two is anywhere near the truth; the descriptions of escapism rehearsed in Chapter Three even partly true to fact; the history and assessment of higher education that occupied Chapter Four even distantly related to the truth of the matter; and the realities reviewed in Chapter Five even in some small part correctly stated—if these things are as stated, then one concludes that the issues are clearly joined. They are joined in a confrontation between the generations.

The Generation Gap

Insofar as the campus is concerned, the confrontation of the generations comes down squarely to a challenge to the research university by the existential university. Although there are more persons under twenty-five than over thirty-five in the existential university, both rivals have their younger and older matadors and *aficionados*. The lines of cleavage have not been rationally defined. Instead, differences in life-style have served as symbols for each group, all the more effective because emotional responses are evoked most efficiently when rational processes are not used.

Nevertheless, it may be worth the effort to apply a rational scheme to an irrational confrontation. Perhaps it can be done

without undue distortion of the meanings of the so-called
generation gap on campus.

Among the elements of the confrontation are:

1. The stubborn immobility of the old tolerance, exalting
reason and denigrating feeling, calling for patient postponement of the moment of satisfaction; confronted by

2. the arrogance of the new intolerance, rejecting rational
process and immersing itself in immediate and unmediated experience, indulging each moment to the full, brooking no
delay of satisfactions and demanding immediate and unquali-
fied commitment to the changing values of each moment;

3. the slowness of institutional change; in the face of

4. mounting expectations prompted by easy promises too
often proffered without a realistic time schedule for correcting the sources of moral outrage; confined in

5. the pressure cooker of an incredible future shock that
made the stuff of every moment of experience expendable,
obsolete even as it occurred, the future becoming past almost
before its present had been savored; and therefore

6. the shortness of time before threatening crisis becomes
actual catastrophe; coupled with

7. the possibility that the course of the immediate future
may be determined not by rational men and women through
democratic processes but by preponderant power serving irrational and repressive counterproductive purposes; because

8. an angry backlash is evoked by

9. the nonnegotiable demands springing from instant disillusionment that was born of disappointed instant idealism;
the whole being characterized by

10. the absence of accepted meanings and commonly held
values, without which neither communication nor understanding becomes possible.

The so-called generation gap is not a new phenomenon. It
has been a constant factor all through human history; but
never before has the opposition between the generations been

as decisively important. Always before, there has been time to permit inevitable adjustment to be made—sometimes evolutionary, sometimes revolutionary, but always with time to complete the struggle without endangering human survival. There is no such leisure now. The confrontation of values that the generation gap symbolizes without rightly expressing, is a struggle for the survival of the human race and all that is of value in human life. It is a struggle, be it noted, in which neither side appears to be giving answers to the human condition that will lead to survival; both sides appear to be bent on winning over each other by destroying themselves as well.

The accelerating pace of events since World War II has widened the gap, deepened the chasm. And the tools of rationalism and democracy that bridged the gap in previous times of peril appear ineffective for our day because each side tends to reject these tools whenever it appears to be losing in the power struggle. At the present time, the older generation has the power. It therefore repeats the accustomed rituals of national self-esteem, trying to evoke support, or at least compliance, from the younger generation. But chanting the liturgies does not win the approval of the disenchanted and the dispossessed. Such invocatory ritual has about the same effect as staging a black-face minstrel show at the Apollo in central Harlem.

And yet, if there is to be a future and *we* are to be in it, the shape of that future will be determined by what we—all of us—choose to do now. Especially will it be determined by what will be held to be precious by today's young adults as they come to power. In fine, all components of the crisis are reducible to the problem of values.

The Crisis of Values

Our difficulties of decision do not lie primarily in the area of technology. It is true that our problems derive to a very large extent from the fact that our technology is a concretion of the value-free scientism that does not and cannot supply the moral and rational controls essential to its direction; but our difficulties are not primarily those of know-how. We can no longer afford the irresponsibility of letting know-how tell us that whatever can be done ought to be done. Runaway technology is not managed for far-visioned purpose.

Neither is our difficulty primarily a matter of tactics and timing, of know-when. Such expertise is readily supplied by know-how *if* technology is required to schedule itself for any purpose. It is done now, in simply carrying out technological processes for their own ends. It is not inconceivable that our know-how could supply the know-when, if only we knew the which.

Paralysis of decision on the spaceship *Earth* comes from the lack of a relevant and commonly accepted know-why from which a definite know-which might be derived. If our value system—our controlling purposes, our goals, our measures and evaluations, our qualitative preferences, our moral choices— were developed to anything like the level of sophisticated excellence we have demonstrated in our technology, all the rest would be a swinging descent in the breeze to a welcome splashdown in a calm sea.

The simile is partly apposite, but not wholly. As our spaceship *Earth* hurtles toward the point in time at which the wrong decision, or indecision, will forever seal our fate, no friendly Houston stands by to relay a computerized program to be fed into the controls. The answers we need are qualitative. They are intricately complex. They are shot through with problems of power and limited or altered by considerations of compassion and of ruthlessness. They deal with the human condition. And *we* have to supply them. With all our know-how, we are immobilized and impotent at the controls. Meanwhile, precious, critically important, irreversible, nonreturning time rushes by. If we miss the narrow reentry window, whether by indecision or wrong decision, there will be no splashdown.

Shooting the moon was child's play compared to salvaging the human condition. For one thing, there were no people between earth and moon. For another, the moonshots had no problem of an obsolescent hardware that some tried to discredit at countdown. And there was no association of old-time arrogants seated on the flight deck, holding all the good jobs, and counseling "patience and fortitude," no clutch of new-time arrogants diverting themselves by dropping asafetida into the air conditioning and endlessly playing loud acid rock on the ship's intercom to protest seniority rules.

The redirecting of higher education, as a critical component of the process of national redirection, is a task measurably more difficult than the technological problems of moon exploration. The redirecting of higher education will succeed only to the degree that action is taken, and taken in the light of a value system that meets the severe demands of the human condition. We have not yet agreed on the value system. Quarreling among the space travelers brings no answer.

Said one sophomore to another as they left the lecture hall, "So Hobbes thought that life was solitary, poor, nasty, brutish, and short. Have I got news for him! The Establishment has completed all of the job except for one thing. We'll do that one. We'll make it nasty."

6

Teaching and Learning

⊸§ "It cannot be doubted that in the United States the instruction of the people powerfully contributes to the support of the democratic republic; and such must always be the case, I believe, where the instruction which enlightens the understanding is not separated from the moral education which amends the heart."
—Alexis de Tocqueville (1835)

"The last few decades have witnessed a serious erosion of any clear sense of mission in American higher education."
—The President's Commission on Campus Unrest (1970)

What values are now being taught in American colleges and universities? How? And what are students actually learning? Are any changes needed to make these institutions positive factors in influencing the human condition?

An Unexamined Assumption

Time was when it could be assumed that teachers were to teach and students were to be taught. It might even have been assumed that students did learn what teachers intended them to learn. Those were the days, also, in which, if a student and a college president faced each other across the president's desk, it could be assumed that it was the student who was in trouble.

The 1960s revealed how specious these assumptions had become. The 1970s witness some changes throughout higher education, changes that reflect a desire to reconsider old assumptions.

The process began much earlier, as the research university and the land grant university challenged the working assumptions of the liberal educational tradition. The first bastion to fall was the working assumption that students must conform to religious teachings if they were to be granted degrees. Indeed, the revolt against dogmatic domination of campus thought had its origins in the Deism of the eighteenth and nineteenth centuries—almost coterminous with the founding of the institutional archetypes themselves. Nevertheless, there was no immediate retreat from institutionally announced objectives. Most colleges and many universities for a long time continued to assert that it was their purpose to teach students to be ladies and gentlemen, that is, to be persons who conformed to generally accepted standards of ethical and religious behavior and belief. Moreover, institutions commonly stood *in loco parentis*, and parietal rules governed the whole of student life. Dismissal from college and other forms of discipline were a generally accepted practice. The whole ethos of the typical institution of higher education was infused with the idea that teachers knew, better than students, the correct life-style. Students were expected to accept that assumption and to be governed accordingly. If they did not so govern themselves, the institution had remedies. If they did, it was assumed that they had learned the proper values.

But the value-free university found itself embarrassed by such assumptions and practices. Tolerance of diversity in ideas led to tolerance of diversity in conduct. And that implied an ethical pluralism, which presaged a vacuum of values. Andrew D. White and Ezra Cornell had thought of themselves as acting to save the faith by bringing it into the orbit of science. They had overlooked a popular belief expressed in

Browning's aphorism: " 'Tis well averred,/A scientific faith's absurd." Faith, for long accustomed to the narrow confines of its familiar corral, wandered off and got lost in the wide-ranging reaches of scientific inquiry.

The conflict between the monolithic and the pluralistic notions of collegiate education was an uneven one, fought on many a front and at widely differing points of advancement and retreat. As late as the years between the two world wars, college presidents could be found who acted through the inertia of tradition as though they were still the arbiters of campus destiny, enforcing accepted campus norms—and many were. It was not until the 1960s that the tidal wave of student uprising overwhelmed the campus, bringing the realization that even though the structure of power had changed little, the locus of power had shifted.

The last of the assumptions to be challenged was the basic one: that teachers are to teach and students are to be taught what teachers believe they should be taught. That assumption still controls most curricular planning and informs most collegiate instruction. It is abandoned with much pain, and slowly. It is the central redoubt of the academic fortress. It is still being defended by many. Educators still assume (with considerable basis in fact) that the collective wisdom of the faculty is greater than that of the student body. They therefore also assume (with somewhat less justification) that students are to be taught, faculty to teach. The process of higher education is thus described: students come to college to be taught what professors want to teach them. The curriculum embodies that opinion. Teaching methods are based on it. Graduation or failure confirms it.

Each of the three archetypes of higher education confirms this basic assumption, although the specifics vary among the three. The liberal educational tradition has aimed to convey to the undergraduate a body of knowledge, skills, and attitudes, of beliefs and values, which were first compiled and systematized as the professional equipment of the clergy. The research university intends to convey to its neophytes the methods, beliefs, and temperament of scientism. The land grant tradition stresses the practical achievements and skills that will make its graduates vocationally and professionally successful. Subcategories and variations of these three principal patterns have appeared as colleges for teachers, public colleges for Negroes, community colleges, and institutes of technology.

And over against the three traditional models and their variants, the emerging existential university is developing a different set of concepts. The starting assumption, the basic impulse of the whole development, is the startling notion that the student knows, better than the teacher, what areas he is ready to explore, and therefore what the curriculum and the instructional process ought to be. This idea is closely intertwined with the student revolt against parietal rules. No longer does the institution stand *in loco parentis*. The courts had established the right of educational institutions to stand in the place of parents, in all respects including disciplining students, in 1866. In 1961, that legal status was reversed; but the spirit of *patria potestas* lingered on. It was successfully challenged by the spirit of *sui juris* in many a campus upheaval. No longer is the student to be forced to live under conditions he did not make or to obey regulations he did not formulate or approve. Students had declared that they knew, better than deans and presidents and discipline committees and governing boards, what the life-style was going to be. They had made that declaration stick. They early assumed a dominant role in the extracurricular life of the institution, and then moved on to claim the right to self-direction in campus governance. They then began to insist on a definitive role in the central matters of curriculum and teaching, and therefore in the hiring, firing, tenuring, and promoting of faculty.

In the existential university, there is an almost complete

reversal of the hierarchy of institutional values, a reversal that corresponds closely to the revolution in campus governance. The irrational, antirational, and nonrational replace reason. Afferent aspects of experience are treasured in preference to the cognitive. Communing replaces communication. Communal activity supplants personal passivity.

Nevertheless—and this is the point of our discussion—the existential university is very much like the three archetypes in that it also aims to induct its participants into a set of attitudes and values that are held to be preferable. In short, all of higher education seeks to teach students a curriculum, however defined, that is alleged to be the embodiment of institutional aims.

This basic working assumption needs to be examined. Does the student actually learn what the institution, in its varying forms, intends him to learn? Or does he learn something else? And how? And why?

On Actual Learnings

For at least half a century, educators have been aware of a trilogy in the learning process, originally identified by William Heard Kilpatrick. They have distinguished among (1) the "primary learnings," i.e., items of knowledge and information—the announced "subject matter" of the curriculum; (2) the "associated learnings," i.e., skills and habits—the manipulatory abilities required to put information to work, both as a learner and a practitioner; and (3) the "concomitant learnings," i.e., the attitudes and value judgments acquired along with the other two categories. Institutions have centered their curricular planning on the first and the second, while emphasizing the third in their catalog self-descriptions and their recruitment brochures. The general run of colleges and universities have given lip service to all three categories of intended learnings. Not always is the teacher-student relationship structured to promote student learnings along lines intended by the institution in any one of the three areas, and seldom is the learning process so structured that the students' actual learnings in all three categories go in the directions announced by the institution.

Consider an example: the old-fashioned "recitation." Yesterday, the professor assigned Chapter 11 in the textbook. If the student has done his homework, he is ready to recite when called on today. The professor goes down the alphabetical list, calling on each in turn, sometimes skipping about at random or reversing the alphabetical order to catch the unwary or the unprepared. And opposite the name of each student in the little black book, the professor enters a mark for the day's recitation. Halfway through the term, there will be a written quiz, with a final examination at the end of the semester. Recitation, quiz, and examination are all designed to stimulate (or force) the student to memorize the subject matter, and to reinforce his memorization by compelling him to review for examinations. The intended learnings appropriate to this process fall almost exclusively in the "primary" category—information and knowledge, "subject matter." There may be some incidental acquisition of study habits and other skills such as verbal dexterity; but if there are any developments in the area of attitudes and value judgments, these developments consist mainly of knowledge about those values rather than the incorporation of intended attitudes and preferences into the daily decisions of the student.

Look at the student, and see whether this is not true. Some students, particularly those with higher intelligence quotients, will have learned from the recitation-quiz-examination sequence that it is easy to get good grades if one carefully does what the professor wants. Farther down the ladder of abilities or of the application of those abilities will be other students who have learned that it is hard to get good grades, but that it can be done. A little farther down the line is the student who learns that, no matter how hard he tries, there is no way to beat the professor's game without cheating. He learns either to accept failure or to cheat. Still farther down are those who, from the beginning of the course, believed that they were not going to get a fair break. They devoted their energies to studying the professor instead of the textbook, and their months of survival became the measure of their success in meeting the enemy.

Very early in his college experience, the student had been made aware of the fact that his standing and progress rest not solely on his individual achievement but also on his achievement compared to all others in the class. He was admitted to college in the first place because he ranked higher than others in his high school class. He is graded in college on a bell curve. The course of study is structured like a competitive game in which, by definition, half of the class must always be below the norm.

All along the distribution of the bell curve there are those who might, perhaps, have been at a higher point on the competitive scale, displacing some other student; but they slipped downward toward failure because they lost interest or missed a crucial point in a linear sequence or got bored. Or perhaps they had no intention of mastering the subject matter in the first place, and only went along for the ride toward a degree. According to professorial whim and compassion, they will be known as "underachievers," or "failures," or "dropouts." Perhaps the most significant single learning that is common to all students in the course is the realization that success consists of beating out one's classmates in performing (or appearing to perform) as the professor wants.

The primarily intended learnings of the course were stated in the textbook and syllabus, in terms of information and knowledge that the professor (with faculty approval and institutional sanction) intended that the student should "master." The associated learnings for the course were seldom spelled out, but they were always implicit. To be able to manipulate the information, recall it on demand, verbalize about it, give evidence that erudition was becoming wisdom—these were the qualities that the skillful professor attempted to educe. It was desired that the student should develop the qualities of a learned man, not merely a scholar. If, in the professor's judgment, the student showed evidence of not merely mastering the subject matter but also of manipulating it with ease and veracity, praise and high grades followed.

As for the third category of learnings, that is, the concomitant attitudes and value judgments that it had been hoped the student might acquire and develop through his classroom experience, the professor knew what was intended; but the classroom situation was not necessarily designed to help the student in those areas. And the student might well have intentions that did not wholly coincide with what the professor had in mind. Moreover, neither the rewards (high marks, dean's list, Phi Beta Kappa, graduation honors) nor the punishments (low marks, probation, flunking out) were geared to reflect the professor's estimates as to student growth in the concomitant learnings. The situation made this inevitable. Concomitant learnings could not be accurately measured in the same manner or to the same degree of accuracy as could the primary and associated learnings. The grading system therefore tended to exclude the concomitant learnings from its purview. In the back of the professor's mind there might be a subjective tendency to add a smidgen to a particular student's grade for the course if that student had managed to convey to the professor an impression that he was growing in the tertiary matters of values and value judgments; but the conscientious teacher always played it fair. He refused to play favorites in "subjective" matters. He graded each student strictly in accordance with the averaged daily marks on his recitations, combined through the objective processes of arithmetic with the results of the quiz and the examination (each properly weighted), in full accordance with a predetermined mathematical formula. As a gentleman and a scholar, he did the honorable thing, playing fair with all the students. He assessed them objectively, on objective bases only. No matter that the so-called "objective" grades represented his own subjective judgment about student performance. At least he was grading student performance, not his own likes and dislikes about a student's value system.

For the student, all of this tended to reinforce his impression that memorizing the subject matter was the main thing, that being able to talk about it intelligently and cogently was a desirable plus, but that acquiring the attitudes and values of the scholar and the gentleman had no definitive effect upon his final grade.

And the net upshot? When the student is graduated, or otherwise ceases to be enrolled at the institution, he quickly forgets most of the subject matter that was mastered in order to pass an examination. He will retain some of the manipulatory skills and work and study habits acquired during the course; but he will have learned to use these mainly under the competitive lash of professorial assignment, classroom recitative, and final examination. He has never learned to study and learn under any other conditions or for any other purposes. The things he will remember best as the years pass are, by the contrariness of the learning process, those things that he undertook to do by his own effort. These are primarily in the third category, values and attitudes, not basically in subject matter or associated skills.

Further in accordance with the contradictions of the learning process, there is no guarantee that the values and attitudes he has learned are those which the institution and its professors had intended. He will fondly recall his undergraduate days and become a loyal alumnus who follows the basketball scores avidly and contributes to the alumni fund. Or he will hate the professor who flunked him and the dean who fired him. Or he will have been inoculated with just enough learning to make him immune to fresh ideas for the rest of his life. Or he will have learned to be rebellious and cynical. Or he will have become skilled in getting by without effort. Or he will have learned to be a convincing four-flusher who values pretense and scorns integrity. Or . . . Thus, it is neither the primarily intended nor the associated learnings that make the lasting impression. It is the tertiary concomitant matters that stay with the student. The learnings in this more permanent area of retention are precisely those that have least to do with institutional measurement and evaluation of the student, with the assignment of rewards and punishments, or even with the structuring of the curriculum and the process of instruction itself.

Thus it comes about that most colleges and all universities have long since abandoned the practice of making graduation conditional upon the alleged "character" of the candidate. Such matters were not "objective," could not therefore be measured and included in a mathematically weighted grade average. And in any case, there was no longer any common agreement on what it was that defined "good" character—in whatever quantity it might be found. In the value-free university, stress was laid on the aspects of experience that could be quantified. Even though qualitative matters probably existed in varying degrees of quantity (intensity?), they could not be measured except as some quantitative standard was used. To reduce quality to a quantitative measurement was a contradiction in terms. Finally, the overriding insistence in the value-free university came to be centered on the "objectivities" of information, knowledge—that is, mastery of data. As to the "subjective" areas of values, there developed a breadth of institutional tolerance verging on indifference. It is true that pious generalizations still continued to appear in institutional catalogs and similar works of descriptive fiction; but neither in the instructional process nor in the grading system did the students' learning of values have a definitive place.

If the foregoing analysis is shifted from the recitation-structured course of study to the lecture hall, the conclusions are not markedly different. The successful student in the lecture course is one who takes careful and copious notes, reads assigned *and* suggested collateral readings, submits a well-researched term paper of his own authoring, crams hard before exams, and works swiftly and unerringly on the true-false and multiple-choice computerized examination. If he does not relish the discipline of taking his own set of notes in the lecture hall, he can purchase for a ridiculously low price at semester's end a complete set of notes taken by a graduate student who was hired for the purpose by an off-campus "bookstore," and whose notes will be superior to his own in any case. For an additional consideration, he can gain access to a series of preexam cram sessions based on the graduate student's notes he has already purchased. He can easily purchase a ghostwritten term paper that is guaranteed to bring him a grade not out of line with his general record at the institution, all properly footnoted (except as to authorship). Under the right circumstances, he can hire someone else to sit for his examination. His resultant mastery of the subject matter is minimal. The skills he has learned have to do with beating the competitive system. The attitudes and values he has learned are not those alleged to be proper to the scholar, the gentleman, or the professional man. He has learned to be a cheat, a thief, a briber, and a suborner. For this, he has to go to college? He will get his degree; but he will look with contempt and cynicism upon the institution that carries on such a ridiculous process.

In the laboratory, the picture changes somewhat. The undergraduate has before him the task of completing successfully a series of set experiments in accordance with the laboratory manual, under the eyes of a laboratory assistant. He has a little greater difficulty in buying or bluffing his way through; but it can be done. Or, he may take advantage of the availability of the graduate assistant (occasionally, of a professor), to learn well the primarily intended learnings of the set experiment. He may even take on some of the mental adjustments of the scientific method and its spirit. If his instructor is a particularly sensitive and dedicated man, the student may find that by repeating the classical experiments in a laboratory under wise and sophisticated guidance he has achieved insights not learned by the rote-memorizer. The laboratory is different from both the recitation and the lecture as an instructional device, because the laboratory gives the student a better opportunity to learn rather than to be instructed. There is, however, no guarantee that the student will see this opportunity or take advantage of it.

The seminar begins to approach a learning situation in which the student *can* learn instead of merely being taught. The supervised project, whether in a group or as one person, likewise provides a much fuller opportunity to learn than does the structured classroom or the large lecture hall. Judicious combinations and permutations of lectures, quiz sessions, rap sessions, individually assigned projects, field experience, reports, library research, laboratory work, practicums, seminars (the list is open-ended) have been tried. Usually some improvement in primary learnings results, at least in the earlier stages of the development of a course, before last year's precedent takes over and the rigor mortis of glassy-eyed routine sets in. Somewhat less frequently, there appears to be some improvement in the associated learnings as well. But for the concomitant learnings, the academic magic wand does not wave.

The truth appears to be that the student, in whatever institutionalized manner he is approached, learns well not what he is taught but what he decides to learn. And nothing is actually learned unless it is accepted as the basis of action—and acted upon. Conversely stated, the important and enduring lessons of an undergraduate's life are precisely those things (facts, information, knowledge, skills, habits, attitudes, ideas, ideals, values) that he incorporates into his life-style and behavior patterns by acting upon them.

The existential university represents an important on-campus recognition of these facts. It rejects the things that the institution has alleged that it teaches. It accepts the realities of what it is that the student actually learns. It begins with the loneliness on the crowded campus as the real basis of student action, and builds on that reality. It rejects the Establishment, the father image. The traditional Establishment, in its obtusity not understanding the situation, or in its busyness not taking time to care particularly about the plight of any one person, or in its bigness and intricacy and bureaucracy failing to give effective expression to the human concerns that lie at the heart of its hopes, continues to insist that the student ought to be in college to be taught what the institution says is valuable. To that insistence, the student replies from his alienation that he doesn't need it. He is learning what he wants to learn in the way he wants to learn it.

Today, he learns to ignore the droning lecture as he contemplates the floating clouds against an azure sky, seen through the winter's accumulation of urban grime on the panes of the half-open window. Tonight, he shares a gallon of cheap wine with five others on his dormitory floor while a stack of hard rock tapes send good vibes pulsating against the walls of the room. Tomorrow, he watches with scarcely titillated curiosity as an activist harangues a noon-hour crowd in front of the Student Union; and as he is elbowed in the excited crowding, he feels mixed emotions—but he *feels*. At the next day's rally, when he is slow to move, he gets clubbed. Suddenly he becomes active. He is "radicalized."

The campus confrontation passes after a week; but the normalcy to which he returns is not the same. Nothing else has changed, but he has. Everything has a different feeling-tone to it. He goes through the rest of the weeks that stretch to the end of the term with a haunting sense of the unreality of structured academic exercises. He looks elsewhere than to the classroom and the lecture hall for what he now begins to call "meaningful experiences." Seldom do these substitute experiences encourage him to master the subject matter of the official curriculum. As for the habits and skills he learns, they may be quite real and very important to him. He senses the immediate and urgent usefulness of composing an eye-catching tight-knit, one-page throwaway that is coherent, concise, and convincing as no assigned theme in freshman composition ever was. He finds that he can work for seventy-two action-packed hours without sleep, whereas he was always nodding off in the classroom. He learns how to operate a mimeograph machine, a walkie-talkie, and a burglar's jimmy. He learns how to organize his peers for collective action, how to stimulate a crowd and lead a mass action of violence without himself appearing to be a provocateur. He has a feeling of significance, of meaning and relevance, about what he is doing. He learns with critical quickness the skills and habits that will serve the objectives and goals that carry meaning for him. He learns what it means to be included in a community of like-minded and like-feeling fellow members of his generation. He learns to savor the interludes of quiet with them, to share common likes and dislikes, common affinities and hatreds. He may, incidentally, acquire some knowledge of facts, facts that are instrumentally useful to him in his newly discovered role with its exciting round of exhausting activities. The facts he learns may even be true: they had better be, because he throws them up against an entrenched opposition in the Establishment, an acknowledged reservoir of limitless information. He learns how to use the library, its periodical section as well as its books. For all this learning, he needs no professorial taskmaster who makes an assignment, quizzes him, and issues a grade. More probably, he finds a maverick from the professorial or graduate-assistant ranks working alongside him, and for the first time he has a feeling of comradeship with a member of the faculty. (He will remember that, next term, when the guy gets busted by the administration and needs a student strike to get his job back.) Through all of this, he does what he does because he feels it has some importance, some usefulness, some meaning. As long as the new-found motivation sustains him, he is an accepted and acceptable member of the existential university, whether he joins a movement or supports an organization or continues as a loner. Through it all, he is most assuredly a learner.

On occasion, the established procedures of the structured learning process can be made to take on some of the intensities of meaning that are commonly found in the existential university. A student is confronted with a new idea that bursts upon him like some newly risen sun, and a happy professor ceases to teach him and begins to preside over the self-education of an interested student. There are some who approach college as freshmen with well-defined goals and high hopes, who find it possible to defer their time of satisfactions and to discover real meaning in the plodding progress of the years of preparation for later performance. For them the professor gives thanks. They carry the class.

Whatever may be the academic milieu or the student's adjustment to it, the clear fact is that real learning takes place not when the professor or the textbook or the syllabus or the curricular plan says it ought to, but when the student himself finds meaning in what he is doing. When meaning and action converge, learning takes place. It is a happy moment for the professor and his institution if the meaning and action (and therefore the learning) are what the faculty and the college intended. In any case, whatever has meaning and is accepted as the basis for action comprises the actual (as opposed to the official) curriculum.

Father Newman knew that when he told the youth of Dublin that he would enable them to climb out of the oppressed working class if they would assiduously acquire the intellectual and moral equipment of the gentry. He relied on the anger of the dispossessed, responding to the compassion of the Establishment of the university, to provide motivation that would fill the lecture halls with young men who had already done a full day's work. That motivation brought the students to the Evening Classes and reoriented the institution in the process.

So, also, with the first eager years of almost any college or university. Its founders and builders have had a purpose, a mission, a goal that was shared by the faculty and was also shared by students who were attracted by what they saw and felt. Learning took place because students found meaning in the tasks to which they addressed themselves. That meaning was directly associated with the important aspirations of their own lives.

Initial enthusiasm does not always fade away at once. Whenever the basic nexus between clearly apprehended meanings and a learning opportunity has been preserved, and that functional relationship is accepted by students as a basis for their student days, higher education has succeeded. Where the connection has been less direct, it has faltered. And where students have seen no connection, learning has become incidental, almost accidental. Only instruction remains.

New or revised techniques of instruction may bring temporary spurts in the learning process. Novel experiences have often evoked new student interest; but when interest flags and effort lags, learning ceases. The key to student interest is found in student feelings. When a student feels that there is meaning for him in what he undertakes, he learns. The possibility of learning is therefore greatly minimized when the student sees no real meaning in the situation as it is structured for him.

Sometimes the learning situation can be restructured so as

to give the students feelings of meaning by simulating life. For example, the generation that has spent, on the average, twenty thousand hours in front of the electronic tube by the time it reaches college age can sometimes be reached effectively—for further rote-learning processes especially—through television. Or, the student who has learned a little and heard much about computers can sometimes be reached by giving him "hands on" experience with the key punch and the console. When he programs a problem himself, feeds it to the computer, does his own debugging and recovers his own print-out, he needs no professorial praise to tell him that he has learned something. Whether his actual learnings will be those that were intended by the institution may be a different matter—as experience with programmed learning machines suggests.

Educators used to debate soberly about "carry-over." Was it possible to teach a student isolated bits of knowledge, fact, insight, or process and then expect him to "generalize" these pieces into a coherent whole? This arid debate is still with us. It is beside the point.

Students, like everyone else, learn in whatever situation and under whatever circumstances only those things that they accept as having meaning for them, and upon which they act. If the meaning is only to enable them to pass an examination and stay in college until graduation, they will learn to do just that. And that only will they learn with any predictable certainty. Such students may later learn how to hold a job and draw a paycheck; but work can be just as dull as study. They will be no closer to learning the meaning of their jobs than they were when, in college, they learned how *not* to learn the meanings of the subject matter as they learned how to pass the course.

Learning is selective. At a given moment, a student is bombarded with competing objects of attention: the instructor's voice, a colorful wall map, a squiggle on the blackboard, the beckoning warmth of a spring day and the slowness of the clock, a quickened pulse occasioned by a dizzying awareness of the girl in the next seat and fantasies of the coming evening, plus the letter that arrived from home just as he departed for class—with no check enclosed. What does he learn? In that moment, he learns about whichever among the competing objects is given his attention. If he takes careful notes, follows up with readings and a rap session and enjoys it, he learns a significant section of prescribed subject matter. If he lets thoughts of the girl preempt the hour, but does not follow up with an effort to make a date, he learns to fantasize about sex. If he cools his anger toward his father, he learns a little compassion or, possibly, slips more deeply into resignation. In each case, he will have selected from that hour the items of experience that had greater meaning for him as the basis for his action. These items he incorporates into the fabric of his person. He learns.

Equally important in that same hour, he learns how *not* to learn from the other items that competed for his attention and acceptance, and which were elided or rejected. Learnings can be, and are, negative as well as positive.

These selected learnings, both positive and negative, are carried forward as part of his person, his self, his ego. Reinforced by repetition and reward, intensified by experience, these meanings become second nature to him. His value system—his actual value system, not necessarily the formal system of values to which he may give lip service—is being structured, as he acts upon the matters that he holds valuable.

Selected learning is cumulative in its effect. Sometimes a major decision may subsume numerous minor decisions that flow from it. In this respect, there is an important difference in the meanings inherent in the learning situation in a professional school as contrasted with a college of the liberal educational tradition. To be a successful engineer, accountant, pharmacist, physician, lawyer, clergyman, teacher, social worker, or architect one must have a passport to the profession. That passport is acquired through the successful completion of a prescribed course of study and examination. The student in preparation for a profession knows that he is working under someone's assumption that each item in his prescribed learning sequence has value as a part of his preparation for entrance into his chosen profession. Unless the course of liberal studies is also prescribed as preprofessional, he finds no meaning in the liberal educational tradition (except in the instance of preparation for teaching or the clergy). And for the student in an institution that is nonprofessional in its orientation, or who is pursuing studies that are neither professional nor nonprofessional in a multiversity, the ultimate goal of his four years' residence is, in his own parlance, to get a degree. The institution may describe it in more idealistic terms; but if that description is to have meaning for him, he must accept it and act upon that acceptance. The general curriculum in the liberal educational tradition was originally designed to serve the professions of the ministry and teaching. If he plans to be neither, he finds himself in college "to get an education" but confronted with a curriculum designed to serve particular professions. He has no interest in those professions. His instructors may tell him that his liberal studies are intended to prepare him later to make a life, not merely to make a living. He responds that he doesn't intend to wait until after graduation before beginning to live. He intends to learn whatever has meaning for him, and to learn it now. These are not necessarily the things that the syllabus outlines or the professor retails. The more he protests that the liberal arts curriculum has no real meaning for him, the more his professors tell him that these are the real meanings and that he is in college to learn them well—or to get out. Once in a while, a professor actually convinces a student that the announced goals of a liberal education are genuine and valuable objects of his pursuit during his undergraduate years. This can have unexpected results. A classic example is the graduate of Columbia University who, a few years ago, sued the institution for breach of contract, asking to recover his tuition payments because, he alleged, the university had not taught him wisdom—whereas the catalog advertised that wisdom was the objective of a liberal education. Some observers were cynical enough to comment at the time that the graduate's action in bringing suit was prima-facie proof of the validity of his claim that, indeed, he had not been taught wisdom.

Can Values Be Taught?

There is no question as to whether or not a college student will learn something during his college days. The real question is: *what* will he learn? From the perspective of the institution, the critical questions have to do with the degree of correspondence between what the student actually learns and what the institution declares he ought to learn.

If the disparity between the actual student learnings and institutionally prescribed learnings is measured in terms of subject matter only, as is the case in practically all undergraduate instruction, the institution has little difficulty in arriving at its verdict of success or failure. If the secondary learnings are brought under scrutiny, the institution still appears to be able to provide mathematical grades as measures of student performance. But in the tertiary field of learnings, the values, beliefs, and preferences that govern and express life-style, institutional ability to measure student achievement with reliable precision is seldom found, if at all. As a result, within generous limits of tolerance, neither grades nor graduation depends on whether it is concluded that the student has learned desired values.

There was a time when an elementary school teacher graded each child in "deportment." Most schools still report to the parent regarding a pupil's "citizenship." But colleges and universities, particularly in the last decade, have pretty well given up the last vestiges of effort to enforce a set of values or a life-style as prerequisites to graduation. Parietal rules are gone. As long as the student keeps out of trouble with the courts, his continuance at the college is seldom in jeopardy. In backing away from the former responsibilities of dictating a student's life-style, the institution has abdicated responsibility for evaluating the life-style subscribed to by a candidate for a degree.

Probably this phenomenon is not as new as it appears to be. It is the appearance that is new. In the research university, with its value-free curriculum, evaluation of student performance in terms of any system of values other than the neutrality of objectivity has for a long time been anathema. In the college dominated by the liberal educational tradition, pluralism and tolerance have long since replaced the discipline committee in all but the most public matters of personal morality. The nationwide spread of the Berkeley syndrome during the 1960s was actually the conquest of a vacuum. The existential university flourished because it alone was rooted in student demand for a feeling of value and therefore for the experience of values—values, of course, that were diametrically different from and in contradiction to the inherited value systems enshrined in either the research university or the liberal college.

One result of this general shift has been the reinforcement of faculty resistance to formal institutional efforts to manage students' value systems and life-styles. Faculties have not been too happy, in former days, when charged with the responsibility of monitoring student conduct. It was enough to give a student a grade on the work done in one's class, without being made to double as his wet nurse. Leave that to the dean of students—he's hired to watch out for student morals. Moreover, you can't measure a student's growth in terms of a value system and give him a grade on it. Thus, unless there was gross public turpitude (which might reflect on the good name of the institution), a student's values were his own affair. If only those were to be retained in college and ultimately graduated who showed measurable annual progress in practicing the virtues that were esteemed by some founding father, enrollments would be decimated overnight, and nine out of ten college professors would have no one to sit in their classrooms. The institutions became neutral in matters of evaluating students' values.

The consequence is that the existential university has had the field of values pretty well to itself for at least a decade. Faculty resistance to the new value systems came too late to prevent the growth of a new life-style that made its values clearly apparent, and delighted in doing so. Making no apology for appealing to feelings and sentiments—in fact, basing its appeal primarily in those very areas, the existential university succeeded in immobilizing whatever momentum the liberal educational tradition might still have had, and in occupying without contest the areas that the research university had abandoned.

Thus it came about that the great myth of the liberal educational tradition stood naked before those who accused it of hypocrisy—not because that tradition or its adherents had become knowingly hypocritical, but because the institutions did not appear to practice what they preached. Students were told to be alert and tractable. They would then learn to be wise, knowlegeable, effective, compassionate practitioners of the art of inquiry. They would get ready for life. They would be ladies and gentlemen. But students replied that they did not wish to become ladies and gentlemen. The ideals that were precious to the institution were obscenities to them. They accused both the liberal institutions and the research institutions of failure to practice toward them as students the virtues that (it was alleged) were to be instilled in them. Where, they asked, is the understanding and compassion that would be indices of the suspended judgment? In a competitive grading system? Where is the absolute honesty that ought to be the hallmark of believers in truth and the search for it? In secret classified research for the military-industrial complex? Where is the concern for human welfare that should characterize a humane institution? In the low percentages of members of minorities among the tenured faculty? Where is the dignity of the human being? In a computerized multiversity?

If there were answers to these questions, they were unconvincing to the alienated and the rebellious. The existential university had two seemingly irrefutable reasons for rejecting the established institutions. It was alleged that the values of the research university and of the liberal educational tradition were irrelevant and inappropriate to the felt needs of the Now generation. Secondly, it was alleged that, even if these values were in any sense relevant or appropriate, they were not being practiced by the established institutions. So why should they be accepted by students?

In the answers to these questions, as given by the existential university, is to be found the essential spirit of this newest variety of experience on campus: its life-style embodies its beliefs. Substitute for hypocrisy, directness. For evasiveness and postponement, confrontation and immediacy. For courtesy, vulgarity. For the suspended judgment, commitment. For neutrality, involvement. For discipline, liberty. For patience and devotion and dedication, anger and impatience and self-pride. For tolerance, intolerance. For war, love. For sublimation, sex. For the old clichés of art-for-art's-sake and the pursuit-of-truth, the new clichés of experience-for-its-own-sake and enjoyment-as-the-meaning-of-life. Find value and significance in doing and being *now* what is presently possible, rather than in preparing for some distant day of fulfillment. Precisely at the moment in history when the march of events had made the Establishment appear unsure of the validity of its traditional values, the existential university asserted the centrality of its contrary values. Never was the sound of a different drum more compelling to the beat of the feet of youth.

This transvaluation of values has clear implications for the survival of civilization and of its institutions. Humankind will survive its present crises only if civilization's laundry list is successfully laundered. Higher education will survive as a part of the culture of the future only if it is recognized as being more nearly a part of the laundering than of the laundered. Both in the larger society and in the academic world, survival will be won only in a process that includes the selection of values that have survival value—and in action that expresses those values.

For the college and university, with their magnificent traditions and precious heritage, it is not a question of whether values *can* be learned by students. Some values, positive or negative, are always learned. The question is not whether values can be learned, but whether the values that are institutionally endorsed can be taught so that they are learned. And if so, how?

The Liberal Educational Tradition

Few have given more cogent expression to the traditional answer for the teaching of values through higher education than the longtime president of Notre Dame University.

> The key and central factor in liberal education is the teacher-educator, his perception of his role, how he teaches, but particularly, how he lives and exemplifies the values inherent in what he teaches. Values are exemplified better than they are taught, which is to say that they are taught better by exemplification than by words.
>
> I have long believed that a Christian university is worthless in our day unless it conveys to all who study within it a deep sense of the dignity of the human person, his nature and high destiny, his opportunities for seeking justice in a very unjust world, his inherent nobility so needing to be achieved by him-

self or herself, for one's self and for others, whatever the obstacles. I would have to admit, even immodestly, that whatever I have said on this subject has had a minuscule impression on the members of our university compared to what I have tried to do to achieve justice in our times. This really says that while value education is difficult, it is practically impossible unless the word is buttressed by the deed.

If all this is true, it means that all those engaged in education today must look to themselves first, to their moral commitments, to their lives, and to their own values which, for better or worse, will be reflected in the lives and attitudes of those they seek to educate. There is nothing automatic about the liberal education tradition. It can die if not fostered. And if it does die, the values that sustain an individual and a nation are likely to die with it. [New York *Times*, January 8, 1973, p. 85.]

It could be wished that this position were held by a great many others as tenaciously as it is practiced by the fearless chairman of the United States Commission on Human Rights (now dismissed). And all educators and educational administrators who labor in secular institutions while sharing Father Hesburgh's sentiments must look with wistful yearning toward what appears to them to be the congenial ethos of the church-controlled institution that encourages teachers and administrators to exemplify fully the values they seek to teach. The liberal educational tradition is more easily defended and more persuasively exemplified in a liberal sectarian milieu than in a secular institution. It might also be presumed that student self-selection makes the compelling example of the practicing theologian somewhat more effective in a university under religious aegis than in one of the public institutions with its secular controls and its nonpartisan commitments of indifferent toleration for all religions and none. Since the Supreme Court holds that religious freedom demands that the state and all its instruments, including its institutions of education, must be equally impartial toward any and all religions and no religion, the conscientious teacher-educator in the public institution feels some reticence when he contemplates exemplifying the role that, had he been in a sectarian institution, he would have assumed to be normal and normative. Since ethics generally derive from theology and religion, the educator's enforced inhibition of his religious commitment in the public institution tends to foster a widely tolerant noncommitment toward ethical standards and values as well. It may be that some of the colleges and universities founded and built by orders of the religious and by Protestant denominations are still in a position to take the stance advocated by Father Hesburgh. It is much less clear that publicly controlled institutions have the legal right to do so. And it is abundantly clear from the record that the great majority of institutions of higher education in the United States, whether under private or public auspices, are not overwhelmed by an army of teacher-educators whose daily lives reflect the quality and depth of committed exemplification of man's dignity and high destiny for which the president of Notre Dame calls.

Moreover, the contemporary campus mood is not receptive to the methodology of teaching-by-example in the transmission of value systems, even if the particular values of the liberal educational tradition were to be accepted as setting educational objectives. Whether it be the noninvolvement of the value-free university or the commitments of the liberal educational tradition, neither value system appears to have a compelling acceptance on the contemporary campus. The existential university with grand nonchalance brushes both aside. If students were to assume that they came to college not only to learn from professors (a very large assumption at this time) but also that they came in order to learn to be like their professors, then both the ends and the means of the liberal educational tradition would have a fighting chance for student acceptance. There is no such prevailing assumption on today's campus.

Students assume that they are in college or university for a wide variety of reasons; but to learn to be like their professors does not lead the list of motivations. To learn how *not* to be like their professors is a much more likely objective; and how to beat the system while finding oneself in spite of it more nearly describes student conceptions of educational objectives. If anything was made clear by the tumultuous 1960s, that much is indisputable. Whether the slacking off in student unrest and the apparent easing of campus tensions as the 1970s progress will actually mean a return by students to a former position of tractability, even teachability, is a large and unanswered question.

The Technology of Human Behavior

In the early 1970s, it appeared that the dominant mood of fear and frustration invited some boldly aggressive proposal that might galvanize the fearful and release the frustrated. Old values were shaken. Where was the new answer? The time was ripe for a man who could speak with compelling authority.

In his *Beyond Freedom and Dignity*, one of the nation's foremost living psychologists challenged the assumptions and discarded the conclusions of most of contemporary education, not excluding higher education. "It is nearly impossible to change an educational establishment," wrote B. F. Skinner; but he saw little hope for the survival of contemporary society unless the whole of education were radically changed.

> What is wrong is the educational environment. We need to design contingencies under which students acquire behaviour useful to them in their culture—contingencies that do not have troublesome by-products and that generate the behaviour said to "show respect for learning."

Skinner argued that pretty much the whole range of the sciences rested on a false assumption that he labeled "autonomous man." Instead, he said, man should be understood to be what he has become as the results of his experience in his environment have cumulatively brought him to his present state. To bring man to any other state, you do not appeal to his dignity or exhort him to act as though he were free, i.e., "autonomous." You manipulate his environment and you lead him to act in the light of foreseen consequences of present behavior. Since the environment itself is almost totally of man's making, it can readily be remade so as to control the present for the purposes of an intended future. Since a person does not act upon the world, but rather the world acts upon him, the supreme objective of mankind is to reshape the culture in such a way that all men are led to do what they should do for the beneficent purpose of creating a better environment that builds better men.

Instead of the unseen hand of Adam Smith or dialectical materialism as Marx saw it, Skinner would have us put our faith in the belief that man's destiny can be determined by adopting appropriate social and psychological environmental controls. Among these controls, of course, is education. Instead of Hesburgh's teacher-educator who elicits morality by the contagion of his example, Skinner proposed a school environment so structured that only benign reactions of learners are possible.

Skinner ascribed a role to the environment in matters of human behavior similar to that of Darwin's notion of natural selection in the evolution of species.

> The environment not only prods and lashes, it *selects*. Its role is similar to that in natural selection, though on a very different time scale. . . . It is now clear that we must take into account what the environment does to an organism not only before but after it responds. Behaviour is shaped and maintained by its consequences.

To improve human behavior it is necessary to improve the environment that, by providing the consequences to each action or inaction, controls or determines what each action or inaction is to be. Thus, there is no such thing as "autonomous man," the self-willed psyche, independently existing as an entity over against the environment. Free will does not determine choice. Man does not rule his destiny, nor does God. It is the environment that makes man and writes history.

There is, of course, nothing fundamentally new in Skinner's general argument. Behaviorists have always tended to reject the notion that man is, in any real sense, the captain of his soul or the master of his fate. Karl Marx espoused a form of behaviorism, presented it as the key to man's control over the course of history, and thereby provided an ideology that is now subscribed to in all Marxist countries. Skinner's variety of behaviorism differs from Marxism, however, in several significant ways. Chief among these differences are the values espoused and the methodology proposed. Skinner's values turn out to be those of the nineteenth-century American gentleman, in other words, middle-class individualism. In its value system, Skinner's Utopia is a throwback to Bellamy. Skinner's methodology is only dimly limned in this book; but insofar as it is sketched, it lays down the pattern of societal controls not unlike Pavlov's salivating dogs.

Immediately upon its publication, *Beyond Freedom and Dignity* was subjected to a barrage of discussion and attack in the news media and soon after in relevant journals. A common theme ran through much of this critique: a revulsion against the proposal that critics interpreted as advocacy of totalitarian controls. They feared that a totalitarian society would result.

Perhaps Skinner might have avoided some of the vehemence that rejected his thesis if he had explicitly acknowledged the similarities between Marxism and Skinnerism. For example, he might have admitted that Marx also believed that human beings are creatures of their own actions as directed by their environment, that free will is an illusion, that dignity can come to a person only when he lives in a world that dignifies humanity rather than demeaning men. But there is a curious twist, an almost fatal flaw, in Skinner's analysis that prevents him from calling attention to this similarity to Marxian dialectical materialism. It is, precisely, the opposite error from that which vitiates Marxian analysis. Where Marx sees individual man only as a member of an economic class, Skinner is totally uncurious about the processes and nature of society. Concentrating on individual persons, he says nothing about what happens because men are treated in groups and frequently treat themselves as group members. Although he wants to see us produce a world of civilized, that is, socialized, persons, Skinner leaves his readers ignorant as to the ways in which social process operates, as he sees it.

But if Skinner had acknowledged his affinity to Marx, he would then have had to analyze the differences as well. That would have led him into a rejection of Marx's inverted Hegelianism and down a number of roads that, it would appear, are uninviting to Skinner the behaviorist. He would have had to tell his readers just where it is that Skinner's behavioristic technology differs from Marx's economic determinism. And if these steps had been taken, the vehemence of his attackers might have been even more surely targeted. His attack on the concepts of freedom and dignity would have been disclosed not only as a fascist threat but also as a potential apology for communism.

Nevertheless, before the American educator too easily dismisses Skinner, he should contemplate the fact that the education of human beings and the shaping of human behavior are regarded as being inseparable symbiotic functions of environmental manipulation in Marxist countries. Armed with that conviction, the dictatorship forges the character and behavior of the teeming millions in China and Russia.

It is unnecessary to agree with Skinner's entire argument in order to accept his insistence that schools are necessary. If, indeed, each person were entirely free and independent of all others, stood alone without history, had no effect upon any other (as "autonomy" must imply), then what would be the purpose of providing schools and colleges and universities? Each person, since he is "autonomous," should be free to repeat the entire history of the human race in his own lifetime, making his own mistakes and profiting from them. There is no need to pass on to each generation the accumulated lore and culture of previous generations. Not so! say educators. Each person in each successive generation will profit from learning well the lessons already learned by mankind. That is one of the central meanings of education. Of course, man is not "autonomous" in any sense that dissevers him from history and the present or which denies him access to the riches of the generations. So far, then, Skinner and most educators agree.

Skinner's educational methodology is less quickly accepted. The manipulation of man's (school) environment in order that all men may have an improved environment from which all will be improved would seem to bring our society perilously close to totalitarianism. In Skinner's view, it would be an entirely benevolent totalitarianism. What he wants is a culture that "abundantly reenforces those who have been enduced by their culture to work for its survival." He would use total social control to serve the purposes of enlightened individualism. His Utopia is more like Walden Pond than *Looking Backward*. He looks toward

> a world in which people live together without quarreling, maintain themselves by producing food, shelter, and clothing they need, enjoy themselves and contribute to the enjoyment of others in art, music, literature and games, consume only a reasonable part of the resources of the world and add as little as possible to its pollution, bear no more children than can be raised decently, continue to explore the world around them and discover better ways of dealing with it, and come to know

themselves accurately and, therefore, manage themselves effectively . . . all of this is possible.

Acceptance of Skinner's thesis might be easier if there were a guarantee that his benign environmental controls would, indeed, be the ones used; and that if they were used, benign results would ensue. Unfortunately, there is no guarantee on either count. On the contrary, the operational and methodological values he proposes are exactly those which have been rejected by American society, both by its Establishment and by its countercultures. Experimentation on a small scale in numerous Walden II's has, as yet, not validated his hopes. And any suggestion of large-scale application of his theories raises the specter of totalitarianism.

Nevertheless, this much of Skinner's thesis appears to be irrefutable: mankind will not survive unless survival value is built into each decision by which history moves. Colleges and universities ignore this truth not only to their own peril but at the peril of the species.

And this much, also, can be said about Skinner's proposed methodology: if it were totally applied within a closed national system, it would work. It might not produce the particular qualities of human life for which he yearns; but it would direct human behavior. Russia does it. China does it. Whether America should do it depends at least in part on whether Americans are prepared to make the necessary trade-offs in their value system.

Skinner's modest proposal for controlling the natural and psychological environment in order to achieve a Utopian future is, at worst, a probable road to fascism or communism or some other variant of totalitarianism. At its best, it is a recognition that talking about values, even exemplifying them, is an ineffective and dubious means of achieving what can only be attained through a holistic and heuristic effort.

Skinner leaves us with an unanswered dilemma: who watches the watchman? Who controls the controllers? There is no assurance that mankind will have a future worth having if reliance were to be placed in total control of all human behavior by whatever tyrant or savior might manage to seize power. It is this larger question that claimed the attention of another psychologist.

Psychotechnological Biochemical Intervention

Skinner was not alone in responding to the prevailing mood of the early 1970s with a bold proposal. Where Skinner had argued urbanely for the total control of all human behavior through the conscious manipulation of the physical and psychological environments, Kenneth B. Clark urged a more direct and drastic approach to what used to be called the human psyche, especially and emphatically to the psyches of the men in power.

Delivering his presidential address to the American Psychological Association in 1971, he argued that controls over at least a few highly placed persons throughout the world are absolutely essential to human survival. The present crisis calls for the most completely effective controls that can be made possible, over the centers of power and decision-making. No mere manipulation of the environment will suffice. We must zero in on the selected few among mankind's billions who occupy positions of great power, whose thumbs are poised above the push buttons of nuclear destruction. Clark would have the world prevent all aberrations of behavior in its few chosen leaders through "psychotechnological biochemical intervention." This is not science fiction: it is a serious proposal, seriously submitted.

Few laymen would doubt that the sciences required for such intervention are rapidly approaching that degree of sophistication that could make the total control of the behavior of selected persons through such intervention possible. On second thought, what's so wrong in Clark's proposal?

Tranquilizers are voluntarily used by millions of adults. With parental consent, more than a quarter-million hyperactive schoolchildren are being kept in good order by the judicious rationing of little pills with the hot lunch daily. If small children, on whose good behavior only the peace of the classroom depends are to be tranquilized, then why not a few dozen grown adults on whom the peace of the whole world hinges? "Already," Clark assured his listeners, "there are many provocative and suggestive findings from neurophysiological, biochemical and pharmacological and psychological research." He said, "We might be on the threshold of that type of scientific biochemical intervention which could stabilize and make dominant the moral and ethical propensities of man. It is now possible—indeed, imperative—to reduce human anxieties, tensions, hostilities, violence, cruelty, and the destructive power of irrationalities of man which are the bases of wars."

Citing the fact that a very few men in leadership positions of the industrialized nations now have the power to determine, among themselves, the survival or extinction of human civilization, Clark said that, since there is no other way of surely predicting the emotional, personal, and moral stability of these men in power, mankind is morally bound to intervene to insure that power will be used wisely and morally. Therefore, he proposed, as a precondition for assuming or remaining in high office, all candidates and incumbents should be required to accept the use of "the earliest perfected form of psychotechnological, biochemical intervention which would assure their positive use of power and reduce or block the possibility of their using power destructively."

In the published version of his address, the president of the American Psychological Association did not go beyond the threat of nuclear and biological warfare to find justification for his proposal. It is logical, however, to extend his thesis to areas other than international war. What he calls "the personal ego pathos, vulnerability and instability" of world leaders is potentially quite destructive in other areas as well. Witness the effect of erroneous decisions or of indecisiveness of men in power, with reference to the rapidly approaching critical moments in such matters as pollution, overpopulation, the exhaustion of natural resources, the clash of the races, the vulgarization of the culture, and the prevalence of violence in forms short of international warfare. Millions of human beings could be destroyed, reduced to subhuman existence, or kept in inhumane oppression by irrational or immoral decisions of men in power as they make their daily trade-offs between competing values in the economic, industrial, medical, commercial, technological, financial, political, and educational affairs of nations. If psychotechnology is to be used to avert ultimate catastrophe in one form, why not also in others?

How much of Clark's proposal is actually foreign to the mood of contemporary America? The Eagleton episode of the 1972 campaign quite clearly demonstrated that there is a general belief that the electorate is unready to consider for high office a man whose past life is alleged to have exhibited lapses into instability of personality, however innocent and however well-recovered from. From that insight, it is not a very long step to insist that steps be taken to *insure* the emotional and intellectual stability and moral correctness of any man who comes into a position of definitive control—or who continues therein. The truth is that Americans are anxiety-ridden, feel deeply insecure about the present and the future. They fear that matters are getting out of hand. They crave assurance, absolute certainty to offset dread. In a nation where one or another form of medical and psychological treatment is commonly used to insure physical health and mental and emotional stability, it is not impossible to imagine a situation in which this nation of pill-takers might gladly impose psychotechnological biochemical intervention upon its elected leaders, to allay its own apprehensions. An alternative solution to the generalized dread of an unknown future would be a nation in which nobody worried because the entire population had undergone prefrontal lobotomy.

As with Skinner so also with Clark: the unmistakable message is that they advocate Olympian measures because they are convinced that no lesser efforts will suffice. It is to this warning Klaxon that our attention should be turned, not merely to the specifics of their proposals but to the cry *de profundis.*

Elimination

The logical next step beyond controlling either the masses or a selected few leaders has already been proposed. Disconcerted over the failure of all other methods to control the pandemic curse of drugs, and sharing the deep disquiet of the general populace that lives in daily fear of street crime and nightly bolts its doors and sleeps behind barred windows, some highly placed officials have proposed that drug pushers (including addicts who are pushers) should be permanently and irretrievably removed from society. Governor Rockefeller of New York took the lead, recommending to the state legislature that the dangers of the drug traffic be met with heroic measures. Accused pushers, when arrested, are to be given no chance to plead guilty to a lesser crime. They are to be held without bond while awaiting trial. Conviction automatically leads to a life sentence, with no possibility of parole. Security for the rest of us is to come through eliminating some from all social contact for the rest of their natural lives.

It is not difficult to understand the dimensions of the concern that prompts such a proposal. An estimated 600,000 drug addicts, half of whom live in New York City, and because of whom (in some hospitals) three in every hundred new-born infants are addicted at birth, are the potential source of a spreading living death for an entire population. The social desuetude of a people, a large percentage of whom have become slaves to the needle, looms. Instead of *that* form of pharmochemical intervention in human behavior, are not other measures for insuring general and personal well-being to be preferred? And if life imprisonment of drug pushers fails to stop the traffic and its use, then what?

Governor Meskill of Connecticut gives his answer: final elimination—death to all second-offense pushers.

Thus it is that control, in one form or another, is advocated as a necessary part of the answer to the human condition. Control of an entire population through the technology of human behavior, says Skinner. Control of top leadership of the nations through psychotechnological biochemical intervention, says Clark. Control of the viciously criminal deviant through permanent removal from society: by incarceration, says Rockefeller, by execution, says Meskill.

This is not 1984, and these proposals are not malign whimsy. This is 1973, and these are all good men, deeply troubled, casting about for needed answers. Each sees the contemporary scene in a perspective even more bleak than any the present writer has permitted himself to accept. Each is driven to propose a severe remedy of major proportions in an effort to avert crisis. Each would use total attack on a total problem. Each comes dangerously close to proposing totalitarian methods. All four have in mind benign objectives that cannot be served through malign neglect.

Each also appears to abandon hope insofar as traditional educational approaches are concerned. Appearances, in this instance, are deceiving. The proposals made by these four men differ only in degree, not in kind, from established educational practice. Schools, colleges, and universities (at least up to World War I, and in most instances up to World War II) tended to incorporate into their accepted philosophy and regular practice the essential principles that are now drawn out in extreme form in these proposals. Control the environment in order to direct the growth of children and youth? What else was the meaning of parietal rules and discipline committees? Good schools and colleges and universities have always attempted to envelop pupils and students in a "wholesome environment"—until, not knowing how to do an effective job in manipulating the academic environment so as to achieve educative purpose, they lapsed into paternalism and permissiveness under the pressures that have created the existential university. Or, correct the errors of collegiate life by intervening in the intellectual and moral process of collegiate management? The average term of office of American college presidents is reputed to be about the same length as that of the average undergraduate. A principal cause of the revolving-door presidency has been the scandalous intervention in the internal affairs of higher education by off-campus forces and organizations (from the Daughters of the American Revolution and the American Legion to the White Citizens Councils and the Communist party) and personalities (from legislators and governors and Vice-Presidents and Presidents to ward-heel political hacks and badgering fiscal agents; from the late Senator Joseph McCarthy to the current crop of posturing professional patrioteers). Or, you wish to dispose of the misfits and nonconformists by putting them away for life or by taking their lives away? What else have the colleges and universities been doing, as they flunked out whopping percentages of the freshman class, weeded out subsequent misfits, and took pride in thus enforcing "high standards of excellence" on every student—as though students were so many identical empty gunny-bags to be filled with the same quantity of homogenized academics and stamped with approval at the end of the assembly line—if they made it? Ask any member of the *Lumpenbourgeoisie* or the *Lumpenproletariat* who has been involuntarily and permanently severed from academia what his dismissal actually means. That meaning will differ from life imprisonment or execution only in the degree of intensity of the deprivation—not in its finality. The extreme proposals we have been passing in review are not different in essence from measures long used in colleges and universities. They are only more extreme forms of the same thing.

And now that the planet, the nation, and the colleges and universities are facing exigent problems, should educators be shocked to learn that their own time-honored practices are proposed in extreme form as possible solutions to extreme conditions? Rather, educators might reexamine their own philosophies and practices in the light of these extreme reflections. Mirrored in their exaggerated form, the established practices and reigning philosophy of academe seem to be a little incongruous.

And there are redeeming features, even in the extreme forms of proposed remedies. Skinner's environmentally controlled man would appear to enjoy most of the surface characteristics of voluntarism, making his choices with the feeling of freedom in a world where he believed himself to be an object of respect. After all, the Chinese and Russians have done it: their populations always smile happily in the television documentaries their governments so kindly provide for us to view.

Equally, Clark's psychotechnologically biochemically controlled leaders would be the benign benefactors of a secure and happy world; and they would themselves still be as essential as the queen bee to the hive—in equanimity and benevolence, though a prisoner, she dutifully lays a thousand eggs a day; and all the hive contentedly swarms around her.

As to Rockefeller's thousands of the living dead in their maximum security prisons, while they would, unfortunately, be bereft of all hope short of the final release of death, they would at least cease to be an infecting source of a spreading social cancer; and the streets would be safe again for the rest of us. Meskill's proposal would merely use the surgery of finality to remove a cancerous growth from the body politic.

In all these instances, the new reality would be this: mankind moves to avert the grand disaster and achieves a noble destiny by exercising definitive control in decisive ways. These proposals (which are to be recognized as extreme forms of common academic practice), while they differ from academic practice as pneumonia differs from the common cold, should awake us not only to repugnance to the proposal *in extremis* but also to a belated readiness to reconsider the way that colleges and universities have been run. These proposals should impress us not so much by their lack of winsomeness or aptness in the form of their proposed solutions as by their unflinching recognition and clear acceptance of the facts of the human condition. There is in each of these proposals an acknowledgment that bold measures are in order if man is not to be destroyed by men. Out of the depths, a behavioral psychologist, a veteran civil rights fighter, and two high-ranking political figures cry for Herculean solutions to problems that they correctly know are beyond our present capacity to meet.

Those who cannot themselves suggest better answers had best learn from the voices that call for determined action. The times are dire and the time is late. If better solutions than those already proffered are to be found, they need to be discovered without delay, lest worse alternatives triumph. Yes, worse, for there are depths within depths. Hitler rode into power on a wave of fear and frustration when no one else had succeeded in providing the saving vision or the impelling leadership and practical action that might have diverted the world toward some better goal than the reign of brutality.

7

The Clash of Values

ৰ্তই "If one sins against the laws of proportion and gives something
too big to something too small to carry it—too big sails for
too small a ship, too big meals for too small a body, too big
powers for too small a soul—the result is bound to be a complete upset. In an outburst of hubris the over-fed body will
rush into sickness, while the jack-in-office will rush into the un-
righteousness which hubris always breeds."

—Plato (4th century B.C.)

"The primary project of our counter culture is to proclaim a
new heaven and a new earth so vast, so marvelous that the
inordinate claims of technical expertise must of necessity withdraw to a subordinate and marginal status in the lives of men."

—Theodore Roszak (1969)

The age of reason, compassion, and civility in the groves of
Academe has passed. It was caught in the cross fire between
volatile expectations and institutional rigidities, as two or
three student generations moved through the campus in the
1960s and early 1970s. Many of its external trappings and
institutional expressions remain, like tattered regimental pen-
nants, reminders of half-forgotten skirmishes. Many of its
working assumptions, though challenged, are still displayed,
like battle standards in a military museum. Many individuals
who treasure warm recollections of an age that has entered
history ahead of them are still found on campus, like old
soldiers waiting to be pensioned. Workmen have removed

the battered relics of yesterday's confrontations. Graffiti have been erased. Burned-out structures are being rebuilt. Occasionally, a neat bronze marker on a grassy knoll recalls a moment of horror. Is the age of the iconoclasts ended, or does it merely enter a new phase?

New Dimensions of Struggle

A new alignment of power is being established in academe. During the 1960s, student rebels and faculty dissenters demanded that the president take a stand alongside them, opposing the massive influence of the military-industrial complex against which Dwight Eisenhower had warned, and opposing the evils of caste and violence that offended their value systems. They demanded that the president give up his position of tolerant neutrality, assume the posture of power appropriate to his office, and exercise that power in their behalf as they fought for good causes.

For his part, about all that the president could do was to posture. He had become a shadowy surrogate for an off-campus power, more nearly a figurehead for ceremonial occasions who was also heavily burdened with administrative chores and fiscal worries, one who attempted to mediate internal controversies while fending external attacks. The only remnants of real power he still possessed were those which had to do with controls over student life-style. These were sharply eroded by an indifferent or unsympathetic faculty, defied by students, and finally invalidated as the courts called an end to *patria potestas*. His only remaining powers lay in persuasion and discussion, and these were instruments of delicacy that were not suited to the vulgarities of the new day.

Quite early in their campaigns, campus rebels discovered that the college presidency was empty of real power. The incumbent in office became merely the incidental symbol and focus of an attack on what he symbolized.

Portions of the presidential prerogatives were usurped by political figures and bodies during the decade of turmoil. As the Berkeley syndrome grew and spread, governors and legislators and lesser politicians—both those in office and those seeking to unseat them—vied with each other in cropping campus ineptitude to make political hay. Absentee power over the purse and over disciplinary decisions and policy choices sharply restricted the areas of presidential action and seriously threatened the independence of the educational institutions. Under these circumstances, administrators' efforts to meet rebellious on-campus forces with the accustomed tools of reason, compassion, and civility were decried by campus rebels as unresponsive and evasive vacillation. Outside critics used heavy sarcasm to characterize the same actions as weak permissiveness. Caught in the cross fire between campus demands for immediate radical change and public demands for repressive action to prevent that change, a generation of college administrators passed off the scene. (There were notable exceptions, such as at San Francisco State College, where a series of short-term incumbents was followed by a doughty semanticist who slugged it out, toe to toe and epithet for epithet, with the insurgent forces—but he, of course, came in to rescue a situation from which the original subjects of attack had been removed.) The use of police, and of the state militia and sheriff's deputies, to restore order resulted in severe psychic trauma and, in a few notable instances, in bloodshed and death.

Students had become aware that they were fighting a straw man. Accustomed to revolting against an institutional paterfamilias who had stood *in loco parentis* to them, they had found that it was no trick at all to occupy buildings and stop campus procedures at will. But when it was over, they found that in destroying the father image they had invoked outside forces that eliminated their campus sanctuary. In doing away with the legal, psychological, and institutional expressions of administrative dominance on campus, students succeeded only in bringing onto the campus all the control apparatus of the general society. With parietal rules repealed or fallen into disuse, the special privileges and protections of the campus were also lost. No benevolent administration stood between students and police. Student life came under new scrutiny and surveillance, with police supplanting proctors. Courts replaced discipline committees. Instead of probation or expulsion, punishment was a fine or jail sentence. And a felony record had consequences not carried in a notation on an academic record. The norms and customs of the community at large began to be applied to student life-styles, not always with the tolerance the campus had formerly shown. Less empathetic and less indulgent than its predecessor, the new public control of student conduct stood for law and order. It acted with force. And on the campus, reason, compassion, and civility were no longer normative.

Most college administrators had tried to use the fragile instruments of reason, appealing to compassion and understanding, sometimes with humor, in an endeavor to evoke the sentiments of civility in mutual respect. They resorted to the use of police and overt force only when driven to it by the relentless onset of the existential university. Too few administrators fully understood that their appeals to traditional standards would be ineffective because the new breed of students was impelled by a rejection of those very virtues. This time, it was the crew, not Ulysses, who with unstopped ears heard the sirens' song. With Ulysses lashed to the mast, the crew tried to commandeer the ship and head for shore. Presidents who tried to use admonitory words to warn student rebels, or hortatory appeals to their better natures, found themselves swept aside like the defenders of the *ancien régime* before the walls of the Bastille. It would not end until the Terror had run its course. In six short years, the campus sanctuary came to an abrupt end. Campus became merely a part of the political state and the general society.

During the process of change, faculty reactions were mixed. That was to be expected in an academic world in which each professor's right to "think otherwise" is a jealously guarded prerogative. The protective device called "tenure" had been established with great pains and considerable cost, as an institutional safeguard guaranteeing immunity from punishment to each tenured faculty member as he held his own convictions and expressed his own opinions freely. Not to react differently from one's fellows in academe would have been out of character, contrary to the professors' value system. Thus, some men and women in the professorial ranks took their stand in support of their presidents and deans, against the onslaughts of the existential university. Others enlisted (some clandestinely) with the insurgent forces, becoming the elder statesmen (and secret agents and double agents) of the insurrection. Still others tried to seize the moment to establish increased faculty power in place of the waning power of the administration. They found themselves immobilized between the contending forces of students and administrators.

Among those who looked for greater faculty power were some who foresaw that, with the curtailing of administrative power on campus, each faculty would need to be welded into a tightly controlled and self-directed power bloc, if the intrusions of political, governmental, and other off-campus forces were to be parried. The unions were born. It is not improbable that faculty members will have become union members substantially throughout higher education in America with the passing of another decade. Collective bargaining will replace individual negotiation and departmental intrigue. Administrators will be reduced even further in power, as they function as powerless power brokers, shuttling back and forth between the bargaining table and the trustees.

Students, also, will continue to seek power. There is not much meat left on the institutional bone; but contention will not be diminished because of that. Students will not again be brought under institutional dominance, whether by president or faculty or both. Moreover, with the voting age now lowered to eighteen, the average age of college entrance, the ballot is not an academic matter in either sense of the word. In scores of instances, colleges and universities will furnish the potential voting majority or balance of power in their local communities. They will strongly affect local ordinances, police, and courts—the area to which the control of their lifestyles has now passed. They will affect the levying of taxes and the making of municipal budgets as well as the selection of town and city governing boards and officers. They will, at least in some instances, determine who is to be the chief of police and with what vigor or laxity selected laws are to be enforced.

As students come into tighter conflict with faculties also seeking greater power, controversy will become acrid over such matters as hiring, firing, tenuring, and promoting of faculty members. How definitive is student participation to be in these matters? It is not inconceivable that unions of students may be established, to balance the power of faculty unions, carrying on their own negotiations with both faculty and administration—or directly with the trustees and governmental officials—as well as presenting a united front toward off-campus power thrusts. As with the faculties, so, also, with the unions of students: the strike becomes the ultimate weapon. The unions come into control. We are probably not far removed from the day when Federal legislation will be used to set the ground rules for academic unions, as the Wagner Act and the Taft-Hartley Act did for industrial labor.

Whether the unions of students will be controlled by the spirit of the *Lumpen* or will (like much of organized labor after thirty years of the Wagner Act) take on the character of the Establishment as time passes is one of the open questions of the future. The customary divisions among students will probably continue, divisions between "those who do and those who don't and those who don't care." The union of students will quite certainly be more powerful than any of the traditional forms of student government; and the national union of student unions will be at least as powerful as the American Association of University Professors, perhaps equal in power to the emerging Federation of College Teachers. Students, qua students, will come into power over their own lives to an extent never dreamed of in the days before 1960. The new infrastructure of campus life will profoundly affect the learning milieu and importantly determine what value systems will prevail.

Students have always been at a disadvantage in the campus power struggle because they are transients. Student leadership passes. Power tends to rise and fall with temporary issues. The union of students will provide a more permanent officialdom and bureaucracy, spanning the transient student generations, providing continuity, stability, and staying power. It will be interesting to discover, when unions of students will have been established for some years, whether the oncoming generations of new students will then accept them and work through them—or reject them as only one more manifestation of the Establishment in which incoming freshmen have not participated and against which they must therefore inveigh.

The 1960s and early 1970s saw the emergence of race conflict on campus in new forms and with new virulence. Just as the black community was divided over questions of integration versus separatism and black nationalism, so, too, there were varying voices among campus blacks. In its earlier stages, the demand for black studies was little more than an emotion-backed slogan, lacking in structure or content; and the earlier institutional responses tended to be improvised grab bags of offerings rather than a considered curriculum. As ethnic studies come of age, will they become just one more academic division or department or cluster of departments? Or be merged into an enlarged and enlightening common curriculum? Or pass off the scene? As long as the system of racial caste continues to be part of the American scene, it may be expected to find its expression in some form on campus. Whether higher education can expect to be a normative factor in helping to determine the future of American race relations is by no means clear. This question is subsumed with several others in the laundry list of American civilization.

Another factor that will have a controlling effect upon higher education in the immediate and the long-range future is the shift from campus dormitory to off-campus housing. As Census Bureau surveys reveal, dormitory residents remained constant in number (1,800,000) during the five-year period ending in 1972, while the number of students living away from home but in their own quarters increased from 1,400,000 to 2,400,000, of whom about 1,800,000 were married. About 2,600,000 commuters lived with parents or relatives, in addition to those who lived away from home off campus. Not only have the old parietal rules been annulled: the student population simply does not live on campus in anything like its proportions of even five years ago, and scarcely more than one in four undergraduates now lives on campus. Nearly three-fourths of American college and university students are no longer campus wards.

The tendency for racial and ethnic groups to cluster together off campus in separate parts of the city, or in segregated units within mixed residential communities, if it continues, will strongly negate institutional efforts to integrate student populations by means of on-campus dormitories. Institutional efforts to combat racial caste will be, by that fact, greatly diminished in effectiveness. And the ease with which individuals, young families, and communes run their own daily lives free of institutional control or supervision is a significant barometer of the declining influence of the Establishment in nurturing the learning of values. The emergence of a preponderance of the student body as off-campus adults makes more difficult the teaching of anything outside the formal rounds of the classroom. It also makes much easier the alibi of the reluctant professor and the harassed dean of students. An entirely new educational approach to the teaching of values is implied.

Alongside all the foregoing factors that will combine to affect the functioning and purposes of the traditional institutions of higher education is another newly emerging influence that will also have to be reckoned with. The Higher Education Act of 1972 included an amendment, §1202, which requires any state wishing to share in certain aid-to-education funds to establish a "post-secondary education commission." These new state boards are to include representatives not only from the established four-year colleges and the universities, but also from the two-year colleges and the proprietary schools as well. Set up as profit-making ventures, the proprietary schools have not heretofore enjoyed a status equal to that of the not-for-profit institutions. The newly established commissions in each state will require old-line colleges and universities to sit down, on an equal basis of representation and voting, with the proprietary institutions and the community colleges. The price of noncompliance with this statute will be, in any noncomplying state, a drop in Federal revenues. It is expected that all states will comply, with the result that vocational institutes and commercial schools will be on a par of consideration along with the prestigious universities and liberal arts colleges as plans are laid and executed for postsecondary education in every state. What effect will this have on the self-image of the institution that had heretofore thought of itself as serving an elite and now finds itself lumped with *hoi polloi?* More importantly, what is likely to be the effect on the value systems that the several types of institutions seek to promote? Will the ability of an institution to resist or to correct the pressures of the larger society be enhanced? Or will only the financially fortunate few survive the tidal wave of societal controls? In this situation, can any institution afford the luxury of fighting against the values and goals of the general society, even if it desires to do so? Will educators simply swallow their uneasiness and do as they are told by the society that pays the bills, as that society speaks through its elected representatives in Congress and the Executive Mansion and the sprawling governmental bureaucracy?

Decisions of such magnitude and importance will be made slowly and with difficulty. They will be made by institutions in which administrative leadership has been reduced in power and influence, in which faculties with their unions and students with theirs will play an increasing part, and in which students have physically moved out from under institutional control. The institutions that make these decisions will be no less unwieldy and amorphous, and their distinguishing identities that have traditionally given them a degree of internal cohesiveness will be glossed over as they are merged with proprietary institutions and two-year colleges in a least common denominator catchall of consideration.

The power-struggle that, up to this time, has influenced the course of campus life will not necessarily be muted by its becoming part of a larger quarrel between institutions. Existing acerbities may be exacerbated by additional angularities, accusations of favoritism, new alliances and blocs, and all the devices of back-room politics. Surface eruptions on campus may not, for a time, be as great; but the possibilities of campus unrest are greatly multiplied as layer of superstructure is piled on layer of infrastructure, and the voice of a single institution dwindles to an averaged statistic or a footnote in a voluminous report. The fact that many vectors of power have to be reckoned with may tend to make any particular thrust less forceful; and by that fact the mass-membership unions, both of professors and of students, will inevitably come to play a determinative role. The processes of change will not be smooth, easy, or marked by congeniality.

The foregoing dimensions of the power struggle in academe will be affected by the calculus of an array of external forces during the 1970s and 1980s.

Among the external threats to the quality and integrity of academe, the first to claim attention is the prevailing financial squeeze. The general impact of the inflation spiral is known to the public because of the annual announcements of increased tuition charges, now running at from three to seven times their 1940 levels. The unannounced cumulative costs of deferred plant and maintenance expenditures are formidable. Not a few formerly well-manicured campuses now resemble Goldsmith's Deserted Village, due to reductions in maintenance staff and diversion of funds to such purposes as internal security.

Institutions that have extended themselves on "soft" money are especially vulnerable, as shifting Federal policy looks for the "biggest bang for the buck" in order to justify itself to the voters before the next election. This short-term emphasis is illustrated in the drying up of an estimated 40 percent of all basic medical research in order that all available monies may be concentrated on finding a cure for cancer—all diseases and ailments other than carcinomata, and all progress in basic medical knowledge, can wait. The same shortsightedness is illustrated in the environmental sciences by the practical elimination of all Federal funds for basic research. Both of these shifts are understandable in terms of short-run political ambitions. Neither makes sense in terms of an intelligent and comprehensive attack on the fundamental factors that make up the human condition. Only a combination of adequately supported basic and applied research can be said to be an expression of honest concern for the items that make up civilization's laundry list.

Perhaps the clearest illustration of the effect of impermanence of public policy upon higher education is seen in the decimation of the foreign language and area programs, a change that is directed from the White House. While it is true that the initial support and much of the continuing aid for these programs was justified in congressional debate by the then prevailing notions of national defense and security, it is dramatically clear that the abandonment of flourishing programs is motivated primarily by a change in White House intentions, not by an assessment of the needs of the academic community or an understanding of the dangers and limitations of national parochialism. Finally, the time bomb is now being set for the next cycle of campus disturbances as Washington gives a different (and inadequate) response to the needs of the poor who aspire to a college education—a point to which we shall return a little later.

The private sources of support are not keeping pace with inflation and growth. Endowment and current-gift dollars of income support fewer professors, supply reduced numbers of students with scholarships and stipends, buy fewer of the ever more costly books for libraries (at precisely the time when annual acquisitions should be increasing in order to keep pace with the more than 36,000 volumes annually published in the United States alone). The 1972–1973 academic year has seen a stringency in faculty salaries not felt since the Great Depression, as customary annual increments are reduced or "postponed," while the cost of living continues to accelerate its upward spiral. Because of all these pressures, college and university presidents turn more to their budget comptrollers than to their development planners for definitive guidance. Fiscal management, cost accounting, and productivity auditing keep the computer center busy and, for the hapless faculty member, multiply the irritations of volumi-

nous reports, forms, questionnaires, circulars, and directives. It
is an unusual department chairman who manages to keep his
In basket clear. A college president is no longer defined as a
man who goes around with a worried look on the face of the
dean: both are men of furrowed brow.

The cost-squeeze factor is quite likely to be a principal irri-
tant in student circles as well. Those who have been recruited
from homes of poverty with assurances of adequate financial
aid will not take lightly any reduction in their promised scholarships and stipends. Whether black or white, they will view
a reduction in financial aid (or even the threat thereof) as
one more proof of the hypocrisy and evasiveness of the Establishment. When they are told that the budget is straitened,
they will not be mollified. Brave and liberal little Antioch
College is a harbinger of this trend: in the spring of 1973, a
small fraction of the student body (abetted and accompanied
by a few faculty members) forced the administration and faculty to abandon the entire campus for the greater part of the
term, not because student stipends had been cut but because the uncertainty of future governmental appropriations made it impossible for the college to promise to
continue the present level of financial aid beyond the bien-
nium. When direct action in the campus take-over gets down
to the bedrock anxieties of students' personal life (not merely
the reflexive angers provoked by societal ills), as it has done
in the Antioch case, the cost-squeeze factor in academic life
is no academic matter. (From this perspective, it becomes
easier for the white administrator and faculty member to arrive at an honest appraisal of the deep personal anxieties over
survival that provoked the campus blacks during the late
1960s: more than 55 percent of all campus disturbances in
1968 to 1970 were occasioned by one or another aspect of
the race question.) The *Lumpen*, whether white or black, will
not sit still while the colleges and universities try to work out
of their financial difficulties.

But the cost-squeeze factor is not the only source of institutional anxiety. Less publicized, but even more important in the years ahead, is a change in basic population data. Knowledgeable institutional planners have foreseen it; but few institutions have prepared for it. Thirty years of euphoric growth made it difficult to read the warnings correctly. For three decades, the numbers of college-bound students grew—both because there was an increasing population base and because a larger and larger percentage of the population stream entered postsecondary institutions. Total enrollments grew from 1,600,000 in 1940 to 8,500,000 in 1970, a more than fivefold increase. Despite all the trauma of the late 1960s, it was a euphoric period.

The first slackening of enrollment pressures came with the elimination of the military draft, which ended the necessity of seeking academic sanctuary from military service. It was less noticed than it might have been because the size of the age-group was still increasing, so the net change was still a greater number than before. But the postwar baby boom has now peaked. For the remainder of the 1970s, the population stream reaching college age will remain constant; and in the 1980s it will decline slightly. These are not matters of conjecture. The babies are already born. Between now and 1990, the numbers of college-age persons each successive year will not increase: it will decrease after 1980.

Perhaps a greater percentage of the college-age group will seek admission? Not under existing institutional assumptions. There are, of course, some who have "college abilities" but who do not apply or are rejected. They lack adequate preparation, or essential desire, or financial means. Nevertheless, with present institutional practices prevailing, more than half of the population stream does actually flow through the admissions offices of the nation's institutions of higher education. How much of the remaining half could or ought to go to college? Included in that half that does not now enter college are all the dropouts, failures, underachievers who do not fit the niches of traditional academic requirement and performance. Included also are those whose personal expectations do not include a sojourn in academe—unflattering as that may be to the ears of academics. From the general population, the colleges and universities, *as now managed and intended*, may not expect to draw much more than the present 51 percent of effective applicants.

Perhaps the racial minorities may provide a growth factor for college enrollments? Several reasons for a negative response can be cited. The pressures of the civil rights interests of the 1960s have lessened, making it less likely either that Federal programs will be as generous in their financial aid to ghetto children or that the institutions of higher education will continue to be as strongly concerned over their affirmative recruitment programs. Moreover, blacks make up only 11 percent of the total population, so that it would take a nine-to-one ratio of black student growth to offset or replace a decline (or stasis) in white enrollment. That ratio of effective effort by and in behalf of black students is not likely to be exerted over the coming years: it is too great a compliment to the black student to say that he has an effective effort-quotient nine times as great as his white peer. Moreover, much of the former slack in black enrollments has already been taken up. Blacks now enter college at a rate that is beginning to approach that for whites, their totals having quadrupled from a little over 200,000 in 1960 to nearing 800,000 in 1973. Any further increase in the college-going rate of black students could come only by dedicating ever-greater proportions of shrinking financial-aid funds to minority group students—and the "white ethnics" are beginning to demand their fair share of preferential treatment. As the memories of campus upheavals begin to fade a little and the traditional forces of academic exclusiveness reassert themselves (aided by budget stringency), there is little expectation that the nation's campuses will see anything greater than a modest increase in black enrollments.

Academe faces a watershed of decision as to enrollment policy. The opportunity to face that decision is supplied by the population facts we have been reviewing. Between now and 1990, institutions of higher education will either go onto a no-growth basis or they will radically alter their purposes and practices in egalitarian directions. The leveling off of population pressures provides the historic moment in which the choice can be made. Relieved of the added annual pressures due to an increase in the number of eighteen-year-olds, institutions can accept a static future—or they can elect to project patterns of growth based on wider (and possibly different) admissions criteria, which would be legitimate only if there were also an appropriate change in educational aims and methods.

The pressures in favor of growth are formidable. All the assumptions governing faculty recruitment, tenure, and promotion are rooted in the soil of institutional expansion. To be unable to fulfill faculty expectations for the next two decades would be to dampen the academic spirit severely, limiting appointments and promotions to the number of deaths and retirements, as younger faculty waited impatiently for their aging colleagues to make way (and themselves became senile while waiting for a professorship). All the assumptions regarding new programs and institutional vitality have been built around increased enrollments and larger budgets: the liberal use of the pruning knife on aging plantings does not add to the variety of the arboretum or increase the pleasure of gardeners accustomed to open up new acreage each spring. Institutional pride being what it is, and competition for prestige being as real to the academic world as is the struggle for profits in the commercial world, the pressures for growth instead of stasis are thus seen to be both prudential and psychic.

And since the future of higher education will be, to a very large degree, determined by the readiness of taxpayers to supply the necessary dollars, it is in the public arena that the ultimate decisions will be made. Thus, two sets of decisions have to be made simultaneously: the taxpayer's decision that his dollars are needed and that they are used wisely, and the academic decision that the Academy is ready and able to discharge the social function that justifies its tax support. Both sets of decisions have to be made on the fundamental question of intended growth versus no-growth.

If both the general society and the academic world become convinced that elitist services to a constricted number of students are preferable, the no-growth future may suffice for those institutions that survive; but if either the general public or the academicians turn toward egalitarian goals, the survival of academe will depend on acceptance of egalitarianism by both the general public and the institutions. If such agreement is to emerge, it must become clear beyond doubt that the panoply of postsecondary institutions is, in its totality, designed to serve well the needs of more than half of the population stream, that it is indeed admitting an ever-increasing portion of that stream, and that the results justify the expense. The choice between elitism and egalitarianism cannot, therefore, be made by the institutions acting independently of the taxpayers, even though substantial agreement within the campus circle is also essential.

Many of the great state universities (e.g., Minnesota) have, by law, for many years admitted any graduate from a high school within their state borders. The principle of what is currently called "open admissions" is not new: it is "new" only to the institutions that have built their reputations on exclusiveness. This is the historic moment in which higher education, temporarily relieved of the pressures of burgeoning population, may choose to grow for two decades solely in terms of egalitarian goals, reaching out in new directions to serve the needs of youth. That is to say, higher education could, if it desired, begin not only to serve the purposes that tradition and habit have bequeathed (and which are severely challenged or largely rejected by a society of youths that is tomorrow's world in the making), but also to discover and to meet the purposes that might legitimately be embraced by postsecondary education but which an elitist Academy has disdained.

Several changes will be necessary as the academic world moves from exclusiveness to inclusiveness. A greater variety of postsecondary offerings must be provided—a development in which the two-year institutions have been showing the way, but a development that ought not to be limited necessarily to that one type of institution. An enlightened conception of what may legitimately take place within the groves of Academe must supplant the narrowly conceived idea that colleges exist (as one has put it) solely in order that "youngsters may learn how to be taught from books." And in this process, the academic world must emerge as a recognized asset to the general society in coping with the generality of human needs, serving the human condition. All of these changes must be made in terms of excellence, an excellence that is defined appropriately for each type of educational performance. It was John Gardner who pointed out that "a society which has contempt either for its plumbers or its philosophers will find that neither its pipes nor its theories hold water." There is an excellence that is appropriate to each and any honorable field of human endeavor; and excellent performance of an honorable task should elicit respect, just as the education that fits a youth for that task should likewise be respected. Good technicians and good theorists will, as they perform well their tasks, do more to convince reluctant taxpayers that the institutions that trained and educated them are "excellent" and deserving of support than will all the efforts of institutional public relations officers.

In developing the needed variety of postsecondary offerings, there is one fatal blunder that must be avoided, namely, the duplication at the post-high school level of the invidious "tracking systems" of the high schools. Conant's *Slums and Suburbs* pointed out, a dozen years ago, that the nation's high schools were, at least in the larger cities, miserably failing to serve "the concept of equality of opportunity." He warned of "Social dynamite . . . building up in our larger cities," because differentiated "tracks" led to dead-end futures for the students who were steered into the lower tracks. His scholarly, low-key prose did help to increase school expenditures; but more money for more of the same miseducative school practices did not avert the day of reckoning. Diversity of academic offerings cannot be made synonymous with racial segregation—as it was (and is) in the high schools using the "tracking" method.

The same danger exists in the proliferation of the tracking system at the postsecondary level, best illustrated in the three-track system of public higher education in California. In that state, which leads the nation in providing postsecondary public education, admission to each of the three segments of public higher education is determined by rank in high school class and standing on SAT tests: to be admitted to one of the campuses of the university, one must be in the upper 12.5 percent; in the top third for entrance to one of the state colleges; and the junior colleges admit all the others. This has automatically guaranteed that black enrollments in the university would be less than 1 percent; less than 3 percent in the state colleges; and at the 7-percent level in the junior colleges.

The same error was repeated by the City University of New York in setting admissions processes so that its senior colleges remain predominantly white while its community colleges are predominantly black and Puerto Rican. When an effort was made in 1965 to correct the "tracking" practice within the City University, only one of the senior college presidents supported the proposal. Three years later, every campus of the then seventeen units of the university was under siege. The manifest unfairness of an admissions policy that penalized black and Puerto Rican students because the lower schools had not adequately prepared them for academic success—that unfairness was defended in the name of "standards" and "equal opportunity on the basis of achievement." Such a defense was put forward in all of the senior college faculties, and even those administrators who were ready to move toward fairness and equity managed to make progress much too slowly. From neighboring Columbia, and from a highly vocal segment of the alumni of CUNY, came a stout defense of "meritocracy" and a denigration of the "egalitarian" tendencies exhibited in the remedial programs *cum* wider admissions that had been introduced. So severe was the opposition to egalitarian goals that even when so-called "open admissions" became the order of the day in 1970, the basic features of the tracking system remained. The resulting *de facto* segregation within the City University, despite the fact that blacks make up 22 percent of the total undergraduate enrollment, has not been corrected by open admissions. The disproportionate numbers in the two-year institutions (as well as the disparity of black enrollment ratios among the nine senior colleges) have not resulted in equality of educational opportunity. Indeed, open admissions has jumped the white enrollments at a pace even faster than that of blacks; and the tracking system has resulted in a substantial degree of segregation as between the upper and lower levels of the two-track system. There is one small gain in the present admissions policy over that which was proposed by the central headquarters of CUNY in 1969, namely, that the then contemplated *third* track—the so-called "skills centers" that were to have enrolled all who were rejected by the two-year institutions—has withered on the vine. CUNY did not go all the way in aping the three-track system of the state of California.

If, then, the needed variety of postsecondary offerings is to be achieved, while at the same time the invidious and discriminatory tracking systems are to be avoided, great care and an as yet undiscovered quality of leadership will be required. The formerly predominantly white institutions—all of them, of whatever type or identity—must, at long last, begin to do what they should have been doing since the Emancipation Proclamation: they must decide to educate *at least* the same proportions of nonwhites as are found in the general population. More correctly, they must so reorganize and reorient themselves, from admissions to graduation, that the youth of all races will aspire to come and to learn—and will do so without racial restriction and without segregation.

When there are no islands of exception to this general practice, American higher education will begin to be in a position to stop miseducating American youth; the American college and university will have begun to make its necessary attack on racial caste. But if the egalitarian effort at the point of admissions is to be anything more than a charade, all the institutional practices and individual postures are due for radical overhauling. Until the public schools and high schools begin adequately to prepare inner-city children for college pursuits, the campus must carry a heavy load of remedial instruction—particularly in mathematics, reading skills, and writing competence. And as long as racial caste continues to denigrate the black child, the campus must be prepared to deal effectively with eighteen-year-olds who tend understandably to vacillate between underrating and overrating themselves and their performance. In short, it is not enough to strike the restraints of caste off the computers in the admissions office: the campus must, without further delay, become a world without caste.

If the area of attention is shifted from the student body (and an educational experience appropriate to it) to the faculty, another set of equations calls for comment. Egalitarianism, with its attendant pressures, has already arrived on campus at the faculty level. As the civil rights legislation is effectively enforced (and it will be) in terms of the hiring, tenuring, and promoting of women, blacks, and persons with Spanish surnames, an irreversible process of change sets in. The white male with his freshly inked doctoral certification already competes in a job market different from his predecessor of even five years ago. The white male who is already tenured, and who finds that his new colleagues are of unaccustomed hue and gender, does not always respond with pleasant alacrity to the situation. The years immediately ahead will witness an intensification of the competitive struggle for jobs, position, and power as the traditionally white male faculty world yields to the inexorable egalitarian thrust that, at long last, has the full sanction of law. This is a point at which the elitist institution, with its decision in favor of stasis, becomes most vulnerable. It will be unable to survive or surmount the egalitarian pressures it cannot contain. This is also a point at which, in a growing academic world, a graceful transition along egalitarian lines might be devised.

Even under optimum growth assumptions, however, the transition will not be easy. Anxiety over job security and academic prestige will tend to mute the altruism of the tenured white male, while the sharpest kind of interpersonal struggle for acceptance, advancement, and survival will characterize the years of younger faculty members of both sexes and all races. Increasing polarization between the races, sexes, and ages is assured unless new qualities of objectivity and compassion can be supplied. Once again, it becomes a matter of values: prevailing value systems give little promise of supplying what is needed. New levels of glad comradeship become essential, even as the plausibility of the impending organized struggle for power increases. Unions, quotas, formulae, grievance procedures, arbitration, strikes, and lockouts will supplant much of the traditional machinery for appointment, tenuring, and promoting of faculty. The ombudsman will be busier than the vice president for personnel; and the latter will handle more matters of pressing importance than will the academic dean. Conflict will be structured; but it will not be reduced in severity or intensity merely by being contained in new channels. Finally, in this matter of the inadequacy of traditional values for meeting the new egalitarianism, those in academe who lived through the late 1960s should be able to recall enough of those dysphoric days to make them unready to pursue as a matter of choice a course of action that would almost certainly evoke another season of student discontent. Next time around there will be, among the faculty members, those whose academic credentials and predilections were acquired in the existential university.

In the light of all the difficulties that are to be resident on campus for the foreseeable future, faculty members and administrators might ask to be excused for refusing to mount the ramparts against the generality of human ills. That request, if it were made, should be refused. To extend exculpation to those who will not recognize the obligations of academe to be of service to the human condition would be to compound error with collusion. There is no answer to the exigent moment short of a fundamental reconsideration of educational purpose.

If the arguments and data discussed in this book have any degree of validity, the conclusion is inescapable: academic survival, both personal and institutional, will depend on the degree to which higher education and educators are looked upon as being indispensable to a viable future for mankind. To be regarded as indispensable, academe and academicians must demonstrate both to themselves and to the general society that campus performance and public image alike reflect and express the qualities of life that have a right to endure.

Hubris

The struggle for institutional survival could be described exclusively in terms of its surface manifestations, the relative strength of contending parties in the struggle for power, and the strategies to be followed in successive skirmishes. Perhaps a grand strategy could be laid out, into which the skirmishes might mesh.

A less presumptive and possibly more rewarding attempt to state the alternatives of choice would be an examination of the basic value systems that now confront one another on the campus, to see whether it is possible and worthwhile to take sides in that struggle. Both tactics and strategy might be better informed because of such an examination.

The dominant value system of American life is a pragmatic one. It is based in an efficient technology which (or so the argument runs) has made us number one among all the nations of world history. We know how to do almost anything that could be desired; and if the know-how is slightly tardy in maturing in a given particular, we believe that it is only a matter of dollars and time before we can lick that problem, too. This confidence was given a severe test during the dreary years of the Indochina war, and it is being questioned by the continuing crises in human relations as well as in the deterioration of the ecosystem; but the assumption of ultimate success through an omnipotent technology remains.

We take pride, justifiably, in our know-how. We respond with alacrity to any threat to our superiority in technology (as the immediate restructuring of the teaching of mathematics after the launching of the first Russian Sputnik showed). We have come to believe that we can develop and perfect answers to all the problems of disease, poverty, drug addiction, poor housing, racial conflict, hunger, and crime in the streets. Just a little more time and money and effort are needed. We are on the right track, and we can develop the necessary know-how. We sent men to the moon and brought them back, didn't we? And we are now seriously planning for the day when a manned vehicle will land our men on another planet, perhaps Mars. Nobody seems to raise a serious doubt that the know-how will be available when it is needed.

Even those who quarrel with our national priorities, saying that we ought to divert monies from space programs and military hardware to fight hunger, disease, and pollution, seem to share the general assumption that all we need is time and money in order to lick these problems. A little more time, and we will find that cure for cancer, if we pour enough money into it. A little more time, and we can feed the whole world well—if we don't cut off funds for agricultural research and development. Give us the money and we can rebuild our cities, make them pollution-free and viable. Increase the appropriations for higher education, and we know how to put the funds to good use.

Our confidence in our know-how is, of course, a source of great satisfaction among us. But it is more than that. The Greeks had a word for it: *hubris*, overweening pride, a self-confidence that tells us we can do anything, and do it better than anyone else.

And since we can do anything, why not do it? Indeed, technological progress has gone forward to its present extensions and at its headlong pace because we have seldom previously asked ourselves, as a decision-making nation, whether we should or should not do whatever next thing is technologically possible. A new invention leads to the manufacture and marketing of a product or new bit of miniaturized technology for home use. No one asks whether the new product or gadget ought to be manufactured, so long as it pays its own way in competition for its share of the consumer's dollar and meets the minimum standards of the Food and Drug Administration. Only recently, under the impact of the ecological scare, have we as a nation begun to ask whether our know-how was an unmixed blessing.

Abruptly, within the last half dozen years, we have become aware as a nation that overweening pride is no guarantee of general well-being. From the wasted ecology, polluted and poisoned and approaching exhaustion; from the misery of hunger and the devastation of lingering war; from the violence that stalks the streets and the hatred that inflames racial caste; from health needs that far exceed our ability to deliver health services; from all these and many others come the warning signals. Survival will not come from an uncontrolled know-how that is actually destroying us. Survival will come only as a selective use is made of that burgeoning know-how. And that selective use will come only as we are driven to make trade-offs based in the identification of values that lead to survival.

Not too much good will come from an effort to preach life back into a dying value system. As R. H. Tawney and Max Weber demonstrated half a century ago, the value systems to which we still cling in modified form were created to nurture and to sanction the very economic and political system that has, through its unbridled technology, brought us to the present moment. The prophets of nineteenth-century middle-class values and virtues will continue to rehearse their wares in public, telling us what we already know—that we will not get out of our present condition without hard work. But we also know something they overlook—we will not get out unless we know what to do. The old virtues surely need revival; but they must be revived in a form adequate to today's problems rather than last century's. In both of its principal variations, the nineteenth century appears to advocate value systems that are inadequate to the late twentieth century.

That is to say, that neither Adam Smith nor Karl Marx offers the economic and political values adequate to the post-industrial technological age. Both in Marxist and non-Marxist countries, industrialism and its consequent exploiting technology have filled the lakes with silt and algae, poisoned the rivers and the skies with factory effluence, and begun to endanger the dwindling sources of energy. Both Marxist and non-Marxist nations hold nuclear destruction on slender leash, each restrained only by the mutual balance of terror.

From whence is the needed value system to come? Not from the value-free technology that has spawned the problems. Not from the nationalism that has Balkanized the world and equipped it with biological and nuclear weapons of war. Not from the caste system that divides us into camps of bilious hate. Not from a religion that is torn between apocalyptic irrelevance, ecclesiastical pride, and social ineffectiveness. Not from an educational system that attempts merely to survive in society without serving it by remaking it.

The needed system of values will be hammered out on the anvil of experience by whoever can be rallied to the task, in whatever station or place, however institutionally engaged or disengaged, both from within the Establishment and from outside it.

At a few critical times, the university has served as sanctuary for the creative act as new values have been devised to meet new exigencies. Thomas Aquinas found sanctuary first in the University of Paris (where he precariously defended himself against William of St. Amour), then at the Pontifical Curia in Rome, and again in Paris. It was at the University of Glasgow that Adam Smith wrote *The Wealth of Nations*. Defended by the campus sanctuary from prevailing mercantilism and its political and ecclesiastical expressions, he took the value system of his *Theory of Moral Sentiments* and built thereon the political and economic theories that were to guide two centuries of development. Denied his appointment at the University of Bonn, Karl Marx found sanctuary in the reading room of the British Museum, where he rewrote English history to buttress the value system he proposed as the basis for reorganizing all of life.

Despite the external pressures and the internal feuds, it is not beyond possibility that at least a few academic sanctuaries could be found in the Amercian scene today wherein men and women of mettle might restructure political, economic, and social values to provide what our day demands. Granting the degree of unwelcome intrusion of political forces on campus, and taking into full consideration the institutional hostages already given to the American economy and those who profit most from it, the campus still has a respectable sense of the meaning of academic freedom to inquire. Fertile minds and untrammeled spirits might still find sufficient protection as they pushed the inquiries that our century requires. And now that the campus sanctuary is no longer an enclave, removed from the world, it is an even more promising locus for the inquirer into the human predicament. No longer removed from the world, he must be in it; but not of it.

The difficulty is that most men and women who have the necessary spirit of adventure, the essential intellectual equipment and furnishing, and the understanding and compassion to do the job have permitted themselves to get bogged down in the diversionary skirmishes of the day. Or they have remained enslaved to old controversies, such as that between the warring orthodoxies of Smith and Marx, both of which are irrelevant to today's difficulties. Or they have tried, only to find that mountainous labors produced small mice.

Is it possible that the university and college could be the necessary think tanks and *practica* through which the twenty-first century might be born in hope? And is it not probable that, unless this does happen, neither the institutions of higher education nor the people they are supposed to serve will survive?

To bring us one step closer to the frame of mind in which the constructive task might be successfully addressed, it will be useful to explore a little more carefully the manner in which the conflict of values is carried out as a clash of symbols.

Iconoclasm

The use of symbols to evoke a following and to induce obedience to authority is not a new device. The cross, the crescent, and the star of David each represents an entire conception of the meaning of life and of the universe. Allegiance to the symbol implies obedience to and acceptance of the authority that the symbol represents.

Outsized photographs and paintings carried in processions, Gargantuan idealized statues in public squares, and friendly little statuettes for household use commonly remind the masses of the significance of the Great Leader. In the United States, custom permits this excess of emblazonment for living persons only during political campaigns; but we know as well as anyone that when a man can be shown larger than life, it is easier to believe that he is great. Even in our democracy, we have permitted ourselves to select a few great figures and give them magnificent perpetual representation in the memorials to Washington, Jefferson, and Lincoln in the nation's capital. The heroic faces on Mt. Rushmore attract the patriotic tourist. We know as well as the Chinese that one picture (or piece of statuary) is worth a thousand words.

But what one man venerates, another may denigrate. Denigration may begin as a boyish prank, merely expressing childish ebullience. For example, when the monumental seated statue of Washington B. Duke, benefactor, was unveiled at the entrance gate of Trinity College in Durham, North Carolina, the assemblage gasped and was then convulsed on seeing the results of clandestine undergraduate waggishness: the venerable gentleman could hardly be venerated while his lap was overflowing with empty whiskey bottles.

Denigration may sometimes be due to thoughtlessness, as when a devout Christian uses a cute little statuette of the smiling Buddha for a paper weight—as though a Buddhist were to use a small crucifix as a letter-opener. Or a returning prisoner of war may neglect to salute the colors on his reception at home, only because he is anxious to embrace the wife from whom he has been separated by years; he meant no disrespect for Old Glory.

But thoughtlessness and momentary forgetfulness are in a class quite different from deliberate denigration. Statues are pulled down and beheaded, walls are covered with graffiti, paint is smeared on objects too large to move, cigarette burns deface portraits (early suffragettes used umbrellas to spear museum-displayed dignitaries). Books are burned, flags trampled on, effigies hung. Denigration of symbols is a powerful tool of social conflict. It has a name.

When the emperor Leo III from Constantinople issued an edict in 726 banning the veneration of sacred pictures, he could not have known that he was contributing a word to twentieth-century English usage. Coming from the province of Asia Minor some two hundred miles south of Constantinople, he shared the convictions of his native region. He viewed the worship of religious symbols and portraits as pure idolatry, a relic of pantheism. No matter that the practice was Hellenic. Or, perhaps, because it was Hellenic, he tried to stamp it out. The Greeks, on the other hand, prized their native heritage. Any edict from the capital that seemed to denigrate things Hellenistic would be an offense to them; and when it centered on their most precious religious practices, they resisted with all their might.

The controversy was looked upon as religious and theological. Actually, it was geographic and ethnic: it was a nationalistic fight against imperial dominance. The Greeks had, from before the dawn of recorded history, worshipped a well-tenanted pantheon of deities and heroes. The religion of the polis had given to each city a special guardian; and to the citizen, access to the whole remarkable panoply of protective beings whose help could be invoked when needed. When the Byzantine emperor Constantine embraced Christianity, his edict of 325 "converted" all subject peoples, including the Hellenes. They came under the aegis of the new religion, but they brought their ancient deities and heroes with them, re-baptized as Christian saints (some imaginary) and archangels. In the new dispensation, the ancient deities and heroes, given new names, continued to function as guardians of the people, performing their accustomed miracles and receiving their customary devotion. The painted representations of these saints and archangels were "icons," i.e., sacred pictures. For four centuries after the Hellenes had been "converted" by imperial edict to the new religion, they had continued to venerate their icons. They refused to obey a Syrian emperor who ordered them to quit; and in that refusal they were led by the local clergy, who relied on painting icons and selling them to the faithful to put bread and butter on the monastic table. Thus, nationalistic pride and grass-roots economics combined to resist imperial oppression.

Three times, by edict, Leo III tried to destroy the practice of the veneration of icons. He dispatched the imperial navy. He used the army. His successors in office kept up the running fight for 120 years. Finally, the empress Theodora repealed the ban on the worship of sacred pictures and the controversy was forgotten. But it had served its nationalistic purpose. Having resisted the emperor for more than a century over the symbolic question of the use of symbols, Greek nationalism had grown strong enough to persevere until freedom was won for the Greek nation.

And thus it came about that anyone who attempts to destroy established practices, beliefs, ideals, customs, and institutions is called an iconoclast. History has its little irony in the fact that the original iconoclast was an emperor, not a helot. Cromwell, when he came to power, was to repeat that irony; but Cromwell was never noted for his sense of humor.

In contemporary America, the iconoclasts are not found among the leadership of the Establishment. They come from the ranks and the *Lumpen*. In academia, they congregate in the existential university. They reject prevailing authority and therefore they hold in contempt and obloquy any and all expressions of the Establishment. By the ironic reversal of history, icons today are shattered, smudged, torn to tatters, and defaced not by the emperor but by the helots.

Today's icons are denigrated both because veneration would imply subservience to established power and because the act of veneration is, in itself, held to be ridiculous. To destroy the power of the established order, perhaps to destroy both Establishment and order, prevailing beliefs, ideas, ideals, habits, customs, practices, and institutions must be brought into disrepute.

A principal spokesman for Students for a Democratic Society (SDS), Carl Davidson, laid down the pattern of iconoclasm for his organization in the late 1960s. Speaking in confidence to his own membership, he declared the purpose and method of the SDS to be essentially iconoclastic. The university was to be "a crucible of the new working class." To that end, the movement must become an "effective 'desanctification' program against the authoritarian institutions controlling us." In his unpublished manuscript, he went on to say:

> The purpose of desanctification is to strip institutions of their legitimizing authority, to have them reveal themselves to the people under them for what they are—raw coercive power. This is the purpose of singing the Mickey Mouse Club jingle at student government meetings, of ridiculing and harassing

student disciplinary hearings and tribunals, of burning the Dean of Men and/or of Women in effigy, etc. People will not move against institutions of power until the legitimizing authority has been stripped away. On many campuses, this has already happened; but for those remaining, the task remains. And we should be forewarned: it is a tricky job and can often backfire, de-legitimizing us.

As iconoclasm became a favorite device of the spreading Berkeley syndrome, Davidson's strategies of destruction through ridicule and profanation did not go unanswered. In the wake of the first heavy season of troubles at Columbia University, the Cox Commission's *Report on Crisis at Columbia* said:

> The survival—literally the survival—of the free university depends upon the entire community's active rejection of disruptive demonstrations. Any sizeable group, left to pursue such tactics, can destroy either the university by repeatedly disrupting its normal activities or the university's freedom by compelling the authorities to invoke overwhelming force in order that its activities may continue. The only alternative is for the entire community to reject the tactics of physical disruption with such overwhelming moral disapproval as to make them self-defeating.

Brave words, bravely spoken. But who listened?

As the 1960s approached their concluding years, any gathering of college presidents was a depressing congeries of weariness, quite devoid of sparkle and good humor. College authorities were tired, tired from long days and longer nights of round-the-clock dialogue. Many were bewildered, bewildered by the onslaught of an iconoclasm they did not understand because they believed that they were being wrongly victimized. Too many were harassed, harassed by the recurring disruptive demonstration and the continuing threat thereof, yet reluctant—deeply reluctant—to yield to an almost masochistic demand that force be invoked to restrain iconoclasm. None appeared to have convincing answers to the generation of iconoclasts, contemptuously disdainful practitioners of the art of disruption, so deeply dedicated, so strongly self-convinced. Words from the *Bhagavad-Gita* came to mind:

> For the uncontrolled there is no wisdom, nor for the uncontrolled is there the power of concentration; and for him without concentration there is no peace. And for the unpeaceful, how can there be happiness?

But the truth of that day appeared not to lie with ancient seers—not, at least, for the dysphoric generation. The times had written a macabre script, which was to be acted out by a small and impervious guild of the *Lumpen,* actors who, in self-hypnosis, played each scene to its tragic fullness. Empathy and compassion were unable to write different lines or supply an alternative plot for a happier drama. The generation of lemmings demanded its hour of tragedy.

Unhappy college presidents and deans were unable to stand outside themselves and their situations and, with dispassionate eye, find redeeming truth in the vehemence and vulgarity of iconoclasm. Many administrators, in fact, shared the hopes and aspirations of the iconoclastic generation—or so they themselves believed, at any rate; but the channels of communication were cut off. Iconoclasts no longer wanted a dialogue: they wanted confrontation. Educational administrators who were singled out for derision and contempt, spit upon in public or pelted with overripe garbage, subjected to a running barrage of pamphleteering and street language, ridiculed in the student press, tended to take the whole thing personally. Too seldom did they realize there was nothing personal in the attacks on them—not at first, that is. The personal attacks came as a by-product of mounting confrontation. As the strategy of "desanctification" was elaborated, it became necessary to defame the officeholder in order to demean the office. Presidents had become no longer persons. They were icons, to be destroyed.

The existential university is not inherently arrogant, contemptuous, and contentious, any more than its campus rivals are essentially haughty and disdainful. The postures of the bellicose were dictated by the seeming necessities of tactics and strategy: one cannot speak softly and pleasantly through a bullhorn. In short, campus iconoclasm is a by-product of the human condition, not of its essence.

But what fine sport it is to smash icons! One can't get at "The Man," so one throws a half-brick through a plate-glass window. The Now generation calls it "trashing." One cannot get at the seat of power, so one takes it out on the symbols of power, namely, whichever person or institution or piece of property happens to be accessible. Graffiti smear the walls. A president is mousetrapped as he gives thoughtful consideration to a set of nonnegotiable demands. Pop bottles are thrown at firemen responding to a false alarm. Policemen are shot from ambush. Human dung is smeared on the front door of the administration building. Paper bags filled with urine fall on unsuspecting pedestrians from a quickly vacated upper-story window. None of these things happen because the particular object of disfigurement, disrespect, or attack necessarily deserves the treatment, but because paranoia demands at least symbolic expression.

In its turn, authority has a way of wrapping itself in the flag, appropriating values to support its own purposes and to perpetuate itself in power. Veneration of the values then becomes synonymous with acceptance of the authority because the Establishment has attempted to arrogate to itself the inherent merit of the values. Thus, a President of the United States wraps himself in the dignity that properly belongs not to him but to his office, and accuses his critics of a lack of patriotism when they differ with his policies. A college president is hurt or takes offense when the tools that have served his purposes well (respect, civility, common decency) are derided in four-letter cadence by a student group that is flailing its way through a thicket of enraged despair.

As long as the needs of the human condition are served well by stasis, the confusing identification of authority and values serves human needs; but when—as in our present time—the needs of humanity are volatile and dynamic, the most useful authority is that which is at least equally dynamic. A static authority cannot stand when its supporting value system is swept away. The inevitable result is anomie, a state of society in which normative standards of conduct have weakened or disappeared. And anomie invites tyranny to cure disorder, completing the circle from old authority to new oppression without remedying the human condition.

Iconoclasm, as it presents itself on the American campus today, is revealed not merely as a counterculture, an alternative life-style. It is a thoroughgoing rejection of an authority that has not responded to the dynamics of the human condition and a complete rejection of the value system by which that authority seeks to perpetuate itself in power. That is why the age of reason, civility, and compassion has passed from the groves of Academe. That is why the unresolved struggle for power threatens to support the iconoclastic effort rather than to permit differences to be reconciled in a democratic sharing of power. That is why the campus appears to be an inhospitable sanctuary for the creative act of compassion. And that is precisely why the future is precarious.

8

Beyond Iconoclasm

&⸹ "In that protest which each considerate person makes against the superstitions of his times, he repeats . . . the part of the old reformers, and in the search after truth finds, like them, new perils to virtue. He learns again what moral vigor is needed to supply the girdle of superstition. A great licentiousness treads on the heels of reformation."

—Ralph Waldo Emerson (1841)

"It is the first step of wisdom to recognize that the major advances of civilization are processes which all but wreck . . . society. . . . The art of a free society consists, first, in the maintenance of the symbolic code; and secondly, in fearlessness of revision. . . . Those societies which cannot combine reverence to their symbols with freedom of revision must ultimately decay."

—Alfred North Whitehead (1927)

As we move into the 1970s, the campus is a different place. Important changes have been made. Students sit on governing boards; ethnic studies flourish; the pass-fail grade has become popular; rigidities of curriculum and of requirements have been relaxed. More students live as autonomous adults off campus than are found in dormitories; and nearing two of the seven millions are married; parietal rules are passé.

The pressures from the larger society are different. The draft is ended—until the next war. The weary Indochina engagement winds down to its final snuff-out. Several summers have passed without major urban race riots. The Environmental Control Administration has taken a tough stance toward the automobile industry. Some of the grosser instances of air and water pollution are being reduced (with no promise that municipalities, without the needed Federal aid, will be able to handle their mountains of solid waste and neutralize the toxic effects of human waste). The United Nations has begun to talk about setting up a worldwide inventory of ecological danger signals. The three principal nuclear powers have not recently rattled their missiles, and there is a treaty limiting the strategic arms race.

But there is no profoundly different quality in the human condition. Sampling the eastern Atlantic indicates that half the plankton (basic first step in the food chain) are endangered by spilled oil and accumulated plastic refuse. Poverty, disease, hunger, and death still stalk the continents. The Northern Hemisphere is still separated from the Southern by an ever-widening disparity in standards of living and annual income. The Civil Rights Commission, for the third consecutive year, reports "No progress." Unemployment among blacks is still much greater than among whites, and the disparity widens instead of narrowing. City slums continue to decay. Crimes against person and property increase, and there is small solace in the announcement that the rate of increase has fallen a little. The drug nonculture is pandemic. The generation gap remains.

Continuing Dysphoria

The campus mood is still dysphoric. The nationwide mass protests do not recur with each warm invitation of spring; but the absence of major disruption is due less to a new satisfaction than to a deeper distress, the distress of a despair that has ceased to hope and has forgotten how to care. There is a brittle quality lying just beneath the surface of campus pleasantries.

To be sure, much of the old order remains. The invasion of the public entertainment field by big time "amateur" athletics continues to delight the television industry and to provide undergraduate diversion. Students seem to have transferred their anxieties to the infrapersonal areas of self-exploration and to the personal goals of postcollegiate employment. Faculty members, when they lift their eyes from engrossing research, still assume that they are on campus to teach and that students ought to be taught what the faculty has decided should be taught—regardless of what is learned. There are a few promising tentative efforts at interdisciplinary joint exploration, but there is no discernible mass movement of intellectual inquirers away from the tyranny of the discrete disciplines. Campus security precautions have increased and become more sophisticated; but the feeling of safety from bodily harm and petty theft has not come. Drugs continue to be pushed on campus. Academia has "adjusted." It has not really changed its stance.

There has been no reconciliation, no clear meeting of the minds, between the iconoclasts and the Establishment. The existential university and the research university have not begun serious conversations. The liberal educational tradition remains unsure of itself, and therefore repeats with greater emphasis its traditional aspirations, without too much expectation that there will be an affirmative response.

Those who survived the troubled decade may, perhaps, be indulged while they draw a few free breaths; but the time is short until the bell clangs for the next round. The sense of security that comforts some campuses will be deserved only if the passing moment is seized. The mood of self-congratulation that some campuses enjoy is probably premature, as exhibited in words like these spoken in the winter of 1972–1973:

. . . that most of these so-called new concepts and practices have been with us a long time—and that their limited acceptance has been due to their limited usefulness rather than to their limited trial—and that the traditional university has survived and evolved into its present form because it is intrinsically defensible as the major institutional embodiment of human culture and progress in a civilized society. Let me speak today, then, in behalf of the traditional university.

Before a vast complacency settles its pall permanently over the institutions of higher education as a preliminary to the next dysphoric uprising, can weariness and wariness be transformed into a constructive effort?

The Guiding Synthesis

No scissors-and-paste revisions will do. Although, as always, the structures will use many familiar materials, no patchwork job will suffice. If the institutions of higher education are to be adequate to the times, they must be built anew, with newly thought purposes and freshly devised methods.

The guiding synthesis of values for the twenty-first century must be dynamic, holistic, heuristic, and empathetic. The rigidities of rational logic must give way to the necessities of rapid growth in an all-encompassing effort to achieve survival value.

The new synthesis must be dynamic because there is no other way to achieve relevance to a condition of flux. The human condition is changing momentarily and with exponentially increasing speed. Yesterday's values are only partially relevant to today—as we see. They will be outmoded tonight. Tomorrow dawns upon a humanity naked of its protecting pretensions and innocent of the needed cogent wisdom. To all the other trauma of Toffler's *Future Shock*, add one more dimension: the necessity of keeping ahead of exponentially developing knowledge and runaway technology, with a fixed value system. To direct and control the developments without which the human condition cannot be remedied, a quality of dynamism in the guiding synthesis is imperative.

It must be holistic, because no fragmented or fragmenting approach to the human condition can adequately grasp its meaning or understand its needs. Emphasizing the functional relationship between parts and wholes, the new theories of knowledge cannot be broken up into the segments assigned to the several academic disciplines. Instead of the disciplinary approach, the interdisciplinary; and instead of the interdisciplinary, the interpenetration of the disciplines—until all sharp lines of division have been erased and mutual cross-fertilization has bred the hybrids that will be sturdy and fecund enough to survive the traumas of tomorrow. One of the prices that hubristic academic man now has to pay for his self-pride is the humbling of the disciplines that each publishing scholar and scientist has helped to erect as monuments to his personal achievement. The vested interests of the separate disciplines, their refusal or inability to have a genuine commerce of ideas with one another, and their unreadiness to learn from each other have resulted in projecting great follies on the screen of human experience. While the atomism of inquiring and learning has permitted the exploration of selected aspects of knowledge in depth, the accrued information has not necessarily added to man's wisdom to the same degree that it has increased his technics. What is needed is not merely some sort of philosophical reconciliation of the many branches of learning, nor some watered-down general commonplaces. What is needed is to discover anew the common roots and the meanings central to all, so that each branch may thrive and all may bear fruit. While it is impossible for any one man or group of men to master the whole of human lore in a lifetime, the ignorance of the specialist can no longer be condoned. Extrapolation of insights from findings and data correctly assessed in one field of specialization is valid only when such extension is tested and revalidated as amended with the findings, data, and methods appropriate to the field invaded. That is to say, there has been a pragmatic justification to the creating of the several disciplines because the methods and processes appropriate to the data in each field are dissimilar to those appropriate in others. The error has lain not in establishing separate disciplines, but in dissevering them. It would appear that the minimal requirement that must be made of the specialist is that he attempt to understand both the limitations of his own relevance within his own field and the meaning of the variant procedures and assumptions that are the essence of relevance and validity in other areas of human inquiry. Without this appreciation of the genius and meaning of fields of inquiry other than his own, the specialist is neither scientific nor scholarly. He is, however brilliant, an ignorant technician. The holistic effort does not require that any one mind must attempt to master all lore or that any particular discipline is threatened as it is exposed to all others. What it does require is that no discipline develop *in vacuo*. What it does demand is that those who pursue knowledge in any one of the disciplines shall refuse to accept as true any segmented data that have not been examined in their totality of organic and functional relationships—even if that means calling on other disciplines for their contributions in the examination of the same data. In brief, the holistic approach to knowledge demands disciplinary humility in place of departmental *hubris*.

The twenty-first-century synthesis must be heuristic. It must be designed to discover and to unfold rather than to dominate and convince. It must not be eristic—designed more to win an argument than to reveal truth. Its conclusions will always be tentative, subject to correction, best present approximations, constantly replacing earlier conclusions and always being replaced by tomorrow's better insights. Its attitude will include listening and hearing as well as looking and seeing, in order that the sometimes irascible contributions of colleagues from other disciplines (as well as from within one's own) may penetrate the protective pride to inseminate the sterile seed of thought. Cross-fertilization of the disciplines ought not to be a figure of speech.

To achieve any of its purposes, the twenty-first-century synthesis must be empathetic, in both meanings of the term. It must evoke from each person the capacity to stand in another's place, to share and to understand: that is to say, the distinction between the eristic and the heuristic must be carried right on through the whole of the continuing inquiry of life if prejudice and prejudging are not to vitiate man's understanding. Secondly, the synthesis must frankly project the so-called "subjective" meanings (whether affective, connotative, or cognitive) into the field of observation, because there is no other way to arrive at holistic knowledge except by including *all* meanings as data—whether subjective or objective. In any moment of human experience, the given fact is that subjective meanings are present. Not to recognize the subjective aspects of the data is to be less than scientific; and to assume that data consist only of what remains after the subjective meanings have been excised is to project the vice of solipsism onto the allegedly "objective" data. The subjective data must, of course, be examined rigorously; but such examination follows only upon their being explicitly recognized as part of the material under analysis. Only by openly including such matters as value systems, for example, can any inquiry into human affairs pretend to be valid.

Useful beginnings are being made in an effort to establish conversations between differing evaluators of current value systems. Sometimes these efforts have some of the necessary characteristics for the new synthesis. There was, for example, considerable merit in the idea that brought within the covers of one slim volume in 1968 the essays of three men who offered divergent opinions in *A Critique of Pure Tolerance*. The principal value of the publisher's exercise, however, lies in the clarification of differing positions, not in their resolution. The three contributors, Wolff, Moore, and Marcuse, appear to engage in an eristic debate rather than an heuristic meeting of minds.

Discussing tolerance, Herbert Marcuse argues for replacing it with aggressive intolerance, intolerance of whatever impedes the struggle against oppression and suppression. He would use benevolent censorship, even precensorship, to redress the imbalance in power between prevailing mores and ideologies and those that are attempting to break the bonds of conformity. He asserts that tolerance as presently practiced amounts to the demand by the Establishment that *it* must be tolerated (that is, unchallanged) in its position of power, while the radical and revolutionary minorities are denied even that degree of tolerance that would let them give intellectual expression (let alone take action) to their radical and revolutionary ideologies. Marcuse sees tolerance as an instrument of the oppressors, used against the revolutionaries.

> I maintain that there are issues where either there is no "other side" in any more than a formalistic sense, or where the "other side" is demonstrably "regressive" and impedes possible improvement of the human condition. To tolerate propaganda for inhumanity vitiates the goals not only of liberalism but of every progressive political philosophy.

If we want justice and decency in a free society, says Marcuse, there is no alternative other than the dictatorship of an "elite" over the people, fully expressing the intolerance that it feels toward such antisocial goals as wars, colonialism, oppression, and economic and cultural exploitation. In short, those who advocate or defend evil cannot be tolerated.

Paul Wolff defends tolerance as having been the necessary instrument of political and cultural pluralism during the developmental stages. Without tolerance, the fruits of pluralism would never have ripened.

> Pluralism is humane, benevolent, accommodating, and far more responsive to the evils of social injustice than either the egoistic liberalism or the traditionalistic conservatism from which it grew. But pluralism is fatally blind to the evils which afflict the entire body politic. . . .

What must now happen, concludes Wolff, is the replacement of democratic pluralism with its successor, a new synthesis that will serve the needs of a new day. As democratic pluralism has enabled America to confront the problems of distributive justice, now we must develop a set of values that concentrate on the common good. Tolerance does not provide those values. On the contrary, tolerance "obstructs consideration of precisely the sorts of thoroughgoing social revisions which may be needed." Grave social ills will not wither away while they are tolerated. Therefore, says Wolff, instead of resorting to the new intolerance, with Marcuse,

> We must give up the image of society as a battle ground of competing groups and formulate an ideal of society more exalted than the mere acceptance of opposed interests and diverse customs. There is need for a new philosophy of community, beyond pluralism and beyond tolerance.

Unlike Marcuse, Wolff does not spell out details of what the new philosophy of community is to be: he invites to the effort to create that philosophy. Like Marcuse, he believes that the prevailing conceptions of tolerance are inadequate—Marcuse goes beyond that agreement, to declare that the prevailing notions of tolerance are inimical.

Barrington Moore, Jr., agrees with neither of the other essayists. His analysis proceeds along quite different lines, from differing premises to different conclusions, because he writes for a different purpose. He attempts to show that tolerance itself needs to be redefined and freshly understood.

When it is so reinterpreted, Moore believes that it should play a vital role in the structure of human relationships and political processes. He believes not only that "tolerant, rational discussion" is attainable, but that it is desirable. He argues for a free society, and points out that

> it requires rather extraordinary people to make it run. Its members must be remarkably intelligent and well-informed, as well as sufficiently self-restrained to be able to give way in a passionate argument that goes against their interests.

To provide the heuristic quality of affirmative tolerance essential to a free society, Moore advocates a thoroughly rational (i.e., "scientific") approach to all debates about goals and values.

> Toleration implies the existence of a distinctive procedure for testing ideas, resembling due process in the realm of law. No one holds that under due process every accused person must be acquitted. A growing and changing procedure for the testing of ideas lies at the heart of my conception of tolerance tied to the scientific outlook. That is genuine tolerance. It has nothing to do with a cacophony of screaming fakers marketing political nostrums in the public square. Nor does the real article exist where various nuances of orthodoxy pass for academic freedom.

The heuristic readiness of Moore to tolerate divergent expressions of ideas in the search for better statements of truth includes an "objective" method for testing those ideas. That, he would call "tolerance," and let it replace the new intolerance through which Marcuse would attempt to redress imbalances of power, as well as letting the notion of tolerance live on as part of the new intellectual tool kit when Wolff believes it has served its purpose.

A Critique of Pure Tolerance illustrates the manner in which preselected value systems control both the selection of data and the shaping of conclusions in the inquiry after values and the meaning of values. To illustrate the point from a different angle, an example is taken from social science research.

The first illustration is concerned with a problem within the synthesizing effort itself. The second has to do with the manner in which research confronts a problem in the so-called "objective" area, external to the researchers and their particular value systems; but it indicates the same general conclusion, namely, that failure to include "subjective" data vitiates results. The fact (objective fact) is that the subjective judgments are present and may be of some influence in determining the objective reality under observation, as this example shows.

The problem under investigation was: Do the schools serve the purposes of equality? As long as this question was considered to be primarily, perhaps exclusively, a problem with which the educational profession was to deal, the general practice was to proceed from the Jeffersonian assumptions as modified and elaborated by Horace Mann and John Dewey and their followers, and to gather data that tended to prove that schools were an instrument of democratic equality. Schoolmen were pretty generally sure of their course of inquiry and stoutly defended their conclusions.

Of course, schools make a difference! And since an educated populace is essential to the smooth operation of a democracy, and we are a democracy, we will educate everyone. We know what the American child needs to know and to be; we will teach it to all children and youth. Ergo, the free, universal, compulsory, public elementary and high school—until school-leaving age.

And since the American system of rewards and punishments makes economic success a principal gauge of merit, the proof of the educational pudding was to be found in the fact that the more education a person received, the more income he earned during his lifetime. Conversely, the effectiveness of education was to be measured by the degree to which it served as the ladder of upward economic mobility. As long as the data were gathered mainly from the first- and second-generation European immigrants, the case appeared to be fairly well based in fact. Children of immigrants learned to speak and write English, learned American ways of dressing, acting and thinking—were Americanized. They went into the mainstream of economic life and climbed right to the top. It was obvious that the American school was doing its job.

It was also obvious that blacks and other minorities were less successful in getting ahead, because their schooling was inferior. Equalize schooling, and economic equalizing will follow. That the segregated schools were inferior to those for whites, no one could doubt. Financial data proved it. Beyond question. The differentials in expenditure were indisputable. The case was not quite as convincing when Northern schools were examined; but the pernicious differentials were clearly present throughout the nation. Equality of economic achievement would come only as there was clear equality in schooling.

Through the 1930s the controversy was particularly keen. The heightened social consciousness of the nation under economic duress and the increased expectations of the New Deal era gave added urgency to the upward aspirations of those who now knew they were part of that "one-third of a nation" that was "poorly housed, poorly clothed and poorly fed." They were also those who were poorly educated! Educators turned to anthropologists like Boas and social psychologists like Klineberg to buttress the argument that, given excellent education, the children of the deprived and the disinherited would take their rightful place. Myrdal clinched the argument with impressive research data.

The counterarguments continued, as the dreary debate between "nature and nurture" dragged on. The conservatives did not question the economic value of schooling. They merely cited I.Q. ratings and aptitude scores in support of the conclusion that even so effective an instrument as education had its limits. "You can't make a silk purse out of a sow's ear." They did not challenge the assumption that education made a difference: they only argued that environmentalists overstated their case. Whether they might have rallied their forces to contradict Myrdal, we shall never know. World War II engrossed the nation.

Meanwhile, the National Association for the Advancement of Colored People was pursuing its carefully considered plans to attack the system of racial caste. They drew careful aim on education, and step by step forced the caste system to yield, until the *Brown* decision of 1954 marked the end of that beginning. The court did not say that education would bring equality. What it did say was that inequality in education was unconstitutional; and that segregation was one form of inequality. It ordered the public schools to proceed "with all deliberate speed" to put an end to racial segregation.

A decade later, as the milestone Civil Rights Act of 1964 was being enacted, Congress included a stipulation that a study be made of "the lack of availability of equal educational opportunities for individuals by reason of race, color or national origin." The stage was set for a new round of massive research effort.

James Coleman of the Johns Hopkins University undertook to make the study. Reportedly, he began the inquiries with advance confidence that the data would demonstrate serious differentials in educational opportunity between the races, and that from this showing would flow new Federal monies to bring in the day of equality in education as a means of achieving economic equality. "A rising tide lifts all boats."

When the data were in and the analysis completed, Coleman was amazed and educators generally were shocked to learn that by 1965 the actual inequalities between educational opportunities for whites and for blacks, as measured by the yardsticks selected, were inconsequential. The amount of money spent per child was roughly the same. The physical facilities, formal curricula, and most "measurable" character-istics of teachers in the white and in the black schools were found to be approximately the same. There was no correlation between the performance of pupils on standardized tests and the discoverable differentials in the schools. The only signifi-cant difference that Coleman could pinpoint was that in schools where children from affluent homes were present in significant numbers, the general achievement level of all stu-dents tended to be higher.

Coleman concluded: "(1) These minority children have a serious educational deficiency at the start of school, which is obviously not the result of school, and (2) they have an even more serious deficiency at the end of school, which is obviously in part a result of school." Congress poured more funds into the Head Start and Upward Bound programs to offset the "cultural disadvantage" of the preschool and school-age minority child. The basic premise that schooling raises economic achievement and equal schooling makes for eco-nomic equality was not brought into question.

The Coleman report was issued in the summer of 1966. That fall, at Harvard, Patrick Moynihan and Thomas Petti-grew launched a reexamination of the Coleman data, and after six years published their results (Pettigrew having branched off on his own study with colleague David Cohen after the first winter's seminars). *Racial Isolation in the Public Schools* was the answer by Pettigrew and Cohen to Coleman's re-port. Although Coleman had given only three pages out of nearly eight hundred to a discussion of desegregation, Petti-grew, through his reanalysis of the Coleman data, showed that the Coleman report, rightly understood, supported de-segregation.

Pettigrew himself went further. He reminded the nation that there is a difference between desegregation and integration and that desegregation is an uneasy halfway house located in no-man's-land, where it is caught in the cross fire between segregationists and integrationists. Under such circumstances, there is little opportunity for the tender plant of integration to flourish: affirmative affection grows with difficulty in the withering presence of racial hatred and tension.

But Pettigrew was still working with the assumptions that controlled the Coleman study, insofar as the economic effects of education were concerned. (Working with the computer tapes of the Coleman study, he could not easily escape those assumptions, even if he had wished to.) He did come up with the finding (from another source) that there were some differences in the achievement levels of black children as they came out of three different types of schools: black children did best when they came out of congenially mixed schools, not as well when they came from all-black schools, and poorly when their school had been a desegregated institution in which the white children (and their parents) were opposed to the involuntary mixing of the races. Pettigrew was moving away from Coleman's notion that "equality" of schooling could be adequately measured in objective quantities like per-capita dollars and laboratory space. Not in dollars or facilities or curricula or teachers' qualifications, alone, were the measures of school equality to be found. All the "objective" data fell short of informing the whole truth. A school was "equal" for the minority child only when, in addition to all the so-called "objective" factors, that school afforded him equality of consideration and expectation.

But Pettigrew's study was submitted to the Civil Rights Commission, which had financed it; and that commission promptly reached for some quantitative yardstick that could be applied in the effort to assure each minority child of an "equal" education: no black child should go to a school that was more than 50 percent black. Thus, busing. And so the stage was set to take the research controversy into the political arena, where the research findings survived their intended meanings with some difficulty. Meanwhile, the controversy between research teams continued.

Pettigrew appeared to suggest that the working of unmeasured "subjective" factors in the school was an important determinative of comparative learning achievement. There will be no answer to that question until the subjective data are included in the study along with the so-called objective. That is why the volume that Christopher Jencks wrote, with seven coauthors, is something less than successful in its attempt to put the whole controversy to rest. *Inequality: A Reassessment of the Effect of Family and Schooling* (1972) shows an awareness of the fact that unmeasured variables were doubtless present in the study. At several points in the discussion, careful insistence is made to the effect that there are no solid data on which to base an opinion, one way or the other, as to the effect of desegregation on actual learnings of pupils. Jencks does concede that "Black students in truly integrated schools, whatever they may be, might gain more than 3 points on standardized tests." In that somewhat cavalier dismissal of "truly integrated schools, whatever they may be," Jencks brushes aside as fruitless the effort to describe or to measure "integration." He also continues to apply the quantitative yardstick of standardized tests.

It is doubtless true, as the researchers imply, that mass data dealing exclusively with test scores and economic success are not intended to shed light on the qualitative aspects of the results of schooling. Jencks makes a gesture in the direction of adequacy of a researcher's methodology when, in passing reference, he briefly explores the possibility that schools might be classified according to the numerical ratios of the races enrolled, and the test scores of these classifications compared. The continuing error is inevitable under the working assumptions of the researchers: qualitative factors are present *as data* in the schools, and only as they are taken into account can reliable objective conclusions be reached.

On this point, the Supreme Court of the United States has seen the issue more clearly than have the social scientists. The actual language used by the High Court in arriving at and recording its conclusions needs to be read with care, and with full respect for the economy of utterance that appears to imply that iteration carries no additional weight. These excerpts sum up the reasoning and the import of the 1954 *Brown* decision:

> There are findings [in the court] below that the Negro and white schools involved have been equalized, with respect to buildings, curricula, qualifications and salaries of teachers, and other "tangible" factors. Our decision, therefore, cannot turn on merely comparison of these tangible factors in the Negro and white schools involved in each of these cases. We must look instead to the effect of segregation itself on public education. . . .
> We come then to the question presented: Does segregation of children in public schools solely on the basis of race, even though the physical facilities and other "tangible" factors may be equal, deprive the children of the minority group of equal educational opportunities? We believe that it does. . . .
> To separate them from others of similar age and qualifications solely because of their race generates a feeling of inferiority as to their status in the community that may affect their hearts and minds in a way unlikely ever to be undone. . . .
> Segregation of white and colored children in the public schools has a detrimental effect upon the colored children. The impact is greater when it has the sanction of law; for the policy of separating the races is usually interpreted as denoting the inferiority of the Negro group. A sense of inferiority affects the motivation of a child to learn. Segregation with the sanction of law, therefore, has a tendency to [retard] the educational and mental development of Negro children and to deprive

them of some of the benefits they would receive in a racially integrated school system. . . .

We conclude that in the field of public education the doctrine of "separate but equal" has no place. Separate educational facilities are inherently unequal.

It was not, the Court said, differentials in expenditure or facilities or curricula or teachers' qualifications or any other "measurable" or "tangible" or "objective" datum that made the segregated school unequal. It was the fact of segregation itself, which was inherently a declaration of inequality and which told the Negro child that he was unequal to those from whose companionship he was arbitrarily excluded, and which thereby reduced the expectations of his achievement—it was segregation per se that made the schools unequal.

Unless the data gathered in studying the results of schooling on the comparative achievement of the races shed light on the problem as stated by the Supreme Court, no research regarding the comparative results of the education of the races will be valid.

Jencks and his colleagues are aware of this shortcoming in their study. They admit that they carried out "no empirical research on what school administrators and teachers are really trying to do. . . . We did not look in any detail at things like morale, teachers' expectations, school traditions and 'climate.' " And finally they concede:

> The question, then, is how desegregation affects the attitudes of children and adults. . . . Our own prejudice is that in most contexts desegregation will probably increase tension in the short run and reduce it in the long run. But we have no real evidence for this. All we have is a conviction that the debate over desegregation ought to focus on this issue, not on test scores and college entrance rates.

Since the negative findings of honest research are often more important than the affirmative reports, educators and social scientists should be grateful for the honesty with which Jencks and his colleagues point up the irrelevance of their study, and therefore of the Coleman study as well.

When Moynihan (coauthor, Frederick Mosteller) finally came out with *On Equality of Educational Opportunity*, half a dozen years after their study of the Coleman data had begun in the Harvard seminar previously alluded to, the same discrepancies of assumption and conclusion marked their findings. Moynihan's purposes appear to differ from Jencks's, but the assumptions remain much the same: measure the test scores, college entrance rates, and occupational success of the pupils, and you have an index of the limited extent to which schooling actually affects performance. These were also Coleman's assumptions. His findings contradicted the then prevailing assumption of American educators that school was the upward ladder of intellectual and economic mobility. Both Jencks and Moynihan share Coleman's findings to a large extent. None of these three attempts to assess the possible effect of desegregation on the American caste system, or the persistence of caste as a self-fulfilling prophecy.

Knowledgeable educators have long since adopted as their working premise the assumption that the "milieu of association" is a definitively final factor in determining educational performance. In schools where the teacher sees his job as primarily custodial, with little genuine expectation of student learnings at levels of true excellence, the results tend to bear out the presumptions of low achievement. In schools where students know that they are being prepared for inferior status and low achievement in the general society, they tend to validate the controlling presumptions of their schools. But in other schools, where the climate of expectation is high and the mutually reinforcing confidence between teachers and students draws out the superior effort of the student to match the reinforcing encouragement of the teacher, the contrary thesis is proved. Knowledgeable educators have known this for decades. Where the affirmative attitudes of community, parents, and school administrators have coincided with the quiet confidence of dedicated teachers, students have more closely approached the performance standards that their innate abilities have made possible. In refusing to consider the "climate" of the schools, or what the teachers and principals (and students) actually intended to do, the Jencks study missed the essential point of the argument. The Moynihan rehash of the Coleman materials falls into the same error. In all three cases, the limitations placed on the study determined its final results. Where the overarching and underlying fact of caste was entering into the educational equation, all these studies refused to deal with it. They relied entirely on quantitative matters that could be measured with allegedly objective data. They rejected, in advance of their studies, the qualitative factors that actually determine the educational result.

In dealing with the tendentious and tangled questions of race, poverty, schools, and the cities, researchers will find it necessary, at long last, to include qualitative matters of racial caste (that is, attitudes and values, among other things) among their objectively considered data. In short, if research wishes to get at the truth, it cannot push part of the data to one side. Research must become interdisciplinary. Even more, it must become holistic. The truth about humanity and the human condition will evade the researcher until he becomes humane— that is, becomes holistic.

The attitude of mind required for constructing the new synthesis is a critical loyalty to an evolving ideal, a loyalty that attaches to the well-being and future of mankind and which is always critical both of itself and of the present. Never satisfied, though sometimes content, the woman or man whose judgments are informed by this critical loyalty to an evolving ideal will be a contributor to the alleviation of the human condition for the twenty-first century.

The Continuing Search

Among the stated goals of higher education, there has always been a reference, variously stated, to the obligation of the institution toward the rearing of the oncoming generations. Too often this has been interpreted to mean the prolongation of infancy long after adulthood had become a biological and psychological fact. In this respect, good nursery schools were superior to colleges and universities: they discharged their custodial function as baby-sitters or day-care centers, but they also presumed that each child deserved individual attention as a learner. Colleges and universities that took their custodial function seriously also tended to place heavy emphasis on excellence of teaching; and in both these actions, they underemphasized the importance of learning as adults learn. The result has been that far too many baccalaureates have never learned to learn. Their infancy has been given an indefinite extension. They are forever dependent upon some teacher image to instruct them. They are gullible children, not autonomous adults.

The Now generation refused to accept the traditional infantile status on campus. The resultant transformations have been rehearsed in earlier chapters. The next generations of incoming students will be very much like their predecessors in at least one respect: they, too, will not necessarily learn what their elders have prescribed. To meet this circumstance, higher education will need to abandon its dearly held assumption that its function is to teach. This should not mean that faculties turn their attention away from students and concentrate their energies on research or public service. It should mean that faculties become interested not in teaching but in enabling students to learn.

A central concern in the learning process is the quality of the person to be developed, rather than the quantity of information and skills to be mastered. Collegiate learning should be restructured with that in mind. The restructuring should not be undertaken with a view to facilitating cognitive learnings. It will do that, but it will do it less well than if it were honest in the matter. The major learnings, the principal intentions of the institution and of the adult students in it, should be the quality of life. When facts and information and skills and habits become instruments of that quality, they take on inherent and derived meanings that make the learning of them significant. This reversal of the hierarchy of learnings means no routine return to the paternalisms of the traditional institutions—not if it is an honest reversal. It means an active interest in enabling each student to be all that he may become, and that is a far cry from trying to make each student into what the institution and the teacher say he should be.

The restructuring is not something that can be completed once and for all and then embalmed in the catalog. Administrative processes and procedures, for example, have a profound educative or miseducative effect in the learning of values. Once they have been restructured with educative purposes in mind, it cannot be assumed that the job is done. On the contrary, continuing change in the light of changing situations and varied needs is in order. When Solon completed his reforms of government in Athens, he believed he had done a job that would stand for a hundred years. His reforms lasted a decade. He went into exile. But while he was at the peak of his prestige, he was asked to draw up a charter for the governance of a new colony. He obliged. When the charter was completed, it seemed perfect to him. He therefore added a final section that required that any man who proposed a change in the charter should enter the assemblage with a halter around his neck. If his proposal were rejected, he should be hanged on the spot. It is not enough that governance of the institutions of higher education should be perfected. They must always be in the process of being perfected. How else is a student to learn the meanings of governance in a democracy? And whatever is done with one freshman class must be repeated at least annually. Students do not, and will not, learn anything just because the institution in which they enroll declares that they should learn it, nor is the example of previous student generations sufficient. The obligation of the institution is, to the extent that it is capable or can become capable, (1) to eliminate any cause or excuse for iconoclasm and (2) to facilitate the expression of the values of the Beloved Community.

The specifics of restructuring will seldom be the same in two different institutions. They ought not to be the same in any one institution over a period of years. Boards of trustees, presidents and deans and faculties have before them a task much more difficult than that repressive control over a rebellious student body that is urged upon them by apprehensive outsiders. Their task is to take each student generation seriously, to discover what its values are, to enable that generation to discover on its own initiative what better values it will learn, and to provide the situation and resources (including older scholars and teachers) with which each successive generation can hammer out its better destiny.

There are dangers in this kind of freedom. It may be misunderstood, taken for mere permissiveness, and therefore condemned from the outside while it is exploited or misused from within. But these risks are preferable to the certainties of failure that lie like bleached skeletons along the trails we have come.

As with governance, so with curriculum. Last year's lecture notes are not necessarily this year's proper pearls to be cast. To inquire as to where each student now is, is to discover the proper starting point in any learning process. From his own point of entry, a student can learn. When he must use the professor's point of entry, he can only be taught—until he catches up, if that ever happens.

To be sure, there are bodies of knowledge that have been organized logically and which are most advantageously presented in a prepared sequence. Learning, however, seldom starts as a logical matter at a logically chosen point of entrance, nor does it always proceed according to premeasured doses. There is no guarantee that last year's sequences and subject-matter content are the most desirable for next year's students. The United States learned that lesson with reference to mathematics when the Russians launched their first Sputnik. In the social sciences, the necessary shift from descriptive to normative effort, necessary if the search for values is to have any reality, would affirmatively affect the learning process. In the humanistic studies, the task of eliminating or curing the vulgarities and eliciting new values will not be achieved merely by shifting from Poe to paperbacks, although such changes may be in order. The progressive impoverishment of the culture by which each individual diminishes himself will not be checked by cutting each successive generation off from the riches of its cultural heritage; but the student must see for himself the advantages of good English usage over street language if he is to learn to communicate well or to enjoy the freedom of pellucid expression to which he is entitled. In the physical and biological sciences, the speed of new discoveries is so great that few professors are able to keep abreast of current publications in their special fields of competence: the case for a curriculum in flux is patent. And in the as yet uncharted synthesis for the twenty-first century, openness and adventuresomeness are prerequisites.

The profound shift away from the didactic and dogmatic attitude, in an invitation to continuing search, must be seen and felt throughout the entire institution in all it is and does. It must not merely be there: it must also appear to be there. As that shift is made, tomorrow looks a little less unpromising, because higher education has become a time for learning instead of a period of being taught.

The Person

In turning to the condition of each student as the best starting place for his learning, we do not fall into the error of assuming that each person is an individual, entire unto himself. He is not.

Properly used, the words "individual" and "social" are adjectives, not nouns. It is improper to speak of "a social" (except in rural America, where it refers to a fancy party at the schoolhouse or the Grange Hall). So, also, it ought to be considered improper to speak of "an individual." Each person is a center of consciousness, developing both individual and social aspects. The only "individual" would be a Robinson Crusoe without Friday and without memory of any experience with other persons.

We have permitted ourselves the expensive luxury of confusing meanings and of meaning confusion whenever we have spoken of "an individual" to denote a single person. He is not an individual. He is a unique person. If he were "an individual," unrelated to other human beings, he would have become what he is at any moment without reference to any social contacts, group identifications, or other than strictly individualized learnings. No matter what nation, race, religion, economic class, or geographical region he has identification with, his identity itself would be purely and solely himself in complete isolation from all others. But he is not. As a unique individual person, he has learned a great many meanings that attach to him as he relates to others, in one-to-one relationships, as part of a group, as a member of a group that relates in one way or another to other groups, and so forth. He is a unique individual person with social aspects.

He is also a socialized person with individual aspects. Each particularity about himself comes to have meanings attached to it. Especially in the years of childhood and youth—and again in his declining years—he is very conscious of differences in age between himself and others. He is early aware of his identity with a particular gender, and as puberty sets in he becomes acutely aware of sex. He has been born with a particular skin color; but, as with age and sex, his racial identity comes to mean something particular to him only when he learns that there are skin colors different from his—that his caste identity means a great deal in the way in which he is esteemed by others. Not as an "individual" but as a member of a racial caste, he begins to know his personal identity. He is a person, within a caste; and as long as caste patterns prevail, he cannot change that fact, much as he might wish.

He has been born with a particular intellectual potential that is not identical with all others. Experience since birth will have determined much of the way in which he thinks, learns, uses his native capacities. If his mother worked, and "home" was something he was locked out of when he came home from school, his childhood development was different from that of his friend whose mother was with him in infant years throughout his waking hours, and who awaited his return each day as school ended. And since Mother's vocabulary is the single environmental factor most closely associated with intelligence as measured by standardized tests, his I.Q. is in part dependent upon whether he had the constant attention of a cultured mother during his infant years. In all these ways and in innumerable others, the individual and social aspects of each human person are intertwined and interdependent. Neither exists without the other. Each human person is a unique expression of the species, and in that sense is "an individual." But only in that sense.

See, now, what happens when we take the erroneous language-use of the past, using "individual" and "social" as though they were nouns instead of adjectives. We then proceed to erect whole theories and value-systems based on these false abstractions, calling them "Individualism" and "Socialism." The next step is to set these two abstractions over against each other as competitors, to arm them, and to plunge into war—cold or hot.

There are differences, important differences, between social groupings, just as there are important differences between persons. The social differences are entirely manmade. These differences get codified into norms of conduct, partly as matters of convenience, partly as matters of social control. To make group living possible, conformity to social norms becomes an active concern. The human being is molded and manipulated by his experience in a social matrix; and as he becomes expert in shaping or manipulating bits and parts of that social matrix, he acquires both independence for himself and power over others. At every step of the process, he is both an individual and social person. He is never completely independent of his social self, never completely unaware of his individual self. Curiously, he feels "lonely" whenever either the individual or social aspects of his person are unduly diminished. That is why he can be lonely in a crowd—or, conversely, satisfied at times with self-communion (which embraces his social self).

The person is a wondrous fact, delicately held together, sensing, knowing, experiencing, growing, developing. He is very much like others: he is very different from all others. He is a person.

To disregard, to underrate, or to overrate either the individual or the social aspects of each person is to do violence to him. And his needs for recognition of each part of himself vary in accordance with the situation. When he skins his knee at play, he needs very much to know that he is a loved son; but he doesn't feel the same need when he is reminded to wear his rubbers. When a rival gang invades his turf, he very much needs to know that he is a member of a gang that stands with him; but when the cops bust the joint, he needs no group identity to get him messed up. During the day at his job, he needs to know that he is accepted as a man who does his work well; but when he gets home at night, it is good to know that he is a husband and father for whom a warm welcome waits. Let his boss try to mother him or his wife try to boss him, and things get a bit mixed up. Although the personal and social aspects of the human being are intertwined and interdependent, each relationship comes to have its own meanings, its own value. These meanings may, and do, vary in accordance with his own varying mood—whether the mood changes because of how he feels physically (sick or well), or mentally (despondent or exuberant), or because of the fact that he got up on the wrong side of the bed. He is constantly bombarded with sensations of all sorts from his surroundings and from within: the meanings of his perception are sifted through the accumulation of all his experiences up to that moment.

These differences, and the way they are apprehended and interpreted, pretty well sum up what we call "values." These learned preferences do not exist apart from the attitudes and actions of the persons in whom they inhere. Each person develops his own likes and dislikes—from breakfast food to marriage mate. That is to say, he develops a matrix of evaluations. We call that his value system. He has a sense of self-identification when he "feels right" with the values he has come to hold. When he is disturbed about some part or all of that value system, or when something happens to disturb some part or all of his value system, he enters an "identity crisis." He says he has to "find himself," which is another way of saying that he needs to discover for himself a system of values through which experience is interpreted and by which he moves forward to the next moment of experience. In discovering the meanings and relationships (relationships with himself and with others) that he can sustain with least inner anguish, the "lost" person begins to "find himself" again.

When the contradictions are sufficiently reduced to become pleasantly bearable, he begins to have a feeling of "wholeness." Failing such achievement, he may project a desired outcome, declaring himself to be A Man! when he feels quite hollow inside—or he will find one or more of a great many other ways to express his asocial or antisocial sentiments. He may accept the value system that comes ready-made with some new group, and, attempting to forsake his former social self, try to substitute the new identity for the old. He becomes a "dropout." Or he is "converted." Or he finds the equivalent of the French Foreign Legion, and lets someone else worry about when he should get up in the morning.

He comes as a freshman to college—not any freshman: *this* human being. Not any college: *this* college. He must be accepted—if at all—for what he is *and* for what he may become. He ought never to be accepted as Social Security Number 440-61-5398 or as that kid in the second seat of the fourth row. See him for what he is, and help him to see in himself what he may become. Then enable him to become all that he can become. Both as an individual person and as a social person.

Three days ago, he stood in the registration line. He was uncomfortable because his mother had insisted that he wear a jacket and tie on his first big day "up there on the hill." Suddenly, a gale of raucous laughter slapped his eardrums. He knew he was being ridiculed. In rage, he wheeled on his detractors and struck the closest guffawing mouth. (He'd learned to defend himself in street-fighting.) The student just ahead of him in the long line, when he heard the laughter, turned in amusement and joined in the fun at seeing a proudly unhappy fraternity pledge parading by in bizarre undress. Which student will make the dean's list? No, not the dean of men. He made *that* list on registration day. So, see that kid in the second seat of the fourth row not only as you see him, but as he sees himself. You might just be able to be of service to the eccentric and brilliant adult that lurks behind those frightened eyes. That is your job, Professor.

The Larger Framework

In saying that education must be concerned with each person, we do not suggest that we proceed in a social vacuum. Not when we remember that each person has both individual and social aspects. If for no other reason, education must deal with the social aspects of each person in order to deal effectively with him. The social as well as the individual aspects must be part of the learning process.

From conception onward, the fetus, infant, child, youth, adult has never been absent from some sort of environmental influences. He has learned to live with the sun and wind and the seasons. He has also learned to live with his man-made environment, its rules of conduct, permissions and prohibitions, customs, laws, money system, property rights—the whole vast matrix of social invention that impinges on him. He forms habits of conduct that come to his aid without much thought, as "second nature." Language supplants gesture in communication. Thought becomes possible in terms of abstractions and generalizations. If he is fortunate, he will have received faithful guidance from his elders, his peers, and his siblings along the way; but, in any case, he has learned. He sees things in the light of what he has already experienced, so that his perceptions never quite correspond to "objective" reality until the new experience has been given its opportunity to register. All of his past learnings walk with him onto the campus, as they have been structured in his unique formulation of the social aspects of his person. The kid in the fifth seat of the front row has come to you as *he* is; but he is what he is because of *his* experience in American society. All the inimical effects of racial discrimination, poverty, and sectional disadvantage have been part of his social experience, while the kid next to him has a substantially reversed set of social experiences in his past. Not to take these differences into account is to run the certain danger of miseducating. To make paternalistic adjustments where they would hinder or hurt, and not to make empathetic adjustments where they would help, is to fail one's opportunity as a teacher. And not to attempt to educate *both* those kids so that the inequities and iniquities that have been built into their value systems are corrected is to evade the social responsibility of education.

This is where civilization's laundry list gets inserted on the clipboard, on top of the syllabus. It is there for every student. It is there for every educator. The traditional method of dealing with the irritating intrusion of that laundry list is—for the instructor—to tear it off, throw it aside, and tell his students not to be concerned with those things in this class. Our subject is thermodynamics and kinetic theory. Or human biology. Or the Renaissance. Or money and banking. Or English composition. Or Chaucer. If you want to deal with that laundry list, go and take a gut course in sociology. And in sociology, don't expect that there will be an effort to deal with anything more than selected aspects of some of these things in any one course. In criminology, you won't learn about even as closely allied a subject as criminal justice—that comes next semester. If you are troubled about racial matters, don't take the course in minority groups because it is purely descriptive, gives no answers. If you want to stop worrying about the ecology, or want to learn how to worry more effectively, maybe you can find a course in the biology department somewhere. They were talking about it last year. But not in this course.

The student, on the other hand, has his method of dealing with the laundry list. He leaves it right where it is, on top of the unopened syllabus. His real learnings are: (1) that college instruction is not directed to his needs and concerns; (2) that he can get by in this course without really studying; (3) that there are a dozen kids who meet in Cranmer 409 at night and who have a thing going about boycotting the Chase National Bank because it has branches in South Africa. He goes where the action is, and he learns what he acts upon.

The traditional ways are not good enough. They were not good enough to enable the colleges and universities to help keep us out of the mess we are in. They will not get us out.

There are other ways. They can be found by men and women, younger and older, who set out to find them. Working singly, in pairs, in groups, they can devise new patterns of subject matter and new constellations of learning processes. It is being done. But it has to be done by each university, each college, each school, each department—in concert with others —as its own effort. Educators, like students, learn only what they act upon.

There are patterns; models, if you will. They can be studied with profit, if they are not copied. As an example, look at the University of Wisconsin at Green Bay. It advertises itself as "one of the few universities in the world with a focus to all its activities." Whether its achievements match its goals is a matter left to the judgment of history. Its catalog makes stimulating reading. There appears to be a conscious effort throughout the entire institution, in its teaching, research, and community outreach, to "deal with the greatest challenge facing the world." No one goes to Green Bay without knowing that the institution he has selected has a purpose to make him a constructive factor in winning survival for the planet and its people. The stance is encouraging. Atomization of the curriculum and the Balkanizing of experience can be corrected. Learning can become holistic. It can become heuristic. It can become empathetic. It can become dynamic.

It can become all of these things provided that professors, administrators, and students are ready to break a few icons. And provided that they are ready to embark on a new, arduous, difficult, exhausting, and altogether refreshing effort to reconstruct the continually revising future.

Beyond iconoclasm lies construction.

If, as we have been saying, this is true for the generation of student iconoclasts, it is just as true for all the rest of us: those who sit in the seats of power and who plan the progress and continuity of their institutions, as well as those who only draw their paychecks. We have little moral right to demand that the iconoclastic generation cease its destructive efforts and begin to build unless we are prepared to cease our obstructive efforts and do the same. More correctly—unless we are already doing the same.

Prometheus and Adam

One task, integral to all others in the area of values, is the restoration of an ancient symbiosis in redefined terms, freshly appropriate to the twenty-first century.

Western civilization cannot stand alone in the intimacies of today's global consciousness; but unless Western man begins more fully to understand himself, he cannot make effective efforts at rapprochement with the Eastern world or the Third World.

Two principal traditions characterize the West: the Hellenic and the Hebraic. Each has made its particular contribution to the aspirations and capabilities, achievements and failures, of Western history. Each has much to say to the contemporary human condition. Once, they spoke as one voice, giving unity and direction to man's efforts and meaning to his life. Today, they do not speak to each other—only about each other. Life is confused and confusing because values are bifurcated.

Let two myths suggest the peculiar genius of each of the two traditions, not by definitive analysis but by suggestive insight.

According to the Greek tradition, man found himself miserable on this earth, subject to fearful forces, buffeted by nature, living in cold and darkness. Yet, every day the blazing chariot of the sun wheeled across the heavens, to the astonishment and despair of mortals. Constantly man asked himself, why should the gods have fire and man not? Came Prometheus. In one bold act of self-declaration, he defied the gods, lit his torch at the fiery chariot, and brought back to earth the kindling flame. Now man could warm and light his dank cave, cook his food, begin to be master of his own destiny. And who knew what might come from such a beginning? With fire, man could dine on roast lamb. He could smelt iron, make tools, cultivate the fruitful earth, fashion ships to crest the waves, supplant want with abundance. So, according to the Hellenes, began man's audacious journey into the provinces of the gods. Out of darkness and want and misery man clambered toward light. He began to conquer the earth and navigate the seas. He dreamed his dreams of riding the winged Pegasus, of sailing "beyond the baths of all the western stars." The march of science had begun.

The gods looked down from Mount Olympus, saw the arrogant act of Prometheus, and feared for themselves. If man had knowledge of fire, he would find ever new things to do with it. One thing would lead to another; and as his knowledge grew, he might become master of his own destiny, no longer having need of the gods. And if the gods were no longer needed, they would be ignored. Olympian fear turned to anger. In response to the call of Zeus, the gods came together in solemn conclave. Their decision was harsh. For his arrogance in stealing the knowledge of fire from the gods, Prometheus was to be chained to the rock on Mount Caucasus and the eagle assigned to tear out his liver and eat it. As rapidly as the liver grew in again, the winged hound of Zeus was again to tear it out—through eternity.

The succinct meaning of the Greek legend is that knowledge is power and that it comes at a great price: eternal agony.

According to the Hebraic legend, man was not created in darkness and abandoned in misery, to envy his Creator. Man was created in perfection and placed in Paradise, to be obedient. All his wants were supplied, his desires fulfilled, his dreams realized. He needed only to choose well and to act wisely, as God directed. But he did not. He chose ill and acted stupidly. His disobedience to the divine will was his downfall. Adam, of course, had his alibi. And she, in turn, blamed the serpent (who was a proper creature for Paradise when he stood erect). And the serpent, since it was the lowest in the totemic scale, had to carry the blame, losing its upright status, doomed forever to slither on its belly and be bruised by man's resentful heel.

And the Hebrew God? He knew no fear because of what man had done. He knew anger, yes. Man was punished. For his disobedience, man was cast out of Paradise—and at the gates were the guarding cherubim and a flaming sword to prevent his return. By the sweat of his brow would Adam eat bread. He had lost his leisure, his serenity, his pristine bliss. He was forever doomed to be a wanderer and a stranger in the earth, longing for Paradise lost. But God loved man, and in man's suffering, He suffered. And so began the long process of redemption that unfolds in the pages of Scripture.

The succinct meaning of the Hebraic legend is that righteousness, obedience to God's will, is required of man, and that when man sins, a great price is paid: agony of the Eternal.

With the blending of these two traditions, Western man acquired his working tools for the interpretation (sometimes the making) of history. Prometheus provided the know-how and Adam the know-which; and from the blending of science and ethics in a single religious unity, God provided the know-why. Prometheus and Adam became joint tenants of the human condition, working out together the divine destiny.

Adam and Prometheus were unevenly yoked. The two traditions did not readily mesh. The gods of the Hellenes were very like men, acting from humanlike impulse in anger or fear or cupidity. To be ethically directed, Hellenic man would need to transcend his gods. Prometheus had no god-given ethical guidance. Not so with the Hebrews. The God of history might share the sentiments and sorrows and hopes and joys of man; but He transcended them as eternity transcends time. To be ethically directed, man had only to do God's will. He alone knew what man ought to do and not to do, what to be and what not to be. The built-in negation between the two traditions has left its legacy through the centuries in the arid controversy over freedom of the will.

Moreover, the relationship between knowledge and faith was not easily bridged. It tended to rest in a contradiction rather than a completion. Promethean man boasted of his knowledge and relied on untrammeled inquiry to increase that knowledge. Adamic man was forbidden to eat of the fruit of the tree of knowledge. He was to accept the directions of an all-knowing God. Prometheus strode with pride where Adam walked in humility. Prometheus relied on the power of his own knowledge while Adam expected faithful obedience to be rewarded by the Lord of history. The more Promethean man struggled to increase his knowledge and thus his control over the forces of nature, the more did Adamic man remind him that knowledge was a heady brew that led not to progress but to downfall. Science wanted to be free of ethical controls in order to follow its own genius; but religion demanded that ethical controls should dominate all aspects of life.

The two traditions were never smoothly conjoined until Thomas Aquinas devised a single formulation in which the symbiosis was firmly established. As no one else before or since his time, Aquinas wove the strands of the Hellenic and Hebraic traditions together in a seamless fabric of meaning.

He had compelling reasons, both practical and theoretical.

He wanted to save the social structure of his time from impending disaster. The feudal system assigned to each man a
fixed status in life and kept him loyally in it; but feudalism
was threatening to fall apart. Barbarism loomed. Aquinas saw
that each man needed to know that he was where he was
because God's will had put him there; the human condition
was divinely ordained.

Thus, all of law and of ethic were brought under ecclesiastical sanction. The sanctions of religion stood behind temporal
powers, commanding obedience and sanctifying the punishment meted out alike to miscreant and criminal with fine
impartiality. Aquinas accomplished his purpose. He gave
thirteenth-century Europe better than two centuries of precarious life. The seamless fabric of faith and knowledge became feudalism's coat of mail.

When he included knowledge in the synthesis, Aquinas
gave scientific inquiry a place proper to it in the hierarchy of
the disciplines in which theology was queen of the sciences.
Reason and faith, approaching a common truth from opposite
directions, agreed—and must agree, because both were of
God, the sole source of all truth. Promethean man was made
to come down from his audacious assaults on the divine se-
crets, to limit his inquiries to things deemed proper to human
exploration, and to leave to God's revelation the mysteries that
could never be fully explained by human comprehension.
Summarizing the whole gamut of learning, secular and sacred,
in a single synthesis, Aquinas brought the entire body of lore
and all of human experience under a single controlling
perspective. Backed by the awesome temporal and spiritual
authority of church and state, accepted by both secular and
sacred princes, the value system of Aquinas saved thirteenth-
century Europe from civil and religious chaos. It also restricted all scientific inquiry.

Simian man kept probing, as he had always done. John
Scotus Erigena and Duns Scotus were but two of the tower-

ing figures who, from within the Establishment, asked probing questions about the place of reason in the house of faith. Giordano Bruno died at the stake for his impious inquiries, punctuating with his death in 1600 a remarkable pair of centuries in which Copernicus, Kepler, Galileo, Descartes, and Newton deplored the religious strictures on scientific inquiry, each in his particular way contributing to the famous compromise that Descartes formulated. The fixed, static concepts of the Angelic Doctor had been adequate to the task of holding together a disintegrating thirteenth-century society; they were inadequate to the dynamic demands of the sixteenth. What Aquinas had forged as feudalism's coat of mail had become society's straitjacket.

It was Descartes who set about to save the faith when the Thomistic synthesis began to come apart under the new pressures. He proposed a division of the field between theology and science. Religion was to have as its preserve all questions of First Origins and of Ultimate Ends, together with the World of Souls in between. To science went all the rest: the actual world of life between birth and death was opened to free inquiry without let or hindrance. In Chapter Four, we have noted the consequences of the Cartesian compromise, and traced in outline the subsequent developments up to the twentieth century. It was in this last century that the full consequences of dissevering Prometheus from Adam were to be realized in the blinding implosion over Hiroshima. Holding in his hand the secret of ultimate power, Prometheus is unbound: he is rampant.

Whether the ancient symbiosis can be restored freshly in terms appropriate to the twenty-first century is a question that has not yet been answered affirmatively. If it cannot be done, there is little hope of rescuing the human condition from its downward spiral. Hubristic man strides the earth with the power of Prometheus, unhindered by a bewildered Adam.

It is false to argue that technology has taken on a demonic quality, a self-propelling life of its own. Science fiction to the contrary, the computer will never rule man unless we deliberately perfect it for that purpose and intentionally adapt man to his new slavery. Technology is man-made. It can be directed and controlled and used by man for whatever purposes men choose.

If Prometheus were to listen to Adam, he would know what trade-offs to make, which preferences to elect for fulfillment, what values are necessary. That is to say, he would learn these things from Adam, if Adam first were in a position to tell them to him. Unfortunately, there is no guarantee that Adam knows the saving word, and there is considerable evidence that the language he speaks is a foreign tongue to Prometheus. Adam has some catching up to do.

Adamic man has made many changes during the centuries, each change supposedly intended to bring history more perfectly under the divine will. The religion of the Hebrews began in nomadic days, and the ethical controls then devised were elaborated in the Torah. They were fitted to a society that was in transition from nomadic to agricultural ways of life. A little later, prophetic insights inveighed against the iniquities of emerging commercial and city life. Trade was restrained from excesses of exploitation, usurious moneylending prohibited. Powerful religious sanctions were applied to support an ethic that set the guidelines for agriculture and for civic and commercial life. Christianity inherited, and a bibliolatrous church adopted, this simpler ethic; while social developments marched ahead. First- and second-century Christianity also absorbed the then prevalent theme of apocalypticism, beginning the alternation of emphasis between ethic and eschatology that still persists. The Thomistic synthesis for a brief interlude provided a synthesis of ethics and technics, a synthesis that was completely adapted to its day and to no other. The medieval transition from a feudal to a mercantile world, with the necessity of devising a new ethic to fit new conditions, was one of the causes (and results) of the Reformation. The consequent Puritan ethic, congenial to capitalism, was bequeathed to colonial Massachusetts, enforcing firm controls over the developing city and commercial life in an agricultural colony. This ethic, which is the backbone of American virtue, is primarily directed toward personal conduct. It relies on Adam Smith's Unseen Hand to reconcile self-interest and the common good. It is essentially preindustrial and pretechnological. From the seventeenth to the twentieth centuries, the American financial-industrial order developed, under the aegis of an ethic that had been intended for a less complex day. As the twentieth century came in, the excesses of industrialism had been laid bare by a series of prophetic voices from Charles Kingsley to Robert Owen to Ruskin. With Rauschenbusch, the Social Gospel was born, in an attempt to create a religious ethic adequate to finance-industrialism. The efforts of the Social Gospel were to be less than adequate, for at least two reasons: (1) it attempted to meet the fast-moving financial-industrial complex with ethical standards that derived partly from the insights of Judaic prophets in an agricultural society, partly from the rigorous seventeenth-century Protestant ethic that the Puritans and other Calvinists had bequeathed (sometimes softened by the leveling influences of the Evangelicals)—its standards were inappropriate to the age; and (2) the ethic was essentially personal, not social, in its approach—moving by a kind of applicationitis to derive *ad hoc* portions of personal virtues as the solution of social questions. The Social Gospel was inapt in content and inept in method. With the decline of the Social Gospel by mid-century, all that was left of Adam's ethical insights for contemporary American life was the radical prophetic insight that could, and did, condemn an errant nation and its military-industrial complex with its runaway technology and its indifference to human values. Having condemned, Adam had no saving word to guide man's choices toward a new and better day.

Indeed, Adam began to doubt that a new and better day lay ahead. A principal casualty of the Great Depression and World War II and subsequent years has been the idea of progress. That notion had been of the essence of the Social Gospel and of its times. It died a lingering death as a bypassed generation fell on sleep and its successors turned to neo-orthodoxy. Not yet created was an ethic that could frankly and effectively face and give moral direction to the swift-moving Age of Technology, with its new intricacies of social and personal relationships.

And throughout the two millennia of the developing Judeo-Christian tradition, a constantly recurring theme has persisted, almost unchanged in spite of changing circumstance and despite its apparent modifications, namely, the particularistic emphasis of each group. Nationalism has, without exception, tended to identify the citizenry of each nation, exclusively and emphatically, as the Chosen People. Racism has made the same identification for ethnic and racial groups: it is busily today working out a new conception of the Deity to support the purposes of Black Liberation.

Yes, Adam has changed through the centuries. It would appear, however, that this gives him little ground for holding Prometheus in contempt because of the chains that bind the latter. In his own perverse way, Adam has forged chains of his own devising that have, in each successive stage of developing Western history, led him astray and made him impotent. Each time, as society made its transitions from agricultural to commercial to industrial to technological structure and process, Adam could be seen, busily at work, trying to hold things down with the controls fashioned for the preceding era. Each time, chained firmly to the ethic of a former age, Adam has never managed to catch up. But neither has he discarded his outmoded ethic: it has been his security blanket.

The immediate task is to bring both the Greek and the Hebraic traditions together in a common discourse of meanings and terms shaped in our day to serve the necessary purposes of present dynamism. A commonly understood language must be devised, so that Prometheus and Adam can talk to each other—and both can listen. The common search for values is essential to the restoration of the creative synthesis in terms relevant to tomorrow's needs.

There are those who would argue that the religious strand of our common heritage should be abandoned altogether and that, instead, we should frankly undertake the painful and arduous task of constructing an ethic entirely within the perimeters and parameters of science. They would broaden the competence of science so as to take over entirely what the Cartesian compromise had reserved to religion.

Let an example illustrate. Barrington Moore, Jr., attacks the problem in his essay in *A Critique of Pure Tolerance,* discussed earlier.

"The essence of science," he writes, "is simply the refusal to believe on the basis of hope." He presses the point:

> The attempt to derive legitimacy for any set of values from some source external to living humans . . . seems to me both doomed to frustration and unnecessary. It is doomed to frustration because no alternative to rationality, no call to faith no matter how disguised, can in the end withstand the corrosive effects of rational inquiry.

Nor does he flinch from affirming the logical conclusion of this journey away from the house of faith.

> Rather than attempt to revive a dubious ontology and epistemology I would urge that we recognize that God is dead and his metaphysical surrogates are dead, and learn to take the consequences.

When he turns from negative to positive argument, however, Moore can only plead that the problem, in his definition, becomes one of "trying to discover some aspects of what is loosely called the human situation that might provide a suitable point from which to argue." He then moves to the next step of his analysis, saying:

> . . . values are human demands put upon the human environment. To establish them is no task to be performed once and for all. It changes with changing historical conditions. This much of existentialist stress on permanent ambiguity has a firm foundation.

With that statement, Moore appears to be revealing that his principal quarrel with religion is not so much the a priori intellectual furniture in the attic (bad as that is), but the unchanging specifics of the antique ethic that controls life in all rooms of the constricted human domicile.

Whether an ethic for our age must be dynamic in order to be relevant is not an open question. It must be dynamic, not static, changing with the times. Otherwise, it is merely a set of obsolete obstructions to be stumbled over in the dark.

But whether science, acting alone, can construct an ethic adequate to the technological age, like a spider spinning her web out of her own innards, is open to question. It has not yet done so. Scientism presses eagerly and relentlessly forward. *Hubris*, not compassion, describes its ethic. Its only apparent limitation is in the time dimension: it does everything now that it can, just because it can be done. Tomorrow it will go on to do all the things that will then have become possible. The choices of such an ethic are technical and temporal, involving no values other than immediacy and practicability.

In this age of future shock, the proclivity of Promethean man does not and cannot provide an ethic that will have the necessary corrective insights: self-secreted standards tend to be just some more of the same. Instead, with its insistence on having, and exercising, the right to gallop off toward any and all ends of technological proliferation, scientism contributes to the moral and ethical dilemmas of man. It does not curb or guide or redirect: it unleashes.

As the *Lumpen* generation knows, that is one of the reasons why the human condition is what it is. The inadequacy of amoral science is reflected in the alienation and outrage of the existential university. Pride in scientism is the underlying cause of the disfavor in which the research university is held. And that same *hubris* keeps the value-free university from producing an adequate ethic or from being susceptible to ethical direction and control.

Man is not only a creature who acquires the knowledge that becomes power. He is also a sufferer who, if he is condemned to endure suffering, must have hope with which to endure. If final hope is denied, he becomes something less than a man. If final hope were to be denied, man would then be free to abandon himself and the future of his children and grandchildren to misery, suffering, and destruction—without compunction. The science that, as Moore puts it, is "simply the refusal to believe on the basis of hope" cannot produce hope or act on it. Herein precisely lies the crux of the contemporary malaise. The times require a larger degree both of commitment, of competence, and of compassion than is implied in the curtailing of belief to the expanding realm of the already proven and of action to the mean level of the already attained.

The task, therefore, is more difficult than Moore would make it. It goes beyond the province of the proven. It reaches into the hoped-for, in terms appropriate to the human endeavor under human circumstances. Our task is to reach out with reason and in hope toward the improvement of the human condition.

The venture of hope is not to be made on the basis of alleged revelation, nor through the application of tradition. The venture of hope is to be taken on the basis of fact. The fact of our age is that if there were no hope other than the present human circumstance, hopelessness would spell futility. Life would be without meaning. The efforts of science would be as meaningless as any other. The fact that men of science have not yet joined the *Lumpen* means that scientists do hope. Where do they get their hope? Not from science, which is neutral—neither hoping nor despairing. Scientists get their hope from the fact that they are also human beings. Prometheus refuses to be bound by the chains he has himself forged.

Return for a moment to Moore's statement: "The essence of science is simply the refusal to believe on the basis of hope." Translated from philosophical to ethical terms, that means "the refusal to *act* on the basis of hope." We have answered that hope is necessary to man's existence: the human condition demands it. If, in the name of science, man were to refuse to act on the basis of hope, the case for some sort of religion would be irrefutable. Not even Prometheus would be content to be without hope, not differing from the clod.

Faith is not to be defined only in terms of believing based on hoping. Faith is not merely "the assurance of things hoped for." Indeed, that would be no faith—not if it were assured. It would be knowledge, something already possessed. Faith is a venture into the unknown, the unproven. It is an act, not merely a belief. A translation of the ancient passage that is more nearly faithful to the original language as well as more nearly apposite to our scientific day reads: "Faith is *the giving substance to* things hoped for." It is not a passive reception of revelation. It is an active human response to the facts of the human condition, a condition that demands the dimension of hope, a hope that becomes valid only when it is acted upon. If the essence of science is defined as "refusal to believe on the basis of hope," then the essence of a religious ethic adequate to the needs of that science might be "the necessity to hope as a basis for action." Religion and ethic so defined reject apocalypticism and eschatology: the Jesus People are right in wanting to hope, but wrong in hoping falsely. Religion and ethic rightly understood put the burden of practical choice squarely on man (where the myth of Adam asserts that it belongs); but acceptance of that burden becomes possible only when man has hope that the times may be redeemed. That hope is not automatically self-fulfilling. It is precariously held. It becomes a valid hope only when it is accepted as the basis for action.

Man may not survive the crushing circumstance of our day. He has the right to hope that he may survive, provided he acts ethically toward his fellow men and becomes the husband of the natural world. Reverence for life would be hypocritical mockery without such hope. That is part of what the Now generation has been telling us. We do poorly if we respond by denying that hope is a viable basis for action, or by affirming that hope without action is sufficient, or by claiming that hope without reason can be valid.

Just as Prometheus has matured over the centuries, so, in his own way, must Adam. Neither science nor religion should be demeaned or rejected because of humble beginnings. Every adult was first an infant: it is only the person who is arrested in growth at adolescence who is cause for concern. Astronomy is not to be laughed at because it began as astrology. What began as alchemy is not now downgraded because it has become chemistry. Neither is it fitting or necessary to put down all religion for the reason that it was once idolatry, pantheism, and belief in miracle.

Prescientific Prometheus became scientific. So, too—in appropriate terms—must Adam. He must learn to converse with Prometheus, and Prometheus with him. Both must work from scientifically verified bases with scientifically controlled processes and procedures. This should not be too difficult a process for Adam, once he puts his mind to the task. He has long since revised his cosmogony and cosmology in the light of scientific discovery. His theology, ontology, and epistemology have been partially revised; but the process waits for completion. It is his ethic that calls for the most comprehensive attention.

Prometheus, alone, is not to blame for the human condition. By default, Adam shares that onus. Adam, when he turns to his Bible and searches for ethical guidance, finds in the Old Testament an ethic designed to serve the needs of a partly nomadic, partly agricultural, wholly preindustrial and pretechnological society, in which the city is abhorred as a cesspool of sin, and only the virtues of rural community life are praised. Oh, yes, God did have compassion on Nineveh; but, even then, it was because all the people therein could not discern between their right hand and their left. He did concentrate a good deal of His attention on Jerusalem; but that was because His temple was there. And whom did Christ chase from the temple? The money changers, of course. And when the man in search of ethical guidance thumbs his New Testament, he has to deal with an interim ethic designed to serve man's needs during a short period of eschatological expectation. When he looks to the traditions of the Church for ethical guidance, he has to shake off the shackles of the Thomistic marriage of church and state in feudalism or adapt the Protestant ethic, which is intertwined with finance capitalism. Refusing to use faith, depending on reason only, he gets little help from these traditional approaches; but refusing to use reason, relying on faith as it was once for all delivered to the saints, Adamic man has only negative words to speak to the contemporary world. He can only deplore; he cannot prescribe. So, he preaches, and moralizes, and condemns—and remains irrelevant.

Or, in the somewhat more sophisticated circles such as the more liberal theological seminaries, he manages to achieve an intellectual explanation of the contemporary situation, and then sits back to admire his handiwork. Or he achieves a new sense of release by committing himself to action in great hope without sufficient intellectual effort: he comes a cropper.

At every developing stage, Adamic man has forged firm chains in an effort to bind the passing age. He has only bound himself to that age, with chains that have held him there long after the age is dead. He has never succeeded in freeing himself in time to be a participant in shaping a new situation as it was emerging. Thus it is that Adam, champion of hope, desperately needs reason.

In his turn, hubristic Prometheus might be a little less sure of himself. He might begin by contemplating the human condition into which amoral science with its technic has brought us. To Prometheus goes the culpability for the sins of commission: Adam has the honor of the sins of omission.

If Adam and Prometheus could, at least for this one point in time, cease to struggle against one another and begin to concentrate, together, on the human situation, a new symbiosis might be created in that joint effort. The new synthesis of reason and hope in joint thought and concerted action to meet the demands of the present human condition would be doubly dynamic: it would change with the times and it would change the times.

If it were true that reason can now sign the death certificate for hope, that would be because man had called on hope *instead* of using reason, when he should have called upon it *with* reason. And if reason is arrant and errant, it is because man has used it instead of hoping, when he should have corrected and elevated reason with hope. Man's rhetoric of conflict has outrun the grammar of the data. The grammar of reality is, in this instance, compassable not in alternatives but in a paradox.

The truth, whether they admit it or not, is that Adam and Prometheus are necessary to each other. As systole and diastole, though forever opposed, are conjoined in the life-giving paradox of the heartbeat, each completed only in yielding to the other; so, too, are Prometheus and Adam. In life and in destiny, they are inseparably interdependent.

The further truth is that the compassionate deed of liberation that would strike the chains of *hubris* from Prometheus and the chains of traditionalism from Adam would—since each reveres his own faults—be an act of iconoclasm. It would be justified only if it were part of the act of reconstruction.

Urbs Coronata

Where to begin? As good a starting point as any, and the only one we have access to, is the place where we stand.

Seventy percent of the privately controlled institutions of higher education in the United States are located in urban centers and their immediate environs. In addition, every urban area has at least one publicly controlled community college, college, or university in it or near it. It is in megalopolis that America now lives, and it is there that Americans will increasingly be found as the century closes. It is there that all the problems of the contemporary world come to sharpest focus and most urgently demand attention.

Perhaps this might be the right moment in time to propose to the Congress the concept of the urban grant university, patterned somewhat after the controlling ideas of the land grant institutions, but focused on megalopolis. There is adequate precedent for Federal action to relieve the human condition through a nationwide network of institutions of higher education, in the Morrill Acts of 1862 and 1890. With that encouraging precedent, and with the Executive Branch of the government moving to dismantle programs of a previous Administration that were directed toward the alleviation of urban blight, there might be a readiness in Washington to try, in the urban situation, a pattern that has proved itself in the rural countryside over the past century. If the needed

Federal support for higher education is to be found at all, it will not be found for universities that turn their backs on the people of the cities where they are located. It might possibly be supplied to institutions that are clearly expected to be assets in the national effort to make the cities viable.

The urban focus is here suggested not only because that is where the people are and the institutions are, but also because it is in the cities that the future will be creatively won or forever lost.

Readers who have followed the argument of this book up to its present juncture might now, with some reason, demand practical and detailed proposals. The omission is deliberate, for several compelling reasons:

1. No two institutional situations are identical: what would be a revolutionary forward leap at one college would be a retrogressive surrender at another.

2. Carping critics might select one or another of the detailed suggestions as inadequate, and try to reject the whole thrust of the argument on such specious grounds.

3. Those who understand and agree with the main lines of argument should not be denied the pleasure of their own creative efforts in refining, revising, and implementing the ideals they have come to espouse.

4. Finally, the mere enumeration of detailed specifics would prolong this tract for the times to unconscionable lengths, detaining the faithful reader when he should be getting on with the job of educational reformation that waits on his action.

There are, however, a few overriding priorities that are of sufficient importance to demand that they be cited. Beginning with the urban milieu—where the institutions and the people are—academe and polis must interpenetrate each other. The urban university and college have no future apart from the cities in which they are resident: both their sustenance and their reason for existing derive from the metropolis. It is not enough that city government begins to be served well by the expertise on campus, although that is clearly a prerequisite to congenial relationships with officialdom. It is not enough that the financial, business, and commercial interests of the city recognize the valuable services furnished to them and the usefulness of a reservoir of educated applicants for employment, although gifts and moral support may be stimulated by an enlightened self-interest that is judiciously reminded of its indebtedness. It is not enough that the cultural and entertainment riches of the campus be shared with the people of the city, even though that would be a remarkable innovation in many instances. Nor would it be sufficient to find professors and students regularly engaged in *practica* and action research throughout the town, essential though these educational and research activities are. There is not a single aspect of any college or university that could not be opened up to direct and useful educational service to the people and institutions of the city. The model of the land grant colleges and universities should not be copied; but its suggestive insights for the urban grant institution will be overlooked only with disastrous results.

Equally important, academe must welcome the citizenry onto and into the campus, not just to provide a congenial public park (although a few mothers with perambulators might serve to remind the academic world that there *are* people who are not yet seventeen or are over twenty-two). Not only the windows, but the gates of academe must be open. And the urban equivalent of the farmers' short courses should thrive. The citizenry should come to the campus for the *educational* services that the imaginative and openhanded institution devises with the direct participation of the citizenry. These educational offerings, which have traditionally been limited to two categories (recreational and vocational-professional), should increasingly deal with the real needs of urbanites. Without necessarily diminishing the traditional extension and

Continuing-Education efforts—indeed, with an intensification of these programs and services—and without implying or expressing any taint of condescension, academe should rid itself of its snobbish preferences for pedantry and share the riches of the intellectual life with naturalness and generosity. It would be a mistake for the campus scholars to plan a program and offer it to the community. Let the impulse begin the other way around, and let the programs grow in response to community interest with community participation in the planning and executing (yes, even in the teaching).

To some few institutions, these suggestions are old hat. They have been doing these things for many years, or have even abandoned them as they advanced from humbler origins. But to the preponderance of colleges and universities located in urban areas, the idea of opening up the campus in all of its fullness to the general citizenry is repugnant. "That's not what a college is *for!*" they expostulate. To which we reply that a good college can be brought to perform its full educational function when it is reminded that every person has a mind and that a mind—any mind—is a terrible thing to waste.

Within the general context of the university without walls, all of the problems that make up civilization's laundry list clamor for intelligent and energetic address. If academe has nothing to offer, it stands mute and naked, deserving the disrespect and contempt it gets; but if it has anything to offer, it will find new life and meaning in making effective response.

As that response is made, it will include among the highest of its priorities a frontal attack upon the American caste system. Recognizing that pride of race may be valuable, but that racism is vicious, town and gown together must work speedily to excise every vestige of racial caste—both within the campus and throughout the city. In the schools, in jobs, housing, politics, business and finance, science and medicine, religion—the whole panorama of human experience—the city is shot through with the venom of caste. And since academicians are generally very much like the citizenry from which they come, caste is no stranger to the campus. Yet, the campus cannot save itself alone: in matters of race, as in everything else, its destiny is intertwined with the city. By every honorable and legal device, by every persuasive example, by every ounce of intelligence and understanding that can be brought to bear, by every legitimate use of economic and political power, by every resource of the human spirit, black and white together must turn the nation around and live as equals in an open society.

There is an alternative. Academe can relax for a little time, do nothing effective to eliminate caste within its own structure and performance, and wait for the gathering storm.

If we are interested in the survival of ourselves and our children's children, we have no real alternative other than to address ourselves seriously to the human condition. We may bewail our fate—that we were born into this moment, to set the times right. When we have done all our crying and decrying, the situation will not have been changed, except for the worse. The *Lumpen* have demonstrated that much, convincingly.

The human condition sets the educational task. All of us—*all* of us on the planet earth—are so many students. Set before us is a task for which we may have little taste: our fondly held value systems lead us in other directions. There ought to be a place to which one could turn to discover a compelling preference for the things that lead to survival of an humane humanity in an enduring and fruitful earth. And where one could learn—not be taught, learn—what to do, why to do it, and how. Nothing less will suffice. We are all on the same spaceship. There is no hope for any of us unless we find real hope for all.

Higher education could become part of the remedy for the human condition—provided educators move from positivism to normative and heuristic exemplification, without which they and their institutions will continue to miseducate. Nobody is stopping the educator. Nobody but himself, with his vested interests, inertia, timidities, lack of compassion, and his false notion that to be a living human being is a betrayal rather than a fulfillment of his profession. He can change. Not to believe that the educator can change, and not to believe that he can change the institutions he has himself built, would be iconoclastic indeed. That would be to strike at the very reason for the existence of institutions of higher education, to deny the validity of the teaching profession and the viability of its institutions. It would be to make of professors faceless persons who merely profess—who are content to build promising intellectual constructs without practicing the redemptive values they claim to espouse.

Beyond such iconoclasm the creative act waits to be discovered. Our directionless and bewildered hour of history could be the moment, the nonrecurring opportunity, in which despair in the face of peril is transformed by action grounded in realistic hope.

Author's Afterword

I assume full responsibility for what I have written. I have tried to name the authors (and their works) on whom I have drawn or to whom I am consciously indebted. Five friends have contributed their candid criticisms of the manuscript. At my suggestion, they are permitted to retain the anonymity necessary to their situations.

My deep gratitude goes to the Leonard and Sophie Davis Foundation for generously providing the working time that these pages reflect, and to June for her encouragement, forbearance, and empathy during the long months of writing.

BUELL G. GALLAGHER

Granite Springs, New York
June 1, 1973

Bibliographic Note

Readers who wish to go behind (or beyond) the text of this tract, either to retrace my steps or to check my facts and insights, are entitled to a little fuller information than is supplied in the running text.

Any careful reader of *The New York Times* and of two or three news magazines such as *Time* and *Newsweek* will be familiar with much of the data of the troubled decade with which I deal. If, in addition, he is familiar with some of the journals of opinion which chronicle (and assess) events from the vantage point of a selected bias, he will evaluate my reconstruction of history in his own way. Further, if he was himself involved in campus life and events he will write his own corrections and additions with his own pen, dipped in the blood and sweat and tears of his own experience.

Throughout the text, I have made reference to the published writings of others. Let me here rehearse the relevant reference data.

CHAPTER 2: The original formulation of the materials in this chapter appeared in a speech I gave before the American Association for Higher Education at its March 1970 convention and which appeared as "Mandate for Change" in *The Troubled Campus*, edited by G. Kerry Smith (San Francisco: Jossey-Bass. 1970). The closely-packed *Environmental Handbook* which was optimisically subtitled, *Prepared for the First National Environmental Teach-In* (New York: Ballantine. 1970) had made its appearance in January of that year in preparation for "Earth Day," an event which many college and university campuses observed on April 22nd. The *Handbook*'s editor, Garrett de Bell, declared that "The 1970's is our last chance for a future that makes ecological sense." Although I had not then seen the *Handbook*, I found myself arriving at many of its conclusions via my own reading route: Rachel Carson's *Silent Spring* (New York: Crest. 1969); Robert and Leona Rienow's *Moment in The Sun: A Report on the*

Deteriorating Quality of the American Environment (New York: Ballantine. 1967); Paul R. Ehrlich's *The Population Bomb* (New York: Ballantine. 1968); and Wesley Marx's *The Frail Ocean* (New York: Ballantine. 1967). Barbara Ward had started many of us thinking in new dimensions of urgency with her Pegram Lectures at Columbia University in 1965. *Spaceship Earth* (New York: Columbia University Press, 1966), and Alvin Toffler's *Future Shock* (New York: Bantam Books. 1970) effectively convinced me that there is no waiting-time. As I was beginning to structure this tract, Frank Graham, Jr., published his *Since Silent Spring* (Boston: Houghton Mifflin. 1970) and Barry Commoner put a few clinchers in the ecological argument with *The Closing Circle: Nature, Man and Technology* (New York: Knopf. 1971).

Meanwhile, another disturbing series of publications summarized and analyzed the social forces which were increasingly expressing themselves on campus. The President's Commission on Law Enforcement and the Administration of Justice, headed by Nicholas deB. Katzenbach, warned of *The Challenge of Crime in a Free Society* (Washington, D.C.: U.S. Government Printing Office. 1967). Following the urban riots of 1967, the National Advisory Commission on Civil Disorders, Otto Kerner, Chairman, issued its *Report* (Washington, D.C.: U.S. Government Printing Office. 1968) and Tom Wicker contributed a hard-hitting introduction to a special rush-order printing of this report, which E. P. Dutton brought out in cloth and Bantam published in paperback. The impact of the illustrations was scarcely less direct than was the text of the report itself. We knew—we who were on campus—that the time was growing very short indeed. Urban America and The Urban Coalition jointly studied the practical results of the "Kerner Report" and published *One Year Later: An Assessment of the Nation's Response to the Crisis Described by the National Advisory Commission on Civil Disorders* (New York: Praeger. 1969) with forewords by John W. Gardner and Terry Sanford, showing that next to nothing had happened to move a bewildered and frightened nation onto a constructive path. As the 1968 elections drew near, the National Commission on the Causes and Prevention of Violence periodically released sections and previews of its forthcoming report in an effort to get the nation off dead center, its final report appearing as *To Establish Justice, To Insure Domestic Tranquility* (Washington, D.C.: U.S. Government Printing Office. 1969). With that massive report, it also issued twelve supplementary Task Force reports (all of which I have read and none of which can be ignored by any person claiming to be an informed citizen). But the juggernaut of violence continued to roll as the academic years 1968 to 1969 and 1969 to 1970 approached their climactic blood-letting; and the President's Commission on Campus Unrest, chaired by William W. Scranton, brought out its *Report* including special reports on the killings at Jackson State and Kent State (New York: Arno Press. 1970). Those of us who were part of a campus experience during these years welcomed the perspectives and insights of this entire series of studies and reports; but books were for burning, not reading, in those crucial months.

I shall not attempt to list the literature of American race relations during the fast-changing decade of the 1970s. Readers who may wish to understand my own prejudices are referred to my *American Caste and the Negro College* (Columbia University Press. 1938, reissued by Gordian Press, New York. 1966). They should also know that the citation appearing in the text refers to August Meier and Elliott Rudnick, *CORE: A Study in the Civil Rights Movement 1942–1968* (New York: Oxford University Press. 1973). Of the half-hundred books by black authors which might well be listed here, I only report that no white reader who is unfamiliar with them has a right to anything more than an opinion based on ignorance.

CHAPTER 3: As the decade began, Robert Jay Lifton wrote his *History and Human Survival* (New York: Random House. 1961) which should have forewarned the nation—but it would appear that the larger section of those who might have been aware were involved in the movements which are chronicled in *The New Left: A Documentary History* (New York: Bobbs-Merrill. 1969) edited by Massimo Teodori, a compendium which lets the participants speak in their own words as the decade closes. Charles Reich's *The Greening of America* (New York: Bantam Books. 1970) had to wait for my reading until it was in its sixth printing as a paperback. Meantime, I had edited and co-authored *College and the Black Student* (New York: Special Contribution Fund of the National Association for the Advancement of Colored People. 1971). The reference to Étienne de la Boétie is to be found in Harry Kurz's translation of his *Anti-Dictator: The Discours sur la servitude volontaire* (New York: Columbia University Press. 1942). The reference to *Walden II* is, of course, to the book by that title written by B. F. Skinner (New York: Macmillan. 1960). In referring to Frantz Fanon (and quoting his work) I have used Constance Farrington's translation of *The Wretched of the Earth* with its preface by Jean-Paul Sartre (New York: Grove Press. 1963).

CHAPTER 4: I have quoted from John Henry (Cardinal) Newman's *The Idea of a University* as published by Longmans Green & Co. (London, 1923), and from Andrew D. White's two volumes, *A History of the Warfare of Science and Theology in Christendom* (New York: Appleton. 1896). By all odds the most up-to-date and comprehensive survey and analysis of American higher education is the series being published by McGraw-Hill for the Carnegie Commission on Higher Education of which Clark Kerr is chairman. Although I have not followed the Commission's classification, I have drawn heavily on its publications—particularly at points indicated in the text; and in expressing my indebtedness to more than a score of writers and researchers who have prepared the Commission's studies, I quickly absolve them of any responsibility for the interpretations which appear in my pages.

CHAPTER 5: I have intentionally written this chapter without benefit of bibliographic support.

CHAPTER 6: The reference to B. F. Skinner is to his *Beyond Freedom and Dignity* (New York: Knopf. 1971). Kenneth B. Clark's presidential address to the American Psychological Association appeared on the Op-Ed page of *The New York Times* for November 9, 1971. The references to proposals by Governors Rockefeller and Meskill are found in the news stories of *The New York Times*. It is in order to add the comment that in neither case did the legislatures of their respective states accept the governor's recommendations without modification.

CHAPTER 7: James B. Conant's *Slums and Suburbs* was a McGraw-Hill, 1961, publication.

CHAPTER 8: Robert P. Wolff, Barrington Moore, Jr., and Herbert Marcuse contributed to *A Critique of Pure Tolerance* three essays prepared in 1965 and published as a single book in 1968 (with a Marcusean postscript of that year) by the Beacon Press, Boston. The essays are titled, respectively: "Beyond Tolerance" (Wolff), "Tolerance and the Scientific Outlook" (Moore), and "Repressive Tolerance" (Marcuse). The volume is examined in this tract not so much for the validity of its arguments as for the character of its methodology. Likewise, the writers and researchers whose works are cited with reference to the controversy over schools and race are used in my pages not so much as a means of examining the finality or validity of their several contributions as a means of understanding what happens when values are not treated as data. The so-called Coleman Report is *Equality of Educational Opportunity* (Washington, D.C.: U.S. Government Printing Office. 1966), prepared by James S. Coleman, et al., at the request of the United States Office of Education. The U.S. Commission on Civil Rights published *Racial Isolation in the Public Schools* (Washington, D.C., 1967) which had been prepared by Thomas Pettigrew and David K. Cohen. The books appeared almost simultaneously in 1972: *On Equality of Educational Opportunity*, edited by Frederick Mosteller and Patrick Moynihan (New York: Random House. 1972); and *Inequality: A Reassessment of the Effects of Family and Schooling in America*, by Christopher Jencks, et. al. (New York: Basic Books. 1972). Readers who wish to go beyond the question of methodology treated in my pages, to consider the merits of the several positions taken and the various interpretations of data (mostly the *same* data) should turn to the authors themselves; but they will find a sprightly and informative introduction to the controversy in the January 1973 *Atlantic Monthly* by Godfrey Hodgson under the title "Do Schools Make a Difference?"

B.G.G.

Index